Study Commentary on 2 Corinthians

A Study Commentary
on
2 Corinthians

Volume 1: 2 Corinthians 1-7

Peter Naylor

 EVANGELICAL PRESS

EVANGELICAL PRESS
Faverdale North Industrial Estate, Darlington, DL3 0PH,
England

Evangelical Press USA
P. O. Box 84, Auburn, MA 01501, USA

e-mail: sales@evangelicalpress.org

web: http://www.evangelicalpress.org

First published 2002

**British Library Cataloguing in Publication Data
available**

ISBN 0 85234 502 X

Printed and bound in Great Britain by Creative Print &
Design Wales, Ebbw Vale

Contents

Part 1: The apostle's ministry and travel arrangements (2 Corinthians 1:1 – 7:16)

Preface

When I was a young theological student, one of our lecturers informed us that no serving minister could afford to be unacquainted with Paul's second letter to the Corinthians. About forty years later, I would endorse the observation. Tracking through this magnificent epistle, one becomes ever more thankful to the Lord that he chose to include it in the body of writings known to Christians as the 'New Testament'. It tells of strength in weakness, comfort in distress, provision in need, fellowship in loneliness, certainty in doubt, guidance in perplexity, protection in peril and hope for the future. Above all, it tells of the surpassing love of Jesus Christ: if Paul the apostle loved and cared for the troublesome Corinthian church as intensely as he did, he no more than reflected, albeit dimly, the grace of God to his believing people, among whom I certainly and I hope you also find ourselves. The benediction of 2 Corinthians 13:14 reverberates through the centuries, reaching us where we are.

I am most grateful to Evangelical Press for encouraging me to write this commentary; to my wife for her patience (she has long since accepted the role of 'book-widow'); to Anne Williamson, who prepared the manuscript for publication; and to the congregation of the Tabernacle Baptist Church, Wellingborough, for hearing so many sermons (too many?) based on

2 Corinthians when, as their minister, I was writing these pages.

Peter Naylor
March 2002

Introductory matters

In June 1908 an enormous fireball approached planet Earth, exploding with the force of an H-bomb just before it could impact the ground somewhere in Siberia. Air waves and ground shock were detected as far away as Western Europe, and nearly 1,000 square miles of Russian forest were devastated. The mass of the projectile was an estimated 100,000 tons, leading some space scientists to believe that it was a small comet rather than a meteorite. No fragments of the extraterrestrial object remain, and it left no crater.[1]

In the fifth decade of the first Christian century the apostle Paul and his colleagues travelled to the bustling and sinful city of Corinth in southern Greece. Thanks to their hard work, blessed by God, a sizeable church was formed. Because Paul was always a missionary on the move his initial visit was in this case for a period of no more than eighteen months (Acts 18:11), after which he travelled via Ephesus back to his home base at Antioch in Syria (Acts 18:22). Sadly, following his pioneering ministry at Corinth, the church was approached by a contingent of high-powered professing Christians — Jewish in origin — who strove to unsettle the people and alienate them from Paul, and who offered a gospel essentially different from that proclaimed by the apostle (2 Cor. 11:4). The shock was widespread, and Paul, now in Ephesus, to which he had returned on

his third missionary journey (7:5), knew that he had
to do something. For the most part the 'something'
turned out to be the epistle we know as '2 Corinthians', the subject of this study. Rather like the
twentieth-century meteor, there is much about the
Corinthian 'pseudo-apostles' (11:13) of which we are
ignorant (for example, what were their names?). The
important point is that, had they not tried to take
over Paul's territory, 2 Corinthians might not have
been written at all, and certainly would not have
appeared in its present form.

Again, like the tracts of Siberian forest menaced by
the exploding asteroid, 2 Corinthians was shaped, so
to speak, from the outside. Whatever it has to tell
about the contrast between the 'old' and the 'new'
covenants (3:14,6) and about the satanic provenance
of the so-called 'superlative apostles' (11:5; 12:11) —
issues which constitute the core of the letter — it
does so by resisting the latter's considerable velocity
and mass. We trace what was happening in Corinth
those many years ago by this third letter which Paul
wrote to the church (cf. 1 Cor. 5:9) and the second
of the two which have been preserved in our New
Testament.[2]

Although this book does not offer a detailed exposition of the Greek text, considerations of various
Greek words and expressions appear throughout. An
English verse-by-verse translation is provided for the
convenience of the reader, the overall aim being to
explain 2 Corinthians with reference to the real-life
situation addressed by Paul when he wrote, and in so
doing to illuminate the abiding importance of the
letter. This, it may be believed, is what the apostle
would have wanted had he anticipated commentators: he knew that his words were stamped with
the authority of 'an apostle of Jesus Christ by the will
of God' (1:1). Paul was almost certainly aware that
the document would remain in the developing body of

writings to be recognized in due time as our 'New Testament'.

In detail, we need to bear in mind that teaching followed by application was the apostolic method: almost always Paul introduces practical guidelines for his readers by pointing them to supremely important theological principles. For example, this letter clearly states that Christian giving is to be contemplated in the light of the incarnation of the Son of God (8:9): he gave; we give. Even when the world is minded to be generous to the needy, as is sometimes the case, it has no such motivation. It follows that to comment upon God's Word without trying to show its relevance for our own lives would be unbiblical. This is why the various sections of the commentary each fall into three parts: an initial overview, translation and exposition, followed by application. Although this procedure may suggest the breakdown of 2 Corinthians into what seem at first sight to be arbitrary blocks, the sections happen to align more or less with the paragraph divisions offered by the United Bible Societies' Greek New Testament (third edition, 1983),[3] these in turn implying the possibility of a coherent analysis of the letter. References to the contents of the epistle note chapter and verse numbers only.

The canonical Second Letter to the Corinthians has been targeted relentlessly by critics in modern times, and there are not a few learned works which attempt to show that it is a composite document, a dossier of writings which were originally separate. This is in spite of the fact that, in agreement with the early church, today's most radical critics never appear to doubt that everything in the letter emanated in some way or other from Paul. The usual allegation is that his materials were eventually sewn together by one or more of his disciples. The point to be made here is that although the approach will not be ignored, this book makes no attempt to put it under the microscope, it being accepted that the text of 2 Corinthians as we have it is an accurate transcript of the epistle sent to the church at Corinth, possibly in the autumn of A.D. 57, and that there is no need to rescue Paul from himself.[4]

Perhaps critical theories may not interest you. If so, don't worry: you do not have a problem, and there *are* things that we can do without. If this is how you feel, you might care to read what comes next — the section covering the background to the letter — and then skip the notes on the 'patchwork-quilt' hypothesis, Barrett's approach and the identity of the 'sorrowful letter', advancing immediately to 'Paul, Titus and 2 Corinthians'.

The background

Paul's first visit to Corinth occurred during his second missionary journey, and we are given the details in Acts 18:1-17. The visit was pivotal in that the apostle remained there for about a year and half (Acts 18:11), no small period of time for an ultra-busy man. During this stay he was instrumental in establishing a church in the Roman colony. Afterwards, Paul travelled back to Syria, stopping over for a brief period at Ephesus. He promised that, subject to the will of God, he would return and minister in that city (Acts 18:21).

The apostle then sailed directly to Caesarea, and presumably visited the church in Jerusalem (Acts 18:22), after which he moved north by land to Antioch in Syria, where was situated what might be termed his 'home church' and missionary base (Acts 13:2). From there he commenced his third journey (Acts 18:23). Paul continued overland to Ephesus and, true to his word, remained there for a period which turned out to be about three years (Acts 19:8,10; 20:31). It was during this Ephesian ministry that he wrote a letter to the Corinthian church, warning them not to associate with immoral persons (1 Cor. 5:9). The document, which has not been preserved, appears to have been misunderstood by some (1 Cor. 5:10-11). It was at this time that unhappy reports were relayed to Paul by the household of Chloe (1 Cor. 1:11), and that he possibly received a delegation, official or otherwise, in the persons of

Stephanas, Fortunatus and Achaicus, who raised questions requiring specific answers (1 Cor. 16:17). It was in the light of this that the apostle wrote 1 Corinthians, possibly during the Passover of A.D. 57.

During the Ephesian ministry Paul almost certainly made a fleeting visit to Corinth, four hundred or so kilometres from Ephesus by sea. This is presupposed by 12:14, where the apostle says, 'Behold, for this third time I am ready to come to you', and by 13:1: 'This is the third time I am coming to you' — the latter statement being followed by a comment about his previous journey (13:2). In other words, Paul's anticipated arrival will be his third, the second having taken place *after* the first pioneering ministry recorded in Acts 18. It is possible, although unlikely, that this second, painful visit (2:1) occurred before the writing of 1 Corinthians and prior to the riot at Ephesus (Acts 19:23). We do not know.

To go back to the time before 1 Corinthians was written, Paul had sent Timothy from Ephesus by land as his forerunner with instructions for the churches which the apostle intended to visit en route, and with orders for him to proceed to Corinth. 1 Corinthians 16:5-10 shows that the people there were to expect Timothy before Paul's own arrival. We know also from 1:15-16 that the latter intended to leave Ephesus to travel directly to Corinth, continuing from there to Macedonia and thence back to Corinth, but that he changed his plan (Acts 20:2; 1 Cor. 16:5). This original itinerary must have been conveyed to the church, for they knew about it (1:16-17), and would have been devised during the Ephesian ministry. Sadly, because the situation at Corinth deteriorated, Paul felt it essential to alter his route, for which reason some Corinthians were reluctant to forgive him. This accounts for the apostle's self-imposed oath exonerating himself from accusations of irresponsibility:

'But I call upon God as a witness against my soul' (1:23).

It is possible that Timothy did arrive at Corinth after the church had received 1 Corinthians, although this is uncertain in view of the absence of any reference to Timothy in 2 Corinthians, apart from his association with Paul in the opening salutation (1:1). Had the younger man reached Corinth according to plan, and had the apostle known about it, might the latter not have mentioned the fact? In any event, when he had completed his business in Greece, Timothy doubtless travelled back to Ephesus. This is a reasonable inference because when Paul later decided to proceed from Ephesus to Jerusalem via Greece he sent Timothy and Erastus into Macedonia (Acts 19:22).

Before he left Ephesus Paul probably received more adverse reports from Corinth. These led him to pay a second visit. As mentioned, this was a painful experience which obliged him to withdraw rapidly: Corinth and he had to part company for a time because he refused to become entangled with intemperate Christians. Such confrontations, to be avoided if at all possible (2:1; 12:21), would have been something of a personal humiliation for the apostle: had he been instrumental in bringing some of *these* people into the kingdom of God? Paul knew that discussions with worldly-minded and complacent believers are, at best, fruitless.

If this reconstruction is accurate, it can be inferred that information brought by Timothy to Ephesus must have induced Paul to send Titus to Corinth with instructions about setting matters right, the latter then returning north, hoping to meet the apostle at Troas (2:13; cf. 7:6). Only when the situation was known to have calmed down would Paul contemplate another visit to the church. Nor was he surrendering his apostolic and pastoral responsibilities, cowering behind Titus, whom some might have suspected he sent to do his work. Of course, had the apostle made an appearance in the church when many were up in arms against him he would have exercised discipline. But choosing to avoid an explosion if at all possible, he sent his colleague, a man not known for timidity, to prepare the way.

2 Corinthians: a 'patchwork quilt'?

We turn now to the popular hypothesis that the epistle known as 2 Corinthians is a later editorial compilation of materials originally written by Paul. In his influential commentary on the letter, which appeared in 1915, Alfred Plummer suggests that 'It is better to talk of "contents" rather than "plan". Beyond the three clearly marked divisions (i.-vii., viii., ix. and x.-xiii.) there is not much evidence of a plan.'[5] The rationale for this approach lies in the assumption that the epistle as we have it is a composition rather than a unit. That is to say, the thirteen chapters which have come down to us are allegedly the product of untraceable editorial ingenuity in selecting elements from two or more letters of Paul to the Corinthians, binding them together as one unit. Over the years this view has attained the status of virtual dogma among many critical commentators, and it is not unusual to read that 2 Corinthians consisted originally of 1:1 – 9:15 (but excluding 6:14 – 7:1, six verses which, it is often maintained, do not fit into the context and which were originally part of another letter),[6] and separate from 10:1 – 13:10, a block written by the apostle *before* the composition of chapters 1-9. Tasker notes acidly: 'It has become *very fashionable* to maintain that the last four chapters are not part of the letter which Paul wrote from Macedonia when he received the good news which Titus brought back from Corinth, but that they formed the closing part of the "painful" letter to which reference is made in 2 Cor. vii. 8' (emphasis added).[7] To compound the issue, some believe that a third letter, allegedly alluded to in 2:4, may have been conveyed from Paul to Corinth by Titus. In this book it will be reasoned that the epistle to which the apostle refers in 2:4 is our 1 Corinthians.[8]

There are not a few variations on the theme, and one commentator will probably differ from another in interpreting the editorial mind(s) that supposedly gave rise to a hybrid epistle. An underlying problem with all this is that critics tend to transgress the principle sometimes known as 'Occam's Razor', which dictates that theoretical explanations are not to be multiplied or made more elaborate unless absolutely necessary.[9] As someone has remarked, 'If you start allowing more complicated hypotheses than are essential to explain the facts, you can launch yourself into a realm of fantasy where your consequent actions will become misdirected.'[10] For example, I might argue that the reason why the tiger suspected to lurk outside my house remains unseen is because it is terrified by humans; every time it hears footsteps it hides. Another interpretation could be that there is no such animal out there. Which, then, do you think is the better explanation for my mysterious cat? This commentary takes the view that 2 Corinthians is a unit and that the usually conflicting arguments in favour of editorial redaction are cumbersome, unconvincing and unnecessary.[11]

At a deeper level, the question of providence is, as any evangelical ought to admit, a major issue. Although we must meet negative critics by subjecting the letter to as close a scrutiny as possible and thereby seek to explain alleged inconsistencies, awkward breaks and startling changes of emphasis, we should not ignore the time-honoured view that the Word of God has been preserved in its integrity by the one who inspired it in the beginning. For numberless Christians 2 Corinthians has always looked like a single letter. The question has to be asked if the Lord, who cannot lie, would have allowed various shorter epistles from the hand of Paul to have been reduced by unknown scribal activity to the format of a letter which was in the earliest times accorded full canonical status. Is it feasible to suppose that some nineteen or more centuries after Paul scholars have now discovered that 2 Corinthians is not what it was always supposed to be? Conversely, should we not concur with the statement contained in the *London Baptist Confession* of 1689 to the effect that 'The Old Testament in Hebrew ... and the New Testament in Greek ... being immediately inspired by God, and by his singular care and providence kept pure in all ages, are therefore authentic' ('authentical' in the somewhat earlier *Westminster Confession*)?[12] The word 'authentic' was well chosen.

Although the issue of divine providence is never, it seems, addressed by the proponents of the multiple-document theory, it has to be faced. This book assumes as a working principle that any examination of 2 Corinthians must be determined by spiritual and doctrinaire presuppositions at least as much as by exegesis and linguistic analysis. The truth is that what we believe (or do not believe) is a controlling factor, although this does not imply that those with whom these pages take issue are to be downgraded as in some sense unspiritual; we cannot and do not wish to judge. Nevertheless, the orthodox doctrines of biblical inspiration and inerrancy generate a bias heavily in favour of the unity of 2 Corinthians. It is part of the task of the present commentary to give credit to this position.

In view of the many challenges to the authenticity of 2 Corinthians, and in order to illustrate the gravity of the matter, it might be useful to expound the reconstruction offered by C. K. Barrett, an eminent mid-twentieth-century New Testament scholar. His presentation of the multiple-strand theory is as lucid as it is typical, and will give you a good idea of the problems that many believe they can see in the letter.[13]

A typical reconstruction

1. The issues

Barrett writes:

> What happened in Corinth after the writing of
> 1 Corinthians, and how Paul responded to it,
> what visits Paul and his colleagues made and
> what letters he wrote, what other visitors made
> their way to Corinth and what Paul thought of
> them, can be deduced only from 2 Corinthians
> itself. Acts, even if we could use it with unques-
> tioning confidence in its historical trustworthi-
> ness, fails almost completely as a source of in-
> formation. 2 Corinthians, moreover, our only
> source, presents us with a number of literary
> problems of great difficulty, and there is a seri-
> ous danger of arguing in a circle — from histori-
> cal reconstruction to literary hypothesis, and
> from literary hypothesis back to historical re-
> construction. The field is one in which theories
> are more numerous than facts, and clear distinc-
> tions between the two are not always made.[14]

Elsewhere he states:

> The initial problem that confronts the stu-
> dent who would reconstruct the events that lie
> behind 2 Corinthians is that the literary and

historical problems cannot be separated from
each other. If one could be settled first, the solution of the other would be greatly facilitated;
but this cannot be done. Grant certain literary
hypotheses, and historical conclusions follow
almost if not quite of necessity; assume a certain sequence of events, and one is more or less
committed to a corresponding view of the literary phenomena. For this reason, the only satisfactory way to approach the problem of
2 Corinthians is to fasten upon particular
questions and view them from both sides, the
literary and the historical, in as great detail as
possible.[15]

What Barrett means is that alleged discontinuities
in 2 Corinthians and the awkwardness of its mood-
swings (as he sees it) suggest that the epistle must be
regarded as a composite production, especially so as
the reader moves from the first nine to the final four
chapters. If this is the case, we are obliged to reconstruct the travels of the apostle from the time when
he sent 1 Corinthians. On the other hand, if the
historical framework of Paul's ministry to the Corinthians is much as has been advocated in this
introduction, the literary characteristics of the letter
have to be accounted for in some other way. This
commentary takes it upon itself to argue that the
background situation at Corinth demonstrates the
epistle to be seamless.

2. The theory

Barrett is prepared to redefine the apostle's itinerary
following the writing and dispatch of 1 Corinthians,
and this for two principal reasons. First, he is unwilling
to accept the Acts of the Apostles as one hundred per

cent historically accurate. Although there is no need to agree with him, the assumption reinforces the hypothesis of a later reworking of documents sent by Paul to the church at Corinth. Second, Barrett reckons that what he describes as 'discontinuities' and sharp breaks in 2 Corinthians are so violent that they can be explained largely, if not solely, upon the theory of a 'simple partition of the epistle between i-ix and x-xiii'.[16] Although this approach is not an unusual one, this commentary seeks to show that there are weaknesses in the thesis.

None the less, as Barrett admits sensibly, 'Literary and historical hypotheses stand or fall together.'[17] His breakdown of Paul's ongoing relationship with the Corinthians is as follows:[18]

After the apostle's first visit to Corinth he wrote a letter to the church ('my epistle', 1 Cor. 5:9), but it need not be accepted that this letter, by definition prior to 1 Corinthians, has been preserved, even in part, in either 1 or 2 Corinthians. Be this as it may, Paul left Corinth for Syria and came to the end of his second missionary journey. As we know, on his third journey he remained at Ephesus for two to three years. It was then that he wrote what we know as 1 Corinthians, which letter has been preserved in its integrity.

Soon after, or possibly before, this epistle was written, the Corinthian church was penetrated by a company of men who claimed to be apostles and who carried letters of commendation from Jerusalem. Barrett says that all were antagonistic to Paul, and that one individual in particular took the lead in reviling him. These adversaries were present when the apostle arrived in fulfilment of the revised schedule announced in 1 Corinthians 16:5 (cf. 1:15-16). The situation was so intolerable that Paul withdrew northwards. He then wrote another letter from Ephesus which was borne southwards by Titus, and which is alluded to in 2:4. In this tearful letter he rebuked the church. This commentary parts company with Barrett at this juncture: although the apostle must have made a second journey to Corinth from Ephesus, unrecorded in Acts, there is no conclusive evidence that he was confronted by a group of false apostles (11:13) organizing themselves behind an anonymous front-man, and this rather eloquent silence might be a fatal weakness in Barrett's reconstruction.

At any rate, according to Barrett, Paul departed temporarily from Ephesus. Journeying via Troas he met Titus in Macedonia, to be cheered by good news brought to him by his colleague. He learned that the ringleader among the pseudo-apostles would be dealt with by the church and that the latter was coming round to Paul's side. He wrote a fourth epistle, 2 Corinthians 1-9, acknowledging his relief, giving directions about the collection for the Jewish churches, and also expounding his apostolic office and ministry.

Sadly, a fresh disappointment arose in that Titus had returned to Macedonia from Corinth with gloomy news in addition to his good cheer. Notwithstanding the more robust stand taken by some, the false apostles and their ringleader tended to dominate and were attempting to Judaize the congregation. Knowing that drastic action was necessary, Paul wrote a fifth letter, our 2 Corinthians 10-13, to defend his own office, to attack the false leaders and to promise a third visit in which, if necessary, he would not spare the troublemakers. (That there was another letter is demonstrated, so Barrett believes, by the alleged disjunction between chapters 1-9 and 10-13.) After this epistle was sent the apostle left Ephesus and eventually arrived at Corinth, where he remained for three months (Acts 20:1-3). His ministry was effective, to judge by Romans 15:26, which relates that Achaia had contributed to the collection.

One major problem with this intricate reconstruction is its refusal to identify the incestuous sinner of 1 Corinthians 5:1 with the repentant offender of 2:5-8 and 7:12. The anonymous individual in the latter two references becomes the aggressive leader of a Judaizing party active in a church which promised to deal with the individual but which in the event failed to do so. The consequence is a fifth, extraordinarily severe letter.

If, as one would prefer to believe, 2:5-8; 7:12 and 1 Corinthians 5:1 refer to the same person, Barrett's literary and historical reconstructions are weakened drastically. Although there was a Judaizing influence of some sort in the church, there is no evidence to prove that there was a pre-eminent 'super-apostle' who confronted Paul during the latter's second visit, who fell into temporary disgrace after the receipt of the sorrowful letter (2:4), but who, renewing his attack, had to be dealt with by a further communication.

3. The unnamed super-apostle

The question arises as to why 2:5-8 and 7:12 should not allude to the incestuous man mentioned in 1 Corinthians 5:1. Such a connection would explain Paul's words in 2 Corinthians in a logical and understandable fashion. Bearing in mind that someone in the church had sinned grossly and had offended his father, it seems reasonable to interpret 7:12 as a reference both to the guilty son and the sinned-against parent. Why deny the link and introduce two other personalities, a leading pseudo-apostle and (perhaps) Paul, who, it is alleged, had been unjustly treated by this individual when at Corinth on the second occasion?

It is obvious that there had been men in the Corinthian church who were emphatically Jewish. Chapter 11 shows that Paul shared their culture, though not their dogmas, the apostle's flaunting of his Hebrew roots, part of his 'little folly' (11:1), proving beyond doubt that they boasted about their Palestinian origin. For Paul, the tragedy was that the race which, in God's providence, had been a light to the Gentile world was sending out men who were destabilizing the churches, and in this case Corinth, by seeking to persuade Gentile converts to yield to Moses. But to separate out one of these men as a culprit who attacked Paul both to his face and, later, behind his back is surely going beyond the bounds of sensible inference. Arguably, this reconstruction owes too much to a literary analysis of 2 Corinthians that assumes a scissors-and-paste procedure which, it is supposed, collated material from as many as five letters to the Corinthians. In turn, this perception might be indebted to a subjective modification of the doctrines of the inspiration and inerrancy of Scripture.[19]

In sum, it could be that in modern times discussion about the apostle's adversaries has led some scholars to read too much into Paul's words, assuming that personal offence must be interpreted in the context of his anti-Judaizing polemic. Yet it need not be so. When even a single member was ill, the body suffered, and pastor Paul was grieved. At Corinth one individual had infected the church with grievous immorality, this state of affairs being a sufficient rationale for the anguish so evident within 2 Corinthians.

The 'sorrowful letter' (2:4) and 1 Corinthians

To recapitulate, it is often argued that 2:4, where the apostle writes, 'For I wrote to you out of much trouble and anguish of heart, with many tears,' refers to a sorrowful letter intermediate between 1 and 2 Corinthians. Kistemaker, in his excellent commentary, is insistent: 'We know that Paul composed at least four letters,' which he labels 'A', 'B', 'C' and 'D'. Allegedly, 'A' is mentioned in 1 Corinthians 5:9, 'B' is 1 Corinthians, 'C' is the sorrowful letter mentioned in 2:4, and 'D' is our 2 Corinthians.[20] But Kistemaker may be overreaching himself.

In the first place, 'I wrote' in 2:4 has sometimes been taken as an 'epistolary aorist', referring to the actual letter (2 Corinthians) that Paul is writing. Kistemaker is probably correct when he remarks that the apostle alludes to an earlier epistle.[21] Further, the former interpretation does not allow for the force of 'I determined', a true aorist, in 2:1, with which 2:4 should be co-ordinated. Because the apostle decided not to visit the church again in sorrow he wrote a letter prior to our 2 Corinthians. Either this was 1 Corinthians or another epistle.

Secondly, could not 1 Corinthians have been written 'out of much trouble and anguish of heart, with many tears'? Kistemaker queries this: 'The hypothesis that Epistles B [1 Corinthians] and C [the 'sorrowful letter'] are identical cannot be sustained ... we cannot say that the apostle wrote all of I Corinthians out of great affliction, anguish and grief (2:4).'[22] It needs to be said that some others who take this

view introduce 7:8 as evidence: 'Because if I grieved
you by the letter, I am not regretful. If I was regretful...' Was Paul sorry that he had written and sent
1 Corinthians? If not, 7:8 might seem to refer to
another epistle, written later than 1 Corinthians. On
the other hand, was it not the grief of the Corinthians
that distressed him rather than a letter designed to
lance the abscess? A decision here is critical, and we
shall return to the matter.

Thirdly, the thesis of a letter intermediate between
1 and 2 Corinthians is often strengthened by an
appeal to chapters 10-13 of 2 Corinthians. These, it
is argued, fit the description of 2:4 nicely. It is further suggested that 2 Corinthians properly ends at
9:15, the abrupt mood-swing between the first nine
and the last four chapters being indicative of a later
reworking by a scribe desirous of expounding Paul's
links with the Corinthians.[23] However, there are
problems.

First, there is no evidence from those extra-biblical
documents that have come down to us from the early
church to suggest that 2 Corinthians 10-13 was ever
anything other than an integral part of the original
letter. Further, ancient New Testament manuscripts
and versions, and quotations from the church fathers,
are silent about a lost letter supposed to be embed-
ded in the final chapters of 2 Corinthians.[24] This
reticence cannot be accidental. Involved arguments
based on alleged mood fluctuations and abrupt
changes in emphasis, of which Paul was capable,
cannot be allowed to disturb the unanimity of the
centuries. Plummer, a persuasive advocate of the
multiple-letter theory, deserves quotation:

> By far the strongest argument in favour of
> the integrity of the Epistle as it has come down
> to us is that the proposal to make i.-ix. and x.-
> xiii. parts of two different letters *rests entirely*

upon internal evidence and receives no support whatever from MSS, versions, or quotations. That is solid ground; and so long as no documentary evidence can be found in favour of the proposal, those who reject it can do so with reason. But the internal evidence in favour of this hypothesis is so cogent in detail, and so coherent as a whole, and the difficulty from which it frees us is so great, that there will probably always be some who prefer it to the traditional view.[25]

Although this makes sense, one would add that the multiple-document theory necessarily detracts from our understanding of what Paul *did* have to say to the Corinthians. To split the epistle into arbitrary fragments must affect adversely the task of unlocking the mind of the apostle to the Gentiles as revealed in this great letter. Plummer's words have stood the test of time. The fact is that many critics allow the dissection of the letter to control their exposition, a procedure which, if we think about it, is not unreasonable: the circumstances of Paul's relationship with the Corinthians must dictate and be dictated by any explanation of what he writes. It is for this reason that it is virtually essential for an exegetical commentary to give at least some attention to the arguments on either side. But before doing so, let's listen to Robertson Nicoll, who entered into print on the subject as far back as 1903, his common-sense realism tilting the verdict heavily against the composite-document hypothesis:

... the theory which regards chaps. i.-ix. and chaps. x.-xiii. as parts of distinct letters which have been joined together by mistake depends on the concurrence of several improbable hypotheses. We have to suppose not only that

chaps. i.-ix. are a fragment of a longer letter
which has lost its concluding pages, and that
chaps. x.-xiii. are a fragment of a longer letter
which has lost its opening pages, but that in
each case the mutilation happened to come at a
point where a new sentence began a new page.
This is a most unlikely thing to happen. Take
any book or manuscript at random and count
the number of places where the tearing away of
the pages does not leave a clause incomplete.
The number will be small indeed. But the
measure of the improbability of this happening
must be twice repeated before we reach the improbability of 2 Cor. i.-ix. and 2 Cor. x.-xiii. being *both* fragments. For neither 2 Cor. ix.15 nor
2 Cor. x.1 is an incomplete sentence... In fact, it
is not too much to say that the phenomena of
the existing document cannot be explained as
resulting from the mere juxtaposition of two
fragments of other letters. We have to postulate,
in addition, an editor who trimmed the ragged
edges and brought the end of chap. ix. and the
beginning of chap. x. into grammatical sequence
by emendation of the texts which the two fragments presented. And beside all this we have
yet to reckon with the improbability, be it great
or small, that the two fragments belonging to
distinct letters should have become joined together under the mistaken impression that they
were parts of one whole. Under these circumstances we fall back on the *prima facie* case,
which is that the Second Epistle to the Corinthians is an *ens integrum* [= a single entity].[26]

Although what he says is sensible, some virtually
ignore the implications. For instance, Margaret
Thrall, author of the 1994 replacement ICC Commentary on 2 Corinthians, comments merely that

'The epistle has always been transmitted as a unity. But this may be due simply to the circumstance that none of its constituent letters was ever published separately.'[27] She cites Furnish, who, writing in 1984, notes in similar vein that the absence of manuscript or patristic evidence for the partitioning of 2 Corinthians 'suggests only that 2 Cor. never circulated except in its canonical form, and that any redactional combination of originally separate letters must have taken place before the circulation of any one of them'.[28] This is all that their major commentaries have to say on the matter. With respect, is not such cursory treatment inadequate? Our retort, not unsurprisingly, would be that the alleged separate letters were not circulated because they never existed. Yet writing for the Word Biblical Commentary series, Martin remarks that 'No manuscript or patristic authority ever divides the epistle. We have no textual evidence which supports any partitioning.' Then, in conformity with the popular approach, he asserts that 'The probative force of this contention is weakened if the earliest textual evidence post-dates the work of a redactor.'[29] It might be asked, 'What redactor?'[30]

Another objection to the strand theory would be that if chapters 10-13 are a part or the whole of a lost letter, it follows that 2 Corinthians 1-9 does not fit Paul's known programme. At a slightly earlier date the apostle wrote in his 'sorrowful letter' that he intended to come soon to Corinth and that he would not spare (10:1-2; 12:14; 13:1-2). Yet it did not happen. Now, in a slightly later '2 Corinthians', he indicates that the visit never materialized because he did not want further sorrow (1:23; 2:1-2). On this hypothesis Paul exposes himself neatly to those charges of fickleness and inconsistency which he has been determined to repudiate.

Further, it is not true that the 'sorrowful letter' mentioned in 2:4 could not be a recall of 1 Corinthians. It might be, as Guthrie suggests,[31] that the apostle gives us a kind of flashback to his subjective reactions when he wrote the epistle, although in it he concealed his own feelings because he had to write objectively. At that time his own hurt was immaterial. No father in the faith could have penned 1 Corinthians without being smitten emotionally, and the apostle must have known that when the epistle was read out to the church tears would flow. This is why he wept in advance.

Nor does Paul indicate in 7:8 that he regrets having sent the previous letter. What he means is that he was grieved for a time because the church was grieved when it learned the contents. For example, if we identify the anonymous offender castigated in 1 Corinthians 5:1-13 with the repentant sinner of 2:7 and 7:12, the problem vanishes.

Nevertheless, were these two men one and the same? Clearly, the notion that 2:4 alludes to a sorrowful letter later than 1 Corinthians gains strength if there *were* two separate individuals. And it must be admitted that in theory a lost letter, exceptionally sorrowful in content, could have been sent to Corinth after 1 Corinthians yet prior to 2 Corinthians. Paul's reference in 1 Corinthians to an earlier letter, 'I wrote you in the letter ...' (1 Cor. 5:9), and his instructions to the Colossians, '... and that [letter] from Laodicea, that you also read [it]' (Col. 4:16), show that not all Paul's writings were preserved. Even so, 1 Corinthians 5:9 does reveal the burden of the actual first letter to Corinth, and in context enlarges slightly upon what the apostle then wrote. But Colossians 4:16 conveys no hint at all about the content of the Laodicean epistle. In the former case there is an illuminating recall; in the second, silence.

The essential point is that a refusal to identify the sorrowful letter of 2:4 with 1 Corinthians falls into a grey area. Why would 2 Corinthians give instructions about the recovery of a penitent sinner whose identity and specific offences remain concealed and who was not anticipated by 1 Corinthians, written only six months or so before 2 Corinthians? At the least, 1 Corinthians 5:9 does give an outline of the thrust of the original non-canonical letter. We are left in the dark about a matter which, causing the apostle much grief, triggered a document otherwise unknown to us apart from the somewhat vague allusions in 2:4 and 7:8, or which allegedly reappears in part or in total in chapters 10-13. In brief, we are informed about the therapy without being allowed to observe the complaint. Besides, given the transport logistics of the period, the six-month interval appears to be too short; nowadays issues in church life tend to have a longer gestation period, and it might not have been different then. It is safer to assume that the offenders mentioned by the first and second letters were identical.

Furthermore, accepting that the contrast between chapters 1-9 and 10-13 of 2 Corinthians is not fanciful, it ought not to be exaggerated. Although 10-13 constitute a vigorous apostolic defence against the false claims of some at Corinth, this emphasis is by no means absent from 1-9. For example, to judge by 2:6, although most of the Corinthians accepted Paul's decision concerning the offender, a minority undercurrent was unhappy about the way in which the apostle handled the issue. Consider, too, 1:17; 2:17; 3:1; 5:12; 6:12, which all imply an opposition.

Had the Corinthians, most of whom were loyal to Paul, pondered chapters 1-9 carefully, they would have known that the apostle was beginning to grapple with the Judaizing faction. It follows that, far from being an editorial addition tacked on at a later date,

chapters 10-13 may, so to speak, be seen as a welcome, indeed essential, apostolic finale. Having
developed the theme of the superiority of the 'new
covenant', Paul necessarily personalizes the whole
matter. The message is far more important than the
messenger, yet the integrity of the latter has to be
validated if Paul can communicate. This is the burden of the final four chapters.[32]

Nor does it appear from 2:1-4 that the 'sorrowful
letter' dealt with an unnamed offender other than the
person mentioned in 1 Corinthians 5:1. If much of
this allegedly lost epistle appears in chapters 10-13,
why do those chapters not refer to the matter? To
suppose that an intensely personal part of the letter
has been lost and that a less important section was
attached at some later date to '2 Corinthians' (chapters 1-9) is at best precarious. It is all somewhat
baffling.

Finally, the Epistle of Clement to the Corinthians,
generally dated about A.D. 95, thirty-five or more
years after 2 Corinthians, shows that 'a few rash and
self-willed persons' 'have perverted' the church
(1 Clem.1:1; 48:5). The letter is in sum an exhortation to be obedient to the elders and loyal to apostolic teaching. Although this is by no means hard
evidence, it fits neatly with what 2 Corinthians tells
us about the character of the infant church, encouraging us to accept the canonical letter as a unity.

To sum up, it is far better to stay with the traditional view that the 'sorrowful letter' of 2:4 is our
1 Corinthians. Robertson Nicoll writes perceptively
concerning this epistle:

> Critics have strangely overlooked ... the fact
> that chaps. vii.-xvi. of 1 Corinthians are mainly
> taken up with answering the queries which his
> correspondents had put to St. Paul; and that
> the body of the letter proper is contained in

chaps. i.-vi. It is in these earlier chapters that we are to look for traces of mental anguish and depression, and I hold that they are plainly there to be found, and that the note of identification afforded by 2 Cor. ii. 4 is answered by such passages as 1 Cor. iii. 12-15, iv. 11-13, v. 1-6,13, vi. 5,9-11. Had the structure of 1 Corinthians been sufficiently attended to, I cannot think that this objection would ever have seemed forcible.[33]

With regard to the alleged change of mood between chapters 9 and 10, comment will be given when we arrive at 10:1. To anticipate, this commentary will attempt to show that throughout his letter the apostle remonstrates almost at every turn with Judaizers who infiltrated the Corinthian church. In fact, far from being alien to the genius of 2 Corinthians, chapters 10-13 are a fitting and logical climax to the main theme of the epistle, which is that the new covenant is infinitely superior to that of Moses, a waning arrangement grossly misinterpreted by self-appointed false apostles.

Paul, Titus and 2 Corinthians

To return to Paul and Titus, when the latter left Corinth the apostle was in an unusual state of anxiety, not only because of his concern for the Corinthians, but also because of severe difficulties at Ephesus. The upshot was that Paul felt that the time had arrived for him to journey to the coastal town of Troas, there, presumably by arrangement (which we might term 'Plan A'), to meet his colleague (2:12). Finding an 'opened door', he remained long enough to establish a church, although distinctly restless because of uncertainties about Corinth. Fearing the worst, and Titus having failed to arrive, Paul put into motion 'Plan B', and proceeded to Macedonia, possibly to Philippi, a supportive church (Phil. 4:15), trusting to rendezvous there with his assistant (2:13; Acts 20:1). In the event, he was not disappointed. Nevertheless, although he was overjoyed at what he learned (7:6), we can infer that the apostle discovered that there were residual problems.

In detail, it was true that a majority within the church had submitted to Paul's counsels in 1 Corinthians, and that some had testified to the deepest repentance (2:1-11). Even so, others were embittered, accusing him of duplicity, of having schemed to embezzle the collection for Judea, and of vanity and cowardice: he would threaten without striking, promise without performing, and was always on the road to Corinth yet never arriving. Worse, so they said, he vacillated both in his teaching and practice. In his arrangements Paul was a 'yes-and-no' sort of fellow who ought not to be given a hearing among respectable folk.

Thus it was that somewhere in Macedonia the epistle we know as 2 Corinthians was written to express the apostle's relief at the overall success of Titus' mission. The date would have been about the autumn of A.D. 57, six months or so after 1 Corinthians.[34] But — and it is a considerable 'but' — although Paul had reason to rejoice at the reported change of heart at Corinth, he was vexed because of the increasing boldness and influence of the false teachers, parasites who had crept into the church. It is this alternation between joyful relief and stormy indignation which must be allowed to explain the astonishing changes of tone that erupt in 2 Corinthians.

This was Paul's third letter to the church. The first, not extant, gave counsel about certain problems (1 Cor. 5:9); the second was the one we know as 1 Corinthians; and the last, the subject of this study.

The tragedy, startling to us, though perhaps not to Paul, was that the intruders, who undoubtedly claimed apostolic status (11:5,13; 12:11), had succeeded in establishing themselves at Corinth: he saw them more as a symptom of local unspirituality and less as a problem. Going out of their way to discredit Paul, they challenged his commission both in terms of his personal qualifications and of the doctrinal content of his message. Asserting their allegedly superior credentials, they made out that they were men from God who should be heard. Looking at the matter through Paul's eyes, it is clear that he could not have remained silent. This letter, therefore, was written in measure to refute the insinuations made against him by the pseudo-apostles.

But the matter went far deeper than a confrontation between Paul and bogus leaders. Like all men, they would soon be gone. The fundamental question which caused the apostle so much anxiety was whether the churches would evolve as a bizarre Jewish sect with a deviant theology centred on the man Jesus, a community necessarily doomed to oblivion. Otherwise expressed, would the gospel of the grace of God, essentially the key to liberty from sin, death, hell — and the shackles of the old covenant — be hijacked by a stale synagogue format consisting of externals only? There can be little doubt that the opponents of Paul were Judaizers ('Are they Hebrews? I also', 11:22), perhaps being encouraged by some from Palestine ('For if someone comes and proclaims another Jesus whom we did not proclaim...', 11:4:), and bearing letters of approval from their fellow countrymen ('Or do we need — as some do — commendatory letters to you or from you?', 3:1). Reduced to its basics, the struggle between Paul and his opponents concerned justification by faith alone in Christ and the relevance or otherwise of Moses' law for believers.

Further, the integrity of the Gentile mission was being called in question. Evil men were asking if the Lord had actually appeared to Saul of Tarsus, and if the converted Pharisee was a true apostle. If not, the Corinthians should walk away from someone who was more often than not elsewhere rather than exercising a hands-on ministry at Corinth, where — they must have implied — he was most needed. This pernicious scepticism had surfaced with regard to the doctrine of the resurrection (1 Cor. 15:11-12), and Paul probably expected that there was worse to come. He knew that personal vilification was bringing his gospel into peril. Aware that the Corinthian cynics were infinitely worse than petty individuals who wanted a change of face in their pulpit, the apostle concluded that he had to react in the strongest yet wisest fashion to their threat. Because the devil's angels wage war (11:13-15), they must be resisted. Paul picks up the gauntlet.

When we read 1 Corinthians we learn about many problems in the church. There was the need for discipline in the case of a notorious sinner and his adherents (1 Cor. 5). Significantly, in this first letter we do not read about false apostles and an organized opposition to Paul and his message; on the surface matters were not yet so serious. But if we remember that 2 Corinthians was written not so long after 1 Corinthians, it appears that the problems revealed by the second letter had mushroomed rapidly in a fertile soil. The stability of the church must have been volatile ever since the early days. Within a brief six-month period, between the writing of 1 and 2 Corinthians, there had emerged a band of pseudo-apostles, accredited in every superficial manner and ready to tear down Paul, his message and in effect the church. This violent eruption can only be accounted for on the supposition that the Corinthians allowed it to be so. Where there is an underlying worldliness among Christians they can accelerate rapidly away from truth.

The letter which we are to study is not simply an epistle to a local congregation: it is addressed to all the churches in the province of Achaia, including, it may be presumed, Athens and Cenchrea (1:1). It might even be suggested that although 2 Corinthians is not of the same genre as, say, the 'catholic' letters of James, Peter, John and Jude, there are parallels; Paul was busily laying down foundations which he knew must remain.

Bound up with his defence both of the gospel and of himself as its authorized exponent was the need for the apostle to explain the change in his itinerary (1:15-17; cf. 1 Cor. 16:5-9), and to advise the Corinthians of an imminent third visit to the church. This apologia was essential because his opponents argued that if the man was unreliable in his arrangements, so must be his preaching. Their premise was fallacious, but some would listen to anything.

In due course Titus travelled back to Corinth from Macedonia bearing 2 Corinthians, with instructions to set matters right in the church and to expedite the collection for impoverished Jewish believers. All this was in preparation for Paul's third arrival at Corinth a month or so later: he would not travel just yet because he had more work to do in Greece (1 Cor. 16:5; Acts 20:2) and because Titus, as Paul's forerunner, needed time to see the church settle down.

This explains why Titus alone is mentioned as the source of Paul's information, even though Timothy is co-author of the letter (1:1). When the apostle eventually arrived in the south he probably made the church at Corinth his base of operations for a three-month spell of missionary work in the area (Acts 20:2-3), but only after peace had been restored. This can be judged from the fact that the epistle to the Romans was written during this time and because Paul was planning his journey to Jerusalem, to Rome and onwards to Spain (Rom. 15:24-25, 28). In the event, he spent the winter at Corinth prior to proceeding by way of Macedonia to Jerusalem with the collection (Acts 20:3; 21:1-17).

An outline of 2 Corinthians

Because he was aware of the tensions within the Corinthian church there must have been considerable intellectual, emotional and spiritual turmoil in Paul's mind when he wrote this letter. Joy in the Lord and in his people, pastoral tenderness, righteous anger, self-vindication in the interests of the ministry, profound theology and concern for harmony both at home and with churches elsewhere all vie for expression. Each strand interweaves with the others. Because this is how it is we have a problem in discerning a formal structure for the letter, and perhaps it would be a mistake to assume that there *is* a structure. Upon scrutiny, what we discover are episodes and allusions almost without number in a kaleidoscope of apostolic thought. Analysis becomes a hard task, yet this does not mean that 2 Corinthians is without form. Over the years most commentators have tended to agree that there are three interdependent sections.

Part 1 (chapters 1-7)

In this first part of the letter the reader follows Paul from Ephesus to Troas and on to Macedonia. The apostle concerns himself with the immediate past and his strained relationship with the church, expressing his joy because problems at Corinth are, at last, clearing up. In these chapters he contributes to

the healing process but also prepares for his remarks
about the collection (chs. 8-9) and for his attack
upon the false apostles (chs. 10-13).

In essence, we have an introduction and then a
review of Paul's labours for the church up to the
time of writing of 2 Corinthians, with emphasis
placed upon the excellence of the ministry of the
new covenant:

The introduction to the letter (1:1-11)
Misunderstood flexibility (1:12 – 2:11)
The ministry of the new covenant (2:12 – 4:6)
Earthly and heavenly homes (4:7 – 5:10)
The ministry of reconciliation (5:11-21)
Paul's pastoral ministry (6:1 – 7:16)

Part 2 (chapters 8-9)

The reader is introduced by Paul to the churches of
Macedonia and the challenge they present to Corinth
regarding a collection for Jerusalem. The apostle
wants the Corinthians to support a worldwide fellowship of churches in which Gentiles and Jews remain
one:

Macedonian generosity (8:1-7)
Advice to the Corinthians before Paul arrives
    among them (8:8-15)
The impending visit of Titus and two colleagues
    (8:16-24)
Fulfilling promises (9:1-5)
Cheerful giving (9:6-15)

Part 3 (chapters 10-13)

This final section concerns the near future and its anxieties, Paul telling of his hoped-for visit to Corinth and outlining the tensions between him and the false apostles. The church is left in no doubt that, whereas the latter are emissaries of Satan, Paul is an accredited senior servant of the Lord. If necessary, when he arrives he will deal with remaining difficulties, possibly exercising apostolic severity, of which he is capable:

Paul and his 'little folly' (10:1 – 11:33)
Paradise, the 'thorn' and the imminent third visit (12:1 – 13:10)
Greetings, final admonitions and a benediction (13:11-14)

Summary

The distinctiveness with which these divisions stand out shows that the epistle is a triad. Furthermore, in the light of the complicated situation at Corinth, and given the apostle's personality, it would be somewhat strange if he had not written such a letter. In the event, Paul's psychological judgement of his readers never errs, which is why he sometimes writes about himself in a way that is a painful folly for him (he would *never* write such things to spiritual Christians), yet which he appreciates to be necessary given the circumstances. Consider the remarkable statement of 12:11: 'I have become foolish: you compelled me.' The humility, boldness and transparent honesty of this man in the interests of the gospel and of the Corinthian church astonish us.

Although the epistle falls into the aforesaid three sections, it is also the case that chapters 1-9 focus

upon the obedient element within the church, and
that chapters 10-13 are concerned with the minority
who oppose Paul. But it would be facile to insist
upon a rigid twofold division. Polemic sections occur
throughout the earlier portion also,[1] the letter being a
seamless document interlaced with doctrine, encouragement, love, indignation and zeal.

Part 1:
The apostle's ministry and travel arrangements

2 Corinthians 1:1 – 7:16

1. The introduction to the letter

2 Corinthians 1:1-11

The opening salutation
(2 Corinthians 1:1-2)

Paul begins the letter with an assertion of apostolic authority; he means to be heard. Moreover, in that the letter is sent to the Christian constituency in the whole region, he may imply that what he writes has canonical authority; this letter is to be no ad hoc memorandum. It is assumed at the outset that the readers are born-again believers, Paul exhibiting his underlying confidence in their integrity.

1:1-2. Paul, apostle of Christ Jesus through the will of God, and Timotheus the brother, to the church of God which is in Corinth, together with all the saints who are in the whole of Achaia. Grace to you and peace from God our Father and from the Lord Jesus Christ.

In New Testament times a letter normally began with the name of the person sending it, then the name of the recipient and then a greeting. In this respect the apostle is conventional, as in all his epistles,[1] yet with a difference. The common form of greeting displayed in most letters was 'be glad' or 'rejoice'

(Greek, *chairein*), expressing the writer's desire that the addressee should be cheerful.[2] As such, the expression occurs in the letter sent by the Jerusalem Council to the Gentile churches (Acts 15:23), in the letter sent by Claudius Lysias to Felix (Acts 23:26), and in James 1:1. Here, in 1:1-2, custom is waived, the apostolic greeting reminding the Christian readers that they are the recipients not merely of a letter from Paul, but of **'grace'** and **'peace'** from **'God our Father and from the Lord Jesus Christ'**. This is a statement of gospel reality, exactly right for an apostle when, as in this case, he addresses **'saints'**. Mundane forms of expression are transformed by the good news of Jesus Christ.

Notice that Paul terms himself an **'apostle'** and refers to Timothy simply as **'the brother'** ('the' because he is someone of note). The contrast is deliberate because the apostle needs to show that he is writing *ex officio*, as one sent from God and not simply as a servant of the Lord, which Timothy also was. This is an intimation that he proposes to vindicate his high office. Moreover, he is what he is **'through the will of God'**, the meaning being that the heavenly Father authorized and enabled his Son to send Paul to Corinth. True apostleship, an appointment from God, was never mediated through ordination by a church or churches. This is one reason why the office ended when those who bore the title went to heaven.

Each of Paul's letters, with the specific exceptions of Philippians and 1 and 2 Thessalonians, leads with a roughly similar statement, the reason being that in each case the apostle needed to exhibit his God-given credentials. With the Philippian and the Thessalonian churches, where Paul enjoyed immensely warm relationships, the pointed exhibition of status was unnecessary.

Achaia was the region of Greece south of the gulf of Corinth, but even when organized as a distinct Roman province in A.D. 27 it was sometimes linked, at least by Paul, with Macedonia in the north.[3] It is always in connection with Corinth that the name appears in the New Testament, although in 1:1 it is implied that the good news of Christ had radiated from Corinth, the hub of local missionary activity, to other places in the deep south. Certainly, there was a distinct church at Cenchrea, a port only a short distance from Corinth (Rom. 16:1). Paul and his colleagues saw to it that the churches lacked neither internal organization nor any encouragement to be interdependent.

'Together with all the saints' (1:1) indicates that although the letter is to be circulated throughout the region, other churches may not have been party to the troubles at Corinth. Paul does not write 'to the church at Corinth *and* all the saints who are in the whole of Achaia'. Certain matters on his agenda, such as the collection for Jerusalem, will relate to other fellowships, but some issues, such as the emergence of false apostles in Corinth, seem to have been peculiar to that church alone. Paul is precise in his choice of words.[4]

'Grace to you' expresses the apostle's prayerful desire that the Father and the Son might jointly convey to the Corinthians an abundance of un-deserved spiritual blessings. When there is **'grace'** there is **'peace'**, the conscious awareness that all is well. In Hebrew terms, there is *shalôm* in our lives. **'From'** suggests the descent or dismissal of peace from two distinct persons within the Godhead who unite in their gracious activity.[5] Further, as else-where, the term **'Lord'** is applied by Paul to Jesus. This is important because the word is employed by the pre-Christian Greek Old Testament (the 'Septua-gint', or *LXX*) to translate the Hebrew name of God,

Yahweh.[6] To Jesus belongs the name that is above every name (Phil. 2:9). Because Jesus Christ is the Corinthians' 'Lord', one other is their Father.

Application

When his secretary put pen to parchment, the apostle Paul knew that he was dictating a letter to a church which had to a considerable extent risen up against him. Perceived spiritual growth in the lives of not a few of these people was, at best, minimal. How significant, then, to note that our author assumes that, notwithstanding their problems, the Corinthians will not fail to experience grace and peace from God the Father and God the Son! Parents with erring Christian children, pastors with erring members, and even churches with erring pastors, may bear in mind that if those for whom they agonize in prayer (supposing that they *do* agonize) have been brought to a conversion experience, the Lord still loves them and will keep them. They can never be alienated from heavenly peace. Grace abounds.

A benediction
(2 Corinthians 1:3-7)

Whenever it is opportune the apostle opens his other
letters with expressions of thanksgiving for his readers.[7] Here he does not, instead offering the Corinthians what is in effect an Old Testament-type dox-
ology, blessing God for comfort granted to him in
Asia and since his removal to Europe.[8]

There may be three related reasons for this somewhat unusual procedure. First, Paul is aware that
the Corinthians have responded positively to the
epistle we know as 1 Corinthians, and later in the
epistle he will express his joy for the comfort brought
to him by Titus (7:6-7). At this point the apostle
implies his confidence in the church (1:7), for which
the Lord is to be praised. Second, the ploy might be a
warning to the Judaizers and their friends that they
will not escape criticism. They should realize that the
apostle is no less a Hebrew than they are (11:22) and
that he, too, can invoke the God of Israel. And,
thirdly, the church should know at the outset that,
notwithstanding his tribulations, Paul is a man
behind whom the Lord stands. This is why he will
issue a call to prayer for himself (1:11).

1:3-4. Blessed is the God and Father of our Lord Jesus
Christ, the Father of mercies and God of all comfort, who is
comforting us in all our trouble so that we may be able to go
on comforting those who are in all trouble by means of the

comfort with which we ourselves are being comforted by God.

Paul had intended to visit the Corinthian church at a relatively early date but had failed to arrive,[9] the principal reason for the delay being that a premature meeting between apostle and church would perhaps have been a fiasco and certainly a humiliation (12:21). Because Paul could not have failed to discipline those in the fellowship whose morals and manners were atrocious, he desired to relieve them — and himself — of the acute embarrassment of a confrontation (1:23). This is why, even though he knew that he would be taken to task for alleged inconsistency, as proved to be the case (1:17), he held off until he knew that it was the right time to revisit the church. In the meantime, there was nothing to be done with some of them: let their arrogance dissipate.

There was also another, more subtle, reason for postponement: the Lord had permitted Paul to remain for an extended period in Asia in order to endure severe hardship. This was with a view to his being better able to stand by, or **'comfort'**, the Corinthians when, at length, he did come to them. The Lord allocated extra sufferings so that his servant might experience enhanced comfort and in this way be better qualified to offer support. It was no part of Paul's continuing relationship with the Corinthians simply to arrive and proffer apostolic teaching and criticism. Because his was essentially a ministry of encouragement it was deemed needful by a higher authority that he should undergo some extra personal preparation.

This is remarkable. Had Paul not suffered enough? No. Did he need to know more of the divine embrace when passing through a personal vale of sorrow? Yes. When he penned 1 Corinthians, was he not ready — psychologically, emotionally and spiritually — to visit

this large, bustling and wayward church for a lengthy
stay? Not entirely. Even he, the Corinthians' father-
in-God and the great apostle to the Gentiles, needed
to grow a little more before he could tend the gaping
wounds at Corinth. And the Lord saw to it that he
would develop. Paul acknowledges this, and proceeds
in these two verses to bless God for the learning
experience granted to him towards the close of his
notable ministry in Ephesus.

Another point emerges. When we travel through
2 Corinthians it becomes obvious that pseudo-
apostles had risen up in the church. Undoubtedly,
they enjoyed a measure of material affluence and did
not depend upon local financial support. Paul, on the
other hand, needed such support but would not take
it.[10] He promises the Corinthians that if at all possible he will soon come to them, but as a man who
has been sustained through many tribulations. This
is a pre-emptive strike. Were unnamed supercilious
Corinthians really in possession of the moral high
ground, and were they in a position to downgrade
Paul? Were they qualified to discount him as a man
of no worth, unable to compete with their formerly
resident 'apostles'? By no means. We know that Paul
always placed a high premium upon proven loyalty;[11]
now, in an exhibition of complete modesty, he implies
cleverly that the Corinthians are unable to disturb a
servant of the Lord who, so to speak, bears on his
body the brand marks of Jesus (Gal. 6:17). The
apostle is not slow to engage upstart would-be leaders at Corinth.

We may learn from this delayed visit. First, a
pastor should never intrude when men are angry and
arrogant: Paul waits until the church cools off and
returns to its senses. To repeat, a premature meeting
would lead to what 12:21 terms a personal humiliation. More of this anon. Further, if a shepherd of
souls knows nothing of personal suffering he may

well be unfitted for the task of healing broken and
bleeding congregations. So vast were the cataclysmic
issues down there at Corinth that the Lord sent his
apostolic servant on an eleventh-hour crash course
in advanced suffering before releasing him to the
Corinthians. It is also true that those who give much
for the Lord deserve to be heard, which is why Paul
implies that the church should receive him.

The apostle is not ungrateful for the mystery of
providence, blessing **'God, and** [or, 'even', 'also';
Greek: *kai*] **the Father of our Lord Jesus Christ'**.
Although Christ is fully divine (1:2), it is equally the
case that the man Christ Jesus is the mediator
between his Father and sinners. It is strictly in this
restricted sense that the heavenly Father is said here
to be the God of our eternally divine and ever-human
Saviour. No man comes to the Father except through
the Son (John 14:6).

These verses insist that the Father is the unique
and sole source of **'comfort'**, 'comfort' meaning
encouragement and strength for someone in need:[12]
God stands by his people in their weaknesses. Notice
the threefold occurrence of **'all'** (or, perhaps,
'every'):[13] literally, **'all comfort'**, **'all our trouble'**
and **'all trouble'**. There is no distress that can separate us from the experience of God's love. On the
contrary, it is precisely when the Christian is afflicted
that the love of the Father is magnified in his life and
heart. This is a major theme of 2 Corinthians, and
Paul introduces it as he opens the epistle.

Furthermore, sufferings have led the apostle to a
more profound experience of the love of God, and he
rejoices. He does not resign himself to misery, or
rebel against what might have seemed a cruel providence, but blesses God for abundant comfort granted
to him throughout dark days. It should not be otherwise for us.

Notice that Paul deals in present tenses: '... **who is comforting us ... that we may be able to go on comforting those who are in all trouble, with the comfort with which we ourselves are being comforted by God'**. Taking it for granted that the love of God is no stop-go matter, he discovers day by day that unceasing streams of grace flow from the heavenly fountain.

Finally, the comfort and encouragement that God the Father does give are often mediated through Christian fellowship: '... so that *we* may be able to go on comforting those who are in all trouble'. Paul had no desire to be the supremo of any man's faith (1:24), but he recognized that part of his ministry was to support the church by expounding the love of God to them, even when some were ready to strip him of his commission. There is more to the ministry than homiletic prowess, vigorous evangelism and (if necessary) correction.

In short, such was the gravity of the situation at Corinth that the church had to be prepared to receive Paul, and the apostle had to be prepared to meet the church. When 2 Corinthians was written the time was near, and its author was on the point of proceeding south, even though he was not sure about the reception he might receive (12:14; 13:1).

1:5. For even as the sufferings of Christ abound in us, even so through Christ our comfort is also abounding.

The abundant sufferings endured by Paul and others have been more than balanced by lavish comfort. **'Us'** may include Timothy, whom the apostle introduces in the opening salutation. Questions arise. First, 'trouble' in the previous verse (1:4) is expounded in terms of **'the sufferings of Christ'**. Why is this? Second, how can it be that the sufferings 'of' (meaning 'relating to' or 'possessed by' Christ) are experienced by Paul and others?

The apostle cannot mean that the redemptive afflictions of Jesus are replicated by him, instituting him as an auxiliary priest, nor that his undoubtedly high morale in stressful situations should be an example for the Corinthians. In the light of what he teaches both explicitly and implicitly throughout his letters and in Acts, the former view would be un-thinkable and the latter dubious at best. These points need no enlargement.

Nor can the apostle be indicating that his suffer-ings were a term of his original call to apostleship, although at his conversion he accepted affliction as inevitable. The Lord told Ananias that Saul of Tarsus would suffer much 'for my name's sake' (Acts 9:16).

Rather, the truth propounded here is that because there is an intimate union between Christ and the church, those who endure trouble for Christ and for the gospel suffer *with* Christ: because they are in him and he in them, they are partners even in this (Phil. 3:10; 1 Peter 4:13). The loyal Christian drinks of necessity from the Lord's cup (Matt. 20:23). If we hope to share his crown we have to be prepared to bear his cross. There is no alternative even though he is with us all the way.[14] What our Lord predicted, Paul has discovered in his own experience.

The compensation for the apostle is that God's comfort has been mediated to him *through* Christ. This is important. Not concerned with suffering in general, Paul focuses solely upon hardship endured in the line of Christian duty. The risen Lord, who underwent so much during his earthly ministry, will see to it that his afflicted servants lack no overflow of comfort. And this comfort, of which the world re-mains incapable, is infinitely more than sympathy. When the physical system wilts, the Holy Spirit is able to invigorate the inner being: 'Our inner self is, rather, being renewed day by day' (4:16).

1:6. And if we are being troubled, it is for your comfort and salvation; if we are being comforted, it is for your comfort that has effect in the endurance of the same sufferings that we also suffer.

Personal affliction and comfort are relatively unimportant as long as Paul the herald is able to convey the message. The operative word is 'if': **'If** [= 'whether'] **we are being troubled, it is for your comfort and salvation;** *if* [= 'whether'] **we are being comforted, it is for your comfort ...'**[15] 'How shall they hear without a preacher?' (Rom. 10:14). If necessary, the apostle is prepared to endure all for the sake of the elect so that they come to salvation (2 Tim. 2:10), his experience being that troubles are counterbalanced by the Lord's comfort.[16]

Perhaps there is a hint of irony at the heart of this verse. Corinthians who bask in relative affluence do not know the sufferings endured by Paul and his faithful company. Therefore they have sparse awareness of a comfort that generates endurance in suffering. If this is something of the meaning, the apostle tells certain unnamed people in the church to grow up.

Conversely, it is likely that the verse lacks any tinge of gentle mockery, the apostle providing encouragement. In that there is an intimate bond between Christ and his body, the various members are not less united to one another than they are to the Lord. This is shown by 1 Corinthians 12:27: 'Now you are the body of Christ, and members individually'; and by Ephesians 4:15-16: 'the head, Christ, from whom the whole body ... causes growth of the body' (cf. Col. 2:19). Undoubtedly there were many in Corinth who loved Paul and who wept for him, and

he tells them that his consolations must parallel
their consolations. This is why the apostle presents a
golden sequence of cause and effect. When they are
(1) reviled by the world because of their faith, their
sufferings (2) will be compensated by dynamic comfort, and (3) they hold out. If (4) they continue to be
faithful, they will be saved. This is why Paul links
present suffering and comfort to eventual salvation.

1:7. And our hope for you is firm, knowing that even as you
are sharers in sufferings, so in comfort.

Paul must have sorrowed greatly when he wrote
1 Corinthians (' with many tears', 2:4) and because
the second visit he made to Corinth, unrecorded in
Acts, was a humiliation. Finding the church in a
deplorable state, he left for Ephesus in some emotional disarray. Even so, he had no doubt that the
Corinthians were the Lord's and that the Spirit had
moved in their hearts. For them it followed that, in
the words of Philippians 1:6, 'He who has begun a
good work in you will complete it until the day of
Jesus Christ.' Here in 1:7, Paul, although assuming
that the people will persevere to the dawn of resurrection glory, presents a nearer reference, sure that
during their earthly lives these erring but lovable
Corinthians must undergo sufferings not entirely
dissimilar to those borne by him and his compan-
ions. Equally, the apostle's hope for the people remains steadfast in that it is based upon his knowledge of the omnipotence of grace: all share in God-
given comfort.

Paul knew acute misery when dealing with falter-
ing Christians, yet he never despaired. Notwithstanding numerous disappointments, he was never
uncertain about either the ability or the will of God to
sustain those whom he had called. And the apostle
makes the point for a specific reason: he is about to

disclose in 1:8-11 the enormity of the trials so recently endured in Asia. His tactic is to plead for fellow-feeling from the numerical majority within the church who at heart are true to the Lord and to his apostolic servant, in this fashion seeking to marginalize the complacent false teachers. Maintaining his confidence in the church (1:14; 7:16), he tells them in glowing terms what he thinks of them. And this is necessary in view of his imminent explanation of the change in his schedule.

Application

How the Corinthians suffered for their faith is not made clear, although 1:6 implies that the details were known to the apostle: '... the *same* sufferings that also we suffer'. Paul makes the point that when the Lord grants his people misery he will often channel comfort through other believers: God has upheld the afflicted Paul so that he might aid the Corinthians. But exactly how does one sufferer comfort another? By identification? By listening? Undoubtedly so, and yet there is another component: experience. The apostle, retrieved from the brink on numerous occasions, is persuaded that the Lord will similarly deliver the Corinthians. Let them take a long, hard look at Paul and be assured that his God is theirs also.

It is good for younger believers to seek out older saints, and particularly those who have known affliction. Their testimonies to the goodness of God will steady nerves and cheer the heart: 'I have been young, and now I am old; yet I have not seen the righteous forsaken, or his seed begging bread' (Ps. 37:25).

Perils in Asia
(2 Corinthians 1:8-11)

The apostle develops the benediction of 1:3-7. The God who comforts his afflicted servant has actually done so by delivering him from what then appeared to be certain death in Asia, and the Corinthians need to be made aware of this (1:8). Further, Paul's statement of hope (1:7) now focuses upon his expectation that the Lord will lead him into and then out of impending perils in Europe (1:10). Of what use, he implies, are generalizations if they cannot be reduced to specifics? Even though — or because — the Lord overrules, the Corinthians need to be fervent in prayer for the apostle.

1:8. For we do not want you to be ignorant, brothers, concerning our trouble which came about in Asia: that we were burdened excessively, beyond strength, so that we despaired even of living.

Paul wishes to inform the Corinthians about recent afflictions which befell him and his colleagues in **'Asia'** — that is, Roman proconsular Asia with its centre at Ephesus. Significantly, the apostle declines to give details, and we are left in the dark as to how Paul came to despair of life, even though Acts 19:21 – 20:1 (which the Corinthians did not have to hand) allows us some intelligent guesswork. What is definite is that the church is being told about the intensity of an affliction so great that even the apostle, a man not unused to difficulties, realized that he had no hope of survival apart from God's help. The arm of flesh had failed. In this light, what Paul underwent fades from view. His purpose is to magnify the grace of God rather than to display his wounds.

Exhausted beyond the most heroic powers of endurance, the apostle was at a loss to see how he could remain alive.[17] This does not mean that at the time Paul had been reduced to a state of abject hopelessness. Far from it. In 4:8 the same Greek verb occurs again, 'not in despair' *(ouk exaporoumenoi)*, the apostle stating that what is impossible for men is possible with the Lord, for which reason his people may hold their heads high. In 1:8 Paul does not regale the Corinthians with a depressing catalogue of his own miseries but introduces an exposition of *why* he had been brought low. He shows that God is faithful, especially in the most dire circumstances, and that he, Paul, needed to relearn the principle. Also, the apostle is seeking to elicit a response from the Corinthians: a soldier in action, he has been snatched by the Lord from the teeth of the enemy. The church needs to appreciate that their God is like this. And the bogus emissaries of Christ should know that he upholds his commissioned servants, in this case, Paul.

1:9-10. But we had within ourselves the sentence of death so that we might not remain confident of ourselves but in God who is raising the dead, who delivered us from so great a death — and will deliver; in whom we have put our hope that he will yet deliver...

The apostle reveals that **'We had within ourselves the sentence of death.'** The Greek perfect tense behind 'we had' *(eschēka)* may retain the sense of an

aorist, meaning that at the time of writing of
2 Corinthians Paul was *not* under the shadow of a
death sentence: at some previous occasion it had
been removed and it was not something that the Lord
had left with him as a permanent deposit. On the
other hand, the apostle might be suggesting that a
sentence of death stayed with him in that what could
have happened in Asia, but did not, might one day
become a sombre reality: the possibility was always
near. The Greek word translated by **'sentence'**
(apokrima) means an official report or decision, or
even a verdict. The Jewish historian Josephus relates
that Julius Caesar authorized the Roman Senate to
make known to Jewish leaders the details of its
'decrees'.[18] Along with others, the apostle had been
told that he must die, and at the time believed that
he would perish in the very near future. Did Paul
reflect upon Hezekiah, who was told by Isaiah that he
had to set his house in order prior to imminent
death? (2 Kings 20:1).

The Greek text of 1:9 begins with **'but'**, connecting
with 1:8: **'We despaired even of living. But we had
within ourselves the sentence of death so that we
might not remain confident of ourselves ...'** This
powerful word, 'but',[19] discloses the divine tactic: the
Lord knew that, because even a steward of the calibre of Paul had something of the old man in him, he
might rely upon his own abilities to extricate himself
from trouble. This would not do. Therefore, to reduce
the apostle to prayerful faith God gave him notice
that he was as good as dead. How the message was
transmitted is, again, unimportant; the fact that it
was delivered is all that matters.

The Lord's intention was that Paul should continue to be persuaded about the mercies of him **'who
is raising the dead'**.[20] Here, resurrection is not the
final resurrection of the body, but the capacity of God
to bring the object of his favour back from imminent

death (cf. 'in deaths often', 11:23). The expression
'who is raising' expounds a permanent attribute of
the Almighty: the manner in which the Lord rescued
Paul in Asia will be repeated because the Lord is who
he is. This is why the apostle predicts that the Asian
episode was not to be the last: '... **and will deliver**'.

The manner of Paul's anticipated decease must
have been particularly repulsive, hence the descriptive **'so great'**.[21] None the less, having delivered his
servant, the Lord is ready to do so again when the
need arises. Furthermore, the apostle is resilient; he
raises his expectations because the Asian experience
has reinforced his trust. Certain of where he stands
with the Lord, Paul introduces 'deliver' (Greek, *ruo-
mai*, meaning 'to save' or 'preserve') no less than
three times in 1:10. Here is a word in which he
delights.

1:11. ... you also helping together on our behalf in prayer,
that thanks may be given by many people on our behalf for
the gracious bestowal to us through many.

Slightly complicated,[22] this carries over from verse
10. The apostle anticipates that in future days he will
be staring death in the face, yet remains confident
that God will retrieve him from disaster. Of this he is
in no doubt even though he does not deserve to be
rescued. Deliverance is a **'gracious bestowal'** because not even Paul is indispensable. This is under-
scored by the employment of a well-known Greek
word which can be transliterated as *charisma*. And
yet there is a condition: providential resurrection will
be accomplished if and when Christians such as the
Corinthians pray for him. Furthermore, if they pray
for the apostle, fellowship among them and others
elsewhere can only be strengthened.

The required co-operation involves local prayer at
Corinth plus intercession by Christians elsewhere on

Paul's behalf. He is also pleading in his own interest. Compare with Romans 15:30, where he asks '... that you strive together with me in your prayers to God for me'. He is urging the Corinthians to link hands with others at the throne of grace. Further, in order to help to resolve tensions among those to whom the letter is addressed, perhaps the apostle may be implying that they ought to organize special prayer sessions in their own church to bring themselves together in the Lord. As the cliché reminds us, those who pray together stay together. Paul perceives that his afflictions could turn out as instruments for good in uniting Christians at God's throne, individuals who might otherwise feel that they have little in common. **'People'** translates the Greek word for 'faces', the apostle perhaps having in mind countenances raised heavenwards.

So far, so good — but there is a further advantage to be gained by this concert of prayer. When the Lord has delivered his servant there will be united thanksgiving: an interceding people must in due course be a celebrating people.

Application

These verses show that prayer for believers in need is a duty incumbent upon the saints, a uniting activity within the church (life is so much easier when Christians attend the prayer meeting!), a discipline certain to strengthen our hope and expectancy, an avenue leading to shared praise for God's undeserved goodness, and an example of the intermesh between divine promise and Christian intercession. The Lord of glory waits for his people to wait upon him.

2. Misunderstood flexibility

2 Corinthians 1:12 – 2:11

Two or three visits to Corinth?

Paul broaches what was for some the thorny issue of his change of plan about revisiting the Corinthians. Before we look at the text it is important to enlarge upon earlier remarks on the subject of the apostle's relationship with the church and try to reconstruct his movements during the second and third missionary journeys.

An apparent problem is that, according to 12:14 and 13:1-2, it seems that Paul had been in the city on two occasions before writing 2 Corinthians. This is why he says that his expected visit is to be the third. But in the Acts of the Apostles we read about only two visits, the first of eighteen months during the second missionary journey (Acts 18:1-18), and the second during the third journey (Acts 20:2-3), when Paul remained with the church for three months. It is this visit (for Acts the second and for 2 Corinthians the third) about which 12:14 and 13:1-2 speak. The challenge is to discover an intermediate visit, unmentioned by Acts. As has been noted, the usual approach (which this commentary accepts) is to interpret the words, '... not to come to you again in grief', in 2:1 as an allusion, not to the initial visit of

Acts 18, when the church was planted, but to an unrecorded visit during the three-year residence in Ephesus (see Acts 20:31).

The second visit caused Paul much pain because the church was in turmoil. This being so, he decided to rethink his stated arrangements for a return in order to give time for both 1 and 2 Corinthians to do their work; local pastoral needs demanded flexibility. The apostle's overall schedule, then, with respect to Corinth was probably as set out in the following paragraphs.

Following the establishment of the church at Corinth at the time of the second missionary journey, and during the third journey, some time within his three years at Ephesus, Paul wrote a first letter to the Corinthians. His purpose was to instruct them concerning practical holiness and probably to answer questions which they raised (1 Cor. 5:9; 16:17). This first letter has not survived.

At that time the apostle decided to venture a second visit to Corinth with a view to making the church a springboard for an extended ministry in Macedonia, then returning from Macedonia to Corinth (1:16), from there to be assisted on a voyage to Judea. According to this plan the Corinthians would in effect enjoy one visit divided into two parts, with a Macedonian interlude between them.

In the event, Paul altered the arrangement because of sad news from Corinth concerning unhappy developments within the church. These are expounded in detail in 1 Corinthians. That epistle was dispatched bearing the information that Paul would not travel to Corinth directly from Ephesus, but proposed to visit Macedonia first, journeying south to Corinth upon completion of his work in the north. He would arrive later than originally planned, thus denying the church the opportunity to act as his base for a fresh campaign in the Greek peninsula. He writes with emphasis that 'I will come to you when I pass through Macedonia (for I am going through Macedonia). But it may be that I will remain or even spend the winter with you so that you may send me on my journey, wherever I go' (1 Cor.16:5-6). It was this alteration which gave opportunity for an emerging opposition at Corinth to attack Paul, failing to appreciate that he felt the switch in his travel plans to be in the interests of the church.

It needs to be said that a supposed second and unrecorded visit to Corinth during the Ephesian ministry does not contradict the evidence given by Luke in Acts. Moreover, it fits well with both 1 and 2 Corinthians. This thesis is reinforced by 11:23-33, the celebrated account of the apostle's sufferings, which mentions events about which Acts remains largely silent. Indeed, it would have been impossible, and no doubt undesirable, for Luke to have given a compressed breakdown of Paul's complete ministry. For instance, we are not told what happened to him following the two-year stay in Rome (Acts 28:30-31) and, but for data supplied by the Pastoral Epistles and Romans 15:24,28 concerning the proposed journey to Spain, our curiosity would be less satisfied than it is. It follows that there can be no overriding objection to the present interpretation.

Paul maintains his integrity
(2 Corinthians 1:12-14)

Incursions by false apostles (11:13), a revised plan for the next journey to Corinth (1:15-17), a difficult previous visit (2:1) and an underlying worldliness (12:20) have strained the relationship between Paul and the church, notwithstanding recent good work by Titus (7:7). Before Paul launches into an exposition of his ministry, he asserts that in his dealings with the Corinthians his conscience has been unsullied and that the letters which he writes to them are sincere: there is no duplicity. The day is approaching when this will be obvious to all.

1:12. For this is our boasting: the testimony of our conscience, that in simplicity and with sincerity to God, and not with fleshly wisdom but with the grace of God, we have conducted ourselves in the world and especially towards you.

This verse continues from 1:11, as indicated by **'for'**. Paul can claim the prayers and sympathy of the Corinthians because he has suffered on their behalf (1:6) and because he has a pure conscience about his relationship with the church. The Greek word *syneidēsis* behind **'conscience'** means 'self-knowledge', or 'moral consciousness'. To have a bad conscience, which the apostle implies he lacks, means knowing something against oneself, acting the part of one's own jury in returning an unfavourable verdict. The apostle, aware that his intensive dealings within and outside the church have been the unfailing object of general scrutiny, takes care to be honest. This explains his shrewd qualifier, **'and especially towards you'**, 'especially' being elative, not comparative. Paul does not mean by this that, although he is prudent when mixing with non-Christians and ministering in other churches, he is much more on his guard when at Corinth because they present greater hazards. Because he has never failed anyone, and certainly no one within the fellowship, the testimony of his conscience is the trigger for boasting: he exercises his right to exult because he is no humbug. Note that Paul's turn of phrase does not say that he prides himself on his good conscience; rather, he rejoices in an honesty about which his conscience has something to say. Sincerity always yields satisfaction.

Negatively, he has conducted himself **'not with fleshly wisdom'**. Such wisdom is much more than being streetwise and knowing how to survive, denoting a preference for living without God. Men are naturally 'wise' (Rom. 1:22) inasmuch as their sagacity reflects their sinfulness and an opposition to the saving wisdom of God, should they hear about it (1 Cor. 1:21). Paul anticipates 10:2-3, where he declares that he does not 'wage war according to the flesh', even though he is 'walking in the flesh' — that is, moving in a wicked world.

Positively, he lives **'in simplicity[1] and with sincerity to God ... with the grace of God'**. When the apostle boasts that his conscience whispers to him that he is as single-minded as he is sincere, he is quick to assert that these virtues are 'to God', worked out as if in the divine presence. Paul has learned that the branch does not bear fruit by itself (John 15:4). He boasts in the Lord. By God's grace, to which he ascribes praise, he is what he is, an apostle with an unclouded ministry.[2]

His outward holiness is matched by inner sincerity. **'Sincerity'** (cf. 'the unleavened bread of sincerity and truth', 1 Cor. 5:8) is probably a compound word meaning something like 'sun-judgement' (Greek, *eilikrineia*). Dazzling sunshine has the effect of making visible tiny blemishes on the most carefully polished surface. The apostle is untarnished. He must have been a remarkably careful, humble and prayerful man.

1:13-14. For we are not writing things to you other than what you read and recognize. And I hope that you will recognize, even to the end (even as you have recognized us in part), that we are your boast, just as you also will be ours in the day of our Lord Jesus.

Paul continues. What he is when moving among men he is when writing his letters. Always the same person, he has never put on an act, nor has masked his true self with a pretence of bravado. But why does he make this point? Perhaps because he is preparing the church for his campaign against the false apostles, men who make out that, whereas his personality is unimpressive, his letters are admittedly substantial (10:10).

If, then, the Corinthians have to acknowledge that Paul's good conscience is no fiction and that his conduct among them has been irreproachable, let them also admit that his letters are neither ambiguous, hypercritical nor hypocritical. He writes no more than he would tell them if he were present, and refuses to commit himself in such a way that at a later date he will have to go back on what he records.

There is a play here on words that cannot be reflected in English in that the Greek verb for **'read'** *(anaginōskō)* is not dissimilar to that for **'recognize'** *(ginōskō)*, 'to see things as they are'. This may be because the prefix *ana* means 'again': the reader discerns *again* what the writer originally had in mind. Paul's point is that even as recognition and reading are verbally similar, so the Corinthians' experience of him, whether face to face or upon hearing his letters read out, has been uniform. He is ever the same man.

In these verses no translation of Paul's Greek can be without its problems. **'For'**, which opens 1:13, points back to Paul's letters, of which 2 Corinthians is now the third to be received by the church. That his correspondence could be misunderstood is shown by 1 Corinthians 5:9-10, where he clarifies advice given in the earlier epistle. Another apostle divulges that not everyone considered Paul's letters to be easy reading (2 Peter 3:16).

'To the end' does not refer to the end of the world, or to the close of the apostle's ministry and life, but to the end of the Corinthians' lives. Thus, may they be permanently assured that Paul is true both to his Lord and to them in all that he does and writes. May they understand that he and those with him are men for whom they should never cease to thank God. They ought to rejoice in that the Lord has graciously seen fit to send Paul, Timothy and Silas to Corinth. Equally, may they understand as long as life shall last that they, the Corinthians, are not removed from the apostle's affections and prayers, nor will they be. Whatever the fluctuations in his relationship with the church, they stimulate Paul to glory in the Lord.

Suddenly the spotlight moves, and the apostle points his readers to the end of the world, **'the day of our Lord Jesus'**. Then, when Christ judges all men (even as Paul's gospel insists — see Rom. 2:16), the Corinthians and he will rejoice together before

the Lord that a work of grace had been performed
through his ministry in their city. It will be so; the
day must arrive. It follows that the church needs to
acknowledge its problems, to appreciate the
apostle's ministry in its true light, and to back away
from those parasites who seek to undermine him.
Even now, early on in the epistle, Paul fires an
opening shot across the bows of the false teachers'
warship.

'In part' may have either or both of two meanings.
First, the apostle might be saying that part of the
church, but not all, has recognized him for the man
he is, but that there are some who remain potentially
or actually malignant (for this sense of 'in part', cf.
Rom. 11:25; 15:15). Or, he may indicate that none of
the Corinthians has understood him completely: they
all came to know something about him, although
imperfectly (for a similar sense, cf. 1 Cor.13:9,12).
The latter interpretation is probably weak; to assert
that none of the people properly understood Paul
would have been an ill-fitting and probably untrue
reproach. May we not believe that the measure of the
man was appreciated by at least some?

The shadow of care which lies over 2 Corinthians
is being exposed in that Paul confides his awareness
that some at Corinth do not trust him. Even so,
knowing that their dissatisfaction is unfounded, the
apostle will seek to validate his integrity, all the while
confirming his love to the congregation.

Application

In church life an elder must strive to keep a pure conscience, a
discipline more important than anything else. If the man fails
here, it will be noticed, and painful must be his efforts to make up
the shortfall: those who sit in the pew always measure him while

they listen to what he says. Moreover, let his declamations, both in the pulpit and elsewhere, contain no hidden agenda.

Supposing, then, that a church maintains a faithful gospel ministry, the minister(s) and the people should be mutually thankful. Indeed, they ought to rejoice in one another now, even as they certainly will when Christ appears. Let them be grateful that they have been allowed to enjoy such a relationship.

The changed itinerary
(2 Corinthians 1:15-22)

Paul's original plan had been to travel to Corinth from Ephesus, from there to Macedonia, and then back to Corinth. But because of a deteriorating situation at Corinth he felt compelled to alter the arrangement. The apostle anticipates 1:23 – 2:4, in which he asserts that it was for the sake of the Corinthians that he changed the schedule. His immediate point is that the admitted alteration must not be taken as a sign of personal weakness in the face of hostility. On the contrary, his motives reflect the mind of the God whom he serves: even as the Lord reacts differently in different real-life situations, so also does his emissary.

Moreover, in that the apostle presents himself as the reliable servant of a faithful God, he gives further implicit warning concerning the Judaizers who have caused so much harm. Paul deserves to be heard rather than they. Let the Corinthians know, too, that because he has no doubts about their own standing in Christ, by parity they should not question his integrity.

1:15-16. And in this confidence I intended to come to you first so that you might have a second benefit, and to travel by way of you through to Macedonia, and again from Macedonia to come to you, and by you to be sent on to Judea.

Paul points to the original itinerary drawn up during his residence in Ephesus (Acts 19:1 – 20:38). In the light of Acts 19:21 the schedule was probably fixed but then revised prior to the riot in the theatre (Acts 19:29-41) and before 1 Corinthians was sent to Corinth (see 1 Cor. 16:5-6). In 1:15-16 we are given the first evidence that the apostle had planned to make Corinth his base of operations for a tour of Greece as the culmination of the third journey.

The shock to the church, which must have learned in some way about the original intention, perhaps in the 'lost letter' of 1 Corinthians 5:9, quite apart from 1 Corinthians (Paul would never have arrived unannounced and unexpected), must have been considerable. Not unsurprisingly, his enemies were eager to exploit the matter. An explanation was owing to the church. Before he launches into the theology of the new covenant, the apostle has to clarify the issue. This is why 1:15-16 leads into some plain speaking in 1:17.

Paul declares that **'in this confidence'** — that is, with the assurance that the majority of the Corinthians held him in high esteem, as he did them — he intended **'first'** to come to them from Ephesus that they **'might have a second benefit'**. This had been his settled plan of action rather than a vague wish.[3] With the assistance of the Corinthians — **'by way of you'** or 'by means of you'[4] — he would travel north to Macedonia to churches in Philippi, Thessalonica and elsewhere, and subsequently return to Corinth. They would then send him onwards to Judea. Paul emphasizes that the northern journey and the concluding voyage to Caesarea would have been underwritten to a great extent by the Corinthians (some of whom might have travelled with him), and he had every confidence that it would be so.[5]

The two benefits to be enjoyed by the Corinthians were the opportunity for two visits, one prior to

Paul's travelling north and the other on his return
from Macedonia. The Greek *charis*, translated 'benefit' or 'favour', suggests that the apostle would have
arrived at Corinth with a view to proclaiming the
grace of God (cf. Rom. 1:11); he was no pompous
cleric bestowing a blessing upon the laity by deigning
to be among them for a while. Or, because he knew
that he would be meeting old friends, as he thought,
does he indicate that all concerned would be doubly
pleased because of his double visit? This interpretation
is not impossible. Either way, expectations did not
materialize.

1:17-18. Therefore, intending this, did I act lightly? Or those
things which I intend, do I intend according to the flesh, so
that with me there is 'Yes, yes' and 'No, no'? But God is
faithful because our word for you is not 'Yes' and 'No'.

In 1:15 Paul introduced the word 'intended'. As
already noted, the apostle's set purpose was to journey to Corinth directly from Ephesus. In 1:17 the
same Greek verb *(bouleuomai)* behind 'to intend' (or,
'to plan', 'to counsel') occurs no less than three times.
The second and third occurrences should be pin-
pointed to the time of writing of 2 Corinthians, as if
Paul is now claiming that, even as his original plan
was well thought through, his revised schedule has
been (contrary to the expressed views of some) no
less the fruit of responsible and prayerful consideration. This is why we have a question which expects
a negative reply from the readers: was the initial
Ephesus → Corinth → Macedonia → Corinth →
Judea route flippant and thoughtless? No. Is the re-
routing to Ephesus → Macedonia → Corinth →
Judea the reflection of a disordered mind, or of a
man out of communion with the Lord who acts
'according to the flesh', who shouts 'Yes, yes' and

later on 'No, no'? Again, certainly not. Paul rejects the implied charges of frivolity and inconsistency.[6]

The truth is that there has been a careful deliberation in all his plans. The manner in which the apostle lives and moves is as responsible and consistent as is his ministry towards both saints and sinners. Because his gospel is uniform, with no glaring irregularities either in doctrine or application, Paul has seen to it that what he says is backed up by what he does: '**... so that with me there is "Yes, yes" and "No, no"?**' could be compared with our Lord's statement, '"But let your 'yes' be 'yes', and your 'no', 'no'. For whatever is more than these is from the evil one"' (Matt. 5:37). The apostle signifies that he, as the Lord's steward, is no more guilty of both affirming and denying the same principles in his preaching than he is, when out of the pulpit, of promising to do one thing but delivering something else. Depending upon the meaning of 'that' in the phrase, 'that with me there is "Yes, yes" and "No, no"?', either the apostle means that he has not revised his diary to suit his own passing whims, with the unintentional consequence that other people are inconvenienced, or that he does not seek to upset the church, as if a barely concealed inferiority complex had goaded him into a deliberate provocation. According to 1:18, God has overridden Paul's human weaknesses and protects the message as delivered by his chosen messenger: '**Our word for you** [the message of the cross, 1 Cor. 1:18] **is not "Yes" and "No."**' Because God is God, he does not employ cheats and liars.[7] If doctrinal truthfulness must abide as the hallmark of apostolicity, how can Paul let himself be irresponsible in other areas? What would men think about his God?

In short, the apostle is dismayed that some at Corinth have been charging him with fickleness. The turn of phrase in 1:17 is powerful: '**Did I act**

lightly?' pointing to the original, now revised, schedule.[8] The underlying problem is that there has arisen a wayward element in the church. Not unlike the Galatians, they began in the Spirit but work out their discipleship in the flesh (Gal. 3:3). In their immaturity they have impugned the apostle's integrity.

1:19. For God's Son, Jesus Christ — he who has been proclaimed among you through us, through me and Silvanus and Timotheus — has not become 'Yes' and 'No', but 'Yes' has come to be in him.

Paul's developing argument is that a preacher's faithfulness in what he declares will be validated by the way he lives: the sanctity of the good news of Christ irradiates the man who loves and announces it. This being so, and because the apostle is a faithful steward who has no skeletons in his cupboard, Corinthians who query his sincerity because of the relatively trivial matter of a readjustment to his itinerary need to think again. As Acts 20:3 makes clear, when Paul arrived at Corinth he remained with them for three months, a longer stay than might otherwise have been the case. They did not lose out.

How can the apostle show that his lifestyle is spotless? With difficulty, although this becomes the acid test. He knows that, whatever he might state about his own conscience, his critics will remain implacable, ferreting around for whatever they are able to dig up. In their eyes he does nothing right. This being so, Paul's further defence is that all that Silas, Timothy and he have had to say about Christ has been verified by the experience of the Corinthians. Religion is a fragile entity, and there always have been and will be many empty promises issued in the name of the Lord — but not by Paul and his colleagues in their day. These missionaries did not make false statements about Jesus in order to gull their hearers into hasty conversions. Treating the latter as responsible people, the Lord's servants were faithful to the truth. Even if there was urgency, there was never any pressurization. In the event, the converts discovered that their lives had been transformed by the Saviour whom the apostle preached.

At this point in time Paul, Timothy and Silas were the Corinthians' only medium of communication in that (obviously) the latter did not have recourse to Christian literature, taped addresses, or even other churches of long standing, to check on their missionaries. In brief, it was with them as with certain Jews who came to Jesus and admitted that everything that John the Baptist had said in earlier days about the Lord was true (John 10:41).

In that Paul's argument is incontestable and invulnerable, the false apostles are being brought into disarray. Further, those who are wavering between Paul and his rivals are given food for serious thought: it ought to be obvious to them that no man whose preaching has yielded so much good can lead a dubious private life.

Silvanus (or Silas) emanated from the church in Jerusalem. Travelling to Antioch with Paul (Acts 15:22), he accompanied the apostle on the second missionary journey (Acts 15:36-41) and would have met a newly converted Timothy at Lystra (Acts 16:1). Subsequently, he went with Timothy to meet Paul in Athens, the three then proceeding to Corinth (Acts 17:15; 18:1-5). This explains why Paul refers in 1:19 to Silas, Timothy and himself.

The assertion that Jesus Christ is the Son of God almost certainly refers to the eternal sonship of the Second Person of the Trinity. Paul appeals to the Corinthians' undoubted experience of salvation: '... **Jesus Christ ... has not become "Yes" and "No",**[9] **but "Yes" has come to be in him.'**[10] To these people the Lord became all that they had been led to believe he would be (for example, wisdom, righteousness, sanctification and redemption — see 1 Cor. 1:30). In Old Testament terms, 'The Strength of Israel will not lie or repent' (1 Sam. 15:29). The Corinthians tested the content of Paul's preaching by turning to Christ, and found neither it nor (therefore) him wanting.

And Christ has been preached **'through'** the apostle and his associates, rather than 'by' Paul and the others;[11] they have been channels of blessing. So, if the converts trusted the message, should they not respect the instruments? The apostle is saying that God does not commission rogues to inscribe his words on believing hearts. Surely, eighteen months of missionary enterprise at Corinth (Acts 18:11) must have shown that these men were not in that category.

1:20. For as many promises of God as there are, in him are 'Yes'. Wherefore also through him is 'Amen' to the glory of God — through us.

The blessedness of the gospel is expounded in order to prove, yet again, that Paul, a man who had been so signally used by God at Corinth, does not lack integrity. The implication is that his detractors were propounding a slander. The exposition links the Christ whom Paul preached and the many promises contained in what Christians term the 'Old Testament'.

In company with Mary, the mother of Jesus, with Zachariah, with aged Simeon, with Anna the prophetess, with many others who awaited the consolation of Israel, and even with our Lord himself,[12] Paul states that the numerous promises issued by God in past centuries are being realized in the person and work of Christ. Prior to 2 Corinthians, the apostle had written to other churches that 'To Abraham and to his seed were the promises made,' the 'seed' being Christ (Gal.3:16).[13] It is Paul's God-given calling to spearhead the proclamation of this glorious message

among the Gentiles, which is why he writes that
Christ is the God-given **'Yes'**, or fulfilment, of the
assurances issued during the Old Testament period.
In Christ God is seen to be true (John 3:33). This is
the message of the first part of 1:20.

Moreover, Paul's ministry is no trifle. Both in
Corinth and elsewhere the apostle's joyful experience
has been that biblically ignorant non-Jews turn to
Christ, learning ever more about him after their
conversion, gaining some awareness of what the
Hebrew Scriptures contain and, as a result, giving
their hearty assent to all that has been written about
the Saviour. Essentially, Gentile converts become one
with Jewish Christians in their acceptance of the
crucified and risen Messiah. All belong to the true
Israel of God (Gal. 6:16; Eph. 2:11-13).

Note the careful fashion in which the apostle
structures the second part of 1:20. Gentiles and Jews
together have received Christ, and through him
return their corporate **'Amen'** to God, glorifying him
in so doing. This has come to pass, as Paul adds
shrewdly, **'through us'**. Had his colleagues and he
not travelled to Corinth it would not have happened.
Without the messengers there would have been no
message, and without the message there would have
been no faith and no salvation (cf. Rom. 10:14-15). Let
the volatile Corinthians be exceedingly careful before
they shuffle away to follow the teachers of error. Their
debt to the apostle is not inconsiderable.

1:21-22. And he who is confirming us together with you into
Christ and who has anointed us is God, who has also sealed
us and has given the deposit of the Spirit in our hearts.

In essence these two verses are based upon the
doctrine of the Trinity: **'God'** (the Father) is **'confirming'** both the Corinthians and Paul **'into Christ'**, has
'anointed' them, has **'sealed'** them and has bestowed

'the deposit [or, 'pledge'] **of the Spirit'** in their
'hearts'. Paul's language is always well thought out,
and never more so than here.

The controversy between the apostle and his
adversaries could easily degenerate into fruitless
argument about mere details. Paul wants nothing of
this. We need to keep in mind his immediate intention, which is to exonerate himself from the twin
allegations of personal levity and infidelity in allegedly backtracking on his commitment to visit Corinth. Having indicated that God's blessing upon his
ministry in that city and elsewhere must, *prima facie*,
prove that he is not arbitrary and worldly-minded, he
shows that the Corinthians and he share together in
a common spiritual growth.

The point Paul makes is that because his own
fourfold experience of the Spirit (again, anointing,
sealing, being granted the pledge of the Spirit and
ongoing establishment) is on a par with theirs, it is
absurd to suppose that he is irresponsible and a man
of the world, even as he refuses to suppose that the
Corinthians are other than saints. What we read here
is a call for a renewal of confidence in him in the light
of the common gift of salvation from the Father, the
Son and the Holy Spirit. It is as if Paul issues a
challenge: 'Now let's show some sanctified common
sense. I know that the Lord has blessed you abundantly, and is blessing you. I know that you are
neither worldly nor dishonest. Please extend the
same courtesy to me. Then we can talk.'

Nor does the apostle say simplistically that because his readers are Christians they ought to be
reciprocating his confidence. What we are given here
is much more profound than any bland platitude:
before us lies one of the New Testament's grandest
expositions of Christian growth, presented to defuse
a particularly nasty situation in the church.

Paul has informed the Corinthians that God will establish or 'confirm' them without fault (1 Cor. 1:8). Here he indicates that this is happening. Further, it is a continuous process: **'[God] who is confirming us together with you into Christ'**.[14] The meaning is that the union between the Lord and the believer becomes ever more firm in the latter's experience as time goes by, thanks to the grace of God. The saints persevere in faith and holiness.

And the ongoing process of establishment is the inevitable fruit of an assumed earlier event, that of conversion. Remarkably, the apostle says that when they — the Corinthians and he — became Christians, God the Father acted in a manner which should be interpreted in at least each of three ways.

First, they were **'anointed'** (1:21). This word, signifying the outpouring of the Spirit, implies separation and service. In the Old Testament kings and priests were ritually anointed with oil, as were possibly also some prophets. Our Lord was anointed by the Holy Spirit, whence the very frequent title 'Christ' or 'Anointed One'.[15] Apart from 1 John 2:20,27, this is the only verse in the New Testament which describes believers as anointed people. Such rarity has to be significant, emphasizing that Paul and the Corinthians are one because they are in Christ, the Anointed One. This is brought out by a deliberate juxtaposition of 'Christ' and 'anointed', implying that if the Corinthians are in the 'Anointed One', they are anointed. Paul issues a heart-cry to come back to reality.

Second, God the Father **'sealed'** them (1:22). It seems best to understand sealing as the in-breaking of the Holy Spirit at conversion in such a fashion that believers become convinced that they are the Lord's and that he is theirs. In ancient times, as since, letters and documents affixed with a royal or state seal were immune from interference and could not be copied.[16] Similarly, God, having set his seal upon those who are his (2 Tim. 2:19), will preserve the true church as his permanent possession. Ephesians 1:13 and 4:30 develop the truth, showing that this sealing is a 'promise' to us concerning the final 'day of redemption'.[17] The Christian is in possession of a species of official document which, were it able to speak, would warn off predators.

Third, God the Father has placed the **'deposit'** of the Spirit in the hearts of both Paul and the Corinthians (1:22). The Greek term employed here, *arrabōn*, transliterates a Hebrew word meaning 'pledge' or 'earnest',[18] an advance deposit handed over in a transaction to demonstrate good faith prior to the completion of the arrangement.[19] Even so, there is one important difference between the pledge of the Spirit and that handed over in a business deal: in the latter situation the pledge might be returnable in the event of completion, as with the arrangement between Judah and his daughter-in-law, Tamar (Gen. 38), whereas the Holy Spirit can never be withdrawn nor, for that matter, will he ever wish to depart. Paul uses the word *arrabōn* again in 5:5 and Ephesians 1:14, the latter verse developing its predecessor: the sealing of the Spirit and the latter's presence as a unique deposit are one experience. This means that when we are sealed with the Spirit at conversion we receive the initial precursor to the glory that shall be. In 5:5 Paul is more specific, declaring that the *arrabōn* is the Lord's way of assuring us that we are prepared for the final resurrection. If you, Christian reader of this commentary, sense the fellowship of the Spirit, be aware that you *must* rise from the dust of death.

Moreover, this sealing occurred **'in** [or, into] **our hearts'**.[20] The irrevocable pledge has been lodged with both apostle and church so intimately that it is incapable of denial. Nor will it ever be cancelled.

These things being so, how can the two sides, and particularly the latter, not exercise respect for each other in the face of malevolent pseudo-apostles?

Application

Moving in a changing world, Paul always subjected his arrangements to the will of God and was motivated at all times by what he considered to be best for the Lord's people. When we go to church we need to be much in prayer. The needs of others are probably more important than ours. To improvise from an observation passed by an American president: 'Do not ask what the church can give you. Ask what you can give the church.'

Let the pastor proclaim Christ with intelligence and affection. In so doing he will not go far wrong and will probably survive. Paul says that 'The Son of God ... was proclaimed among you,' knowing full well that the church was indebted to him.

With regard to the believer's experience of the Spirit (continuous establishment founded upon anointing, sealing and the giving of the 'deposit'), there is no connection with water-baptism or any other ritual procedure, whether authorized by the New Testament or not.[21] Nor are these benefits granted at some point after conversion to Christ, even though our experience of the fellowship of the Spirit ought to mature as time goes by.

Why Paul did not return to Corinth; the previous letter (2 Corinthians 1:23 – 2:4)

The apostle tells the church in plain terms why it was that he did not return to them directly from Ephesus. An earlier visit, unrecorded in Acts (but see 2:1) was so painful that, had Paul visited Corinth according to plan, he would have exercised discipline, which he was loath to do. Grief must have spread everywhere. So, he wrote the epistle we know as 1 Corinthians instead, trusting that the Lord would use it to bring the erring Corinthians to their right mind. Not that writing was an easy matter, as 2:4 indicates so eloquently. Notwithstanding the criticisms being levelled against him, Paul asserts that the earlier letter, the ink of which was salted with his tears, was intended to show his love for the church. It is implied that, unlike others, he has no desire to dominate the Corinthians' faith (1:24).

1:23. But I call upon God as a witness against my soul, that sparing you I came no more to Corinth.

The apostle has explained that his change of plan does not imply fickleness of character, and has offered a two-strand defence: first, an exceptionally useful ministry has proved his integrity; second, the Corinthians and he are equals in that all have received the Holy Spirit. On these counts they should regard him with esteem.

Paul discloses why he changed his arrangements: **'that sparing you I came no more to Corinth'**. The language is emphatic, the apostle asserting that when he heard about the problems mushrooming in the church he postponed a further visit. Because the Corinthians needed time in which to think matters through and, in his conviction, to learn wisdom and humility, a further journey would stay on hold until and unless he heard better things. Had Paul carried out his initial plan, he would have been obliged to deal severely with the whole church. This he did not want to do, knowing that it would be better for the Lord to melt the hearts of the recalcitrants through the written word (in this case, 1 Corinthians) so that sternness would not be needed. 'Love,' Paul had written in 1 Corinthians 13:4, 'is patient,' and the apostle was ready to wait, avoiding awkward meetings in which he must exercise the rod of discipline (1 Cor. 4:21). His compassion would spare them — not him — the ordeal, not because of personal cowardice but because he had a profound affection for his readers and preferred that they be allowed to lick their wounds privately. Nevertheless, as the apostle dictates 2 Corinthians he perceives that severity might yet be necessary (13:2).

He is aware, of course, that his critics will comment that a claim such as this is worse than ludicrous and that he is a frightened humbug. He puts off coming to Corinth because he is scared to face a confident opposition. Compare with 1 Corinthians 4:18: 'Now some are puffed up, as though I were not coming to you.' Like a rabbit, they allege, it is ever his instinct to run for cover. Anticipating the riposte, Paul backs up his statement by calling upon the Lord to witness the truth of what he says. If lying to a church is a dreadful matter (as in the case of

Ananias and Sapphira, Acts 5:1-11), the apostle
builds upon the sombre principle that to cite Almighty God as an accomplice in an act of perjury
would be perilous. That he does call upon the Lord is
an incontrovertible evidence that his stated reason
for postponing the visit is the truth. He is what he
makes himself out to be, and there has been no
concealed agenda. His oath must silence all strife (cf.
Heb. 6:16). Looking back, we ask what manner of
people they were at Corinth, to whom the apostle felt
compelled to write in such a tone. The state of affairs
there must have been deplorable. Some not only
criticized Paul because of fickleness in altering his
plans and for apparent weakness in dealing with
disciplinary issues (10:1-2; 13:3), but may also have
been jealous because the apostle had, it seemed,
favoured the Macedonians over them.[22]

Thus the apostle calls upon **'God as a witness
against my soul'**, the Greek text commencing with
'But I, for my part' *(egō de)*, as if to say, 'May God act
against me, ending my life if I lie to the church.'[23]
'Against' occurs also in Luke 9:5 and Acts 13:51,
where dust from the feet of God's servants is shaken
off as a protest *against* those who refuse to hear the
word. Here, Paul invites divine retaliation if he is a
liar, and it is likely that he has in mind the frequent
Old Testament oath, 'The Lord do so to me and more
also, if ...', as a precedent.[24] He is conscious that he
has no worries on this score.

1:24. Not that we are lording it over your faith; rather, we are
fellow workers for your joy. For by faith you stand.

Albeit in love, the apostle has aimed a broadside at
the Corinthians. They are wrong to suspect that he is
a man not to be trusted. The calibre of his ministry,
their common experience of Christ and, lastly, his
solemn oath are each sufficient to dispel any lingering

doubts. Together, these three strands of argument are invincible.

There is, now, a residual problem: the potency of Paul's self-defence might induce an unhappy reaction among the Corinthians. They may feel that, although the apostle is trustworthy both in word and deed, he suffers from megalomania and lords it over humble Christians who lack his intellectual capabilities, spiritual experience (cf. 12:1-6) and apostolic status. Although he professes to be one with them in Christ, they may say, no man can write as he has written unless he nurtures an overweening sense of his own importance.

Not for the first time, the apostle anticipates danger. The verse opens almost apologetically — **'Not that we are lording it over your faith'** — and falls into three divisions. Negatively, Paul's colleagues and he do not control the faith of the church. Positively, they are merely **'fellow workers for your joy'**. These observations are capped with a reminder to the Corinthians that **'By faith you stand.'**

First, Paul is not a monarch exercising absolute authority. At best, he is someone to whom has been delegated the office of apostle. For this reason alone he deserves to be heard (cf. 1 Cor. 4:1: 'Let a man so consider us, as servants of Christ and stewards of the mysteries of God'). There is one Lord and one faith (Eph. 4:5), each Christian standing alone before Christ,[25] and certainly not before this converted Pharisee. Although Paul has defined the gospel and possessed plenary authority in matters of discipline, he retains neither the right nor the desire to determine arbitrarily what the faith of the churches will be. He delivers only what he has received (1 Cor. 11:23; 15:3).

Second, the apostle and his band of helpers work together harmoniously so that the Corinthians might be joyful believers rather than downtrodden serfs,

which they would be were they to continue to court
the false apostles, men who parade as mini-
monarchs. May the converts have true joy both now
and for ever.[26]

Third, Paul is no mediator between God and the
Corinthians. Because they relate to the Almighty by
faith in Jesus Christ they ought to assess themselves
by this measure. If they are prepared to think carefully, they must accept that the apostle is no essential link between heaven and earth (see 13:5: 'Jesus
Christ is in you'). Within the intimacy of the disciple-
Lord relationship Paul neither wants nor has any
place.

In this fashion he protects himself. The apostle's
humility is the product of sanctified common sense
and a profound awareness of his call, and he writes
in the realization that his opponents lack both attri-
butes. At the same time as they wrestle to consoli-
date their empire, his desire is to honour the Master
by leading others to serve him. He is nothing.

**2:1. Indeed, I decided this for myself: not to come to you
again in grief.**

This verse connects without a break with 1:24, the
modern chapter division being unfortunate. To understand what is said we need to take into account
1:15-17, which reveals that Paul's original plan to
travel directly to Corinth from Ephesus was not
frivolous but was drawn up after careful consideration of the issues involved. Nevertheless, in the light
of discomfiting intelligence from Corinth, the apostle
writes that he judged it expedient not to come **'again'**
to the church **'in grief'**, a sorrow that in the event
would have been mutual. Not only did he wish to
'spare' the people (1:23), he declined to revisit them
with personal heaviness of heart: to grieve the fellowship through the necessary exercise of discipline

would have been a sorrow for him too. He always prefers to avoid mutual anguish if at all possible, their positive joyfulness remaining his objective (1:24).

It transpires that Paul has neither evaded the issue of discipline nor shirked his duties. Had there been no other way of reforming the church he would have kept to his first plan, enduring the mutual humiliation arising from dealing severely with people whom he loves. Compare with 12:21: '... and lest, having come, my God will humble me again with you, and I will mourn over many of those who sinned previously'. This man cared. Fortunately, there was a better way, that of responsible postponement. We have considered this in the review of 1:23.

Therefore the apostle arrived at a conscious decision to revise his schedule. This is the force of **'I decided'** (or, 'I judged'; Greek, *ekrina*). Compare with 1 Corinthians 2:2, where Paul states his judgement that he would know nothing among the Corinthians apart from Christ crucified. In the second letter the altered plan comes across as the fruit of careful, rational thought, even as is his resolve to proclaim the cross and its true meaning.

Because the earlier grievous visit would not have been the initial missionary campaign in Corinth, Paul, as noted, must be alluding to a second visit, unrecorded in Acts (cf. 12:14,21; 13:1). In the light of 1 Corinthians 16:5-6, which assumes the revision of plans, the judgement to defer and alter the route of the third visit must have been taken before the apostle wrote that letter.

There may be more. Paul sent 2 Corinthians from Macedonia, and the churches of that area, just like Corinth, would have known about the altered travel arrangements. Whereas the southerners complained, our letter contains no hint that the northerners were resentful. Here may be a good example of a group of churches working together on behalf of a single congregation. If one suffers, all suffer (1 Cor. 12:26).

2:2. For if I grieve you — who, then, makes me glad if not he who is being grieved by me?

Paul continues to explain himself. Were he to arrive at the church according to the original programme, mutual grief must be the unhappy outcome, the apostle distressing the aggressive Corinthians and in turn being grieved by their bitterness. No church meeting can end on a high note when the people have witnessed the exercise of corrective discipline, as would have been the case given an unaltered schedule. Nevertheless, such was the apostle's love for these difficult folk that they alone were in a position to uplift his heart.

The reference to a single individual — **'who ... makes me glad'** — may best be interpreted as a general proposition. Paul breaks off halfway, probably in a burst of emotion: **'For if I grieve you — who, then, makes me glad if not he who is being grieved by** [or, 'from'] **me?'** If none of those who have been distressed by his pastoral criticisms is in a position to bring joy to his heart through repentance, nobody else has the faintest chance of success. The position of 'I' is significant : 'for if *I* grieve you ...', as if the apostle implies that there are not a few whom he has made miserable, albeit in a spirit of love, but that he has no intention of adding unnecessarily to their number. A literal 'from me' rather than 'by me' is eloquent:[27] any sorrow that Paul caused the church was something squeezed out of him reluctantly in the line of duty rather than a spontaneous outflow of venom.

Nor can the meaning be that the apostle would be gladdened by the exercise of discipline, returning to his lodging after a stormy meeting where he had taken a vigorous stand, feeling satisfied that he had done what he had to do, even though he had done it reluctantly.[28] Such an interpretation does not fit the context. It is true that godly sorrow as the result of apostolic censure rejoices his heart (7:9), but at this point he contemplates the sullenness of those who would not have received his rebuke had he arrived too soon from Ephesus.

2:3-4. And I wrote this very thing lest in coming I might have grief from them in whom I should have rejoiced, being convinced about you all that my joy is that of you all. For I wrote to you out of much trouble and anguish of heart, with many tears, not that you might be grieved but that you might recognize the love which I have more abundantly for you.

The former of these verses divides into two sections, the apostle developing 2:2 with its reference to the earlier letter, our 1 Corinthians.[29] When Christians are sulky they will not be a blessing to others, and particularly not with respect to those in their church who exercise spiritual oversight. Knowing that there were serious problems brewing among the people, the apostle sent 1 Corinthians in order to lead the church to godly sorrow. This is why Paul declares that **'I wrote this very thing'**.[30] He hopes, of course, ultimately to meet **'them in whom I should have rejoiced'**. But for the moment, and given the prevailing atmosphere, he has no intention of arriving prematurely to precipitate general misery by the application of discipline. He desires and expects better things.

In the second part of 2:3 Paul insists that even if some do not think much of him, most do, and he certainly rejoices in them all without exception: **'… my joy is that of you all'**. He had rejoiced when Titus brought good news from Corinth, and believes that the church will be no less glad after receiving his

written assurance that their welfare is ever his concern. Storms pass and there is no need for them to
meet in sorrow. That must not be. Let goodwill flour-
ish. 'How delightful is a timely word!' (Prov. 15:23).

In 2:4 the apostle displays remarkable candour
concerning the writing of 1 Corinthians. The letter
flowed, so to speak, **'out of much trouble and
anguish of heart'**, and was shrouded by a veil of
tears.[31] As observed in the introduction to this commentary, there have been not a few critics who refer
these remarks to a hypothetical lost letter written
after 1 Corinthians. In response, when we take into
account the content of 1 Corinthians and the severe
problems which it addresses, 2:4 becomes a precise
reference.

In sum, the Corinthian church had caused Paul
much trouble, and his heart was in anguish. No true
pastor — and the apostle, apart from his other qualifications, was a pastor — could have formulated and
sent 1 Corinthians without considerable inner distress. To illustrate, Luke 21:25 uses the same word,
'anguish', as in 2:4 (Greek, *synochē*): 'and upon the
earth *anguish* among nations', to show that one day
the world will have reason to believe that it is in a
hopeless state. When he penned 1 Corinthians Paul
reckoned that from a human point of view the state
of affairs at Corinth was nearly desperate. If this
church fell by the wayside, what future would there
be for the Gentile mission as a whole?

Although he was being maligned, and although
many of the converts were showing scant signs of
spiritual growth, the apostle did not write in order to
display malice and resentment. His refusal to hit
back was because he did not want to do so. Far from
it: **'I wrote ... that you might recognize the love
which I have more abundantly for you.'** This does
not mean that Paul's affection for the Corinthians
was greater than that for other churches; the apostle

did not have favourites. The meaning is intensive
rather than comparative, indicating that this church
was loved so very much, and we can draw parallels
with other occurrences in Paul's letters.[32]

By means of this recollection the apostle seeks to
re-establish his credentials. He requests the people to
believe that they have always occupied a special
place in his heart and that their interests are fore-
most. It was so when he planned to travel directly to
Corinth from Ephesus and, later, when he changed
his route, and it was so when he wrote 1 Corinthians, disclosing the new arrangement (1 Cor. 16:5). It
is so as he develops his attack on some who stir up
disaffection among the fellowship. He writes in the
assurance that love works wonders. Paul is committed to these people and wants them to know it.

Remember also that the apostle was not a lachry-
mose, tear-jerking preacher with limited intellectual
capacity. He was as sober as any Christian man
should be because he had to struggle to serve and
survive. The information given us by the New Testament shows beyond doubt that his emotions never
got the better of him. Just like his Lord who wept at
the tomb of Lazarus (John 11:35), when Paul shed
tears, he meant it.[33] Mindful that the Corinthians
have measured his personality, he writes in this way,
expecting to be heard with respect. If he weeps for
them, ought they not to weep for themselves, particularly as the apostle gives them time to repent and
reform?

Application

In these verses Paul shows himself a true gentleman and a
model Christian. He realized that God understood that he loved
the people and abhorred inflicting pain. Nor did he wish to be a
figurehead.

Sometimes it is asked whether we should love those whom we find it easy to dislike. The answer, of course, is 'Yes'. Although there must have been not a few Corinthians with whom Paul found it hard — to say the least — to maintain bonds of friendship and esteem, he could declare with transparent honesty that if those who grieved him did not give him cause for joy, he would remain joyless. Such was his anxiety and such was his love. Moreover, when he wrote 2 Corinthians his intention was to exhibit his care for the people, not excluding the pompous, the selfish, the condescending, the doctrinally naïve and the outright sinful.

Sometimes it can be the hardest discipline of all to love the unlovely. At this point Paul triumphed. In his relationships he reflected Jesus Christ because he had a pure conscience. Herein lies the secret.

One more thing: never write letters which are designed to harm. 1 Corinthians did cause grief, it is true, and this saddened Paul. But all was for the building up of the church. It ought to be like this with us.

Discipline must not go too far
(2 Corinthians 2:5-11)

These verses focus upon the anonymous individual mentioned in 1 Corinthians 5:1-13. It appears that the church had excommunicated the erring brother in accordance with Paul's directive, and that subsequently he repented. Even so, the people had failed to extend the hand of loving fellowship. Paul teaches that the exclusion of a sinner now robed with shame is no less evil than bringing a persistent offender to communion. Let the Corinthians demonstrate their further obedience to the apostle by opening the door to someone who, it is admitted, has caused grief. If not, Satan will smile.

2:5. But if someone has caused you grief, he has not grieved me, but in some degree — that I might not exaggerate — you all.

The section 2:5-11 looks like a parenthesis. Were we to take a pair of scissors and snip out this part of 2 Corinthians, the context would flow smoothly. Try the experiment mentally and skip from verse 4 directly to verse 12: '... that you might recognize the love which I have more abundantly for you... Furthermore, when I came to Troas to preach Christ's gospel...' (2:4,12).

Why, then, the seven-verse interpolation about the notorious offender? Paul tells his readers that, although the unnamed man has caused damage, discipline, whether in retrospect or in prospect, should not be at the expense of love. In the light of his gross misconduct, the church took 1 Corinthians 5 to heart but has allowed the pendulum to swing too far. They have overreacted by continuing to boycott the penitent brother, thereby piling grief upon grief. Undue severity has become an overkill. The apostle introduces the issue here to reinforce his assertion that it had never been his desire to cause unnecessary misery, and he wishes the Corinthians to be his imitators in this respect. In other words, 2:5-11 and Paul's command that the church should accept the contrite offender back into communion have served his interest in labouring to rebuild confidence between the people and him. Further, this vexatious matter needs clearing up without further ado.

Concerning the details of 2:5, one interpretation might be that the offender had caused much grief **'in some degree'** to Paul but in the main to the entire church (**'you all'**). But let the past be past. In the light of a new day and in spite of their shock concerning this sorry incident (cf. 7:8-9), the apostle refuses to press their sensitivities. Here, **'exaggerate'** translates the Greek *epibarō*, meaning 'to weigh down'. The sense is probably intransitive, Paul not wanting to say too much on the subject — a word or two should suffice. Seeing that the man is penitent, the really important thing is that the Corinthians show discernment and receive him back.

However, a better interpretation would be that the offender never grieved Paul personally. Realistically, the apostle was in anguish because the people were dejected, although not destroyed.[34] He softens the charge against the unfortunate man by indicating that if he, who wrote 1 Corinthians with, so to speak, his own tears, has not been mortally wounded, the church should be sufficiently mature to extend a warm welcome. After all, the offender did grieve them, but only to some extent, 'in some degree'. Because the man is sorry Paul will not, and the Corinthians should not, exaggerate their censures.

As said earlier, this commentary takes the view that the individual to whom the apostle refers is the incestuous brother mentioned in 1 Corinthians 5:1-13. Although numerous writers, both ancient and modern, have challenged this, it may be suggested that for at least two connected reasons the interpretation endorsed here is the most sensible: first, it corresponds well with the situation presupposed by 1 Corinthians; second, it dovetails with the counsel given by 1 Corinthians, with 2 Corinthians generally, and with 7:8-16 in particular.[35]

2:6-8. For such a person this rebuke by the many is sufficient, so that on the contrary you should rather forgive and comfort, lest such a person be swallowed up by overmuch grief. Wherefore I exhort you to affirm love to him.

The incestuous man had become the object of church discipline, described in 2:6 as **'this rebuke'**.[36] The action was therapeutic rather than punitive, not as if he had offended against the congregation and had to be penalized, making some sort of recompense for the injury he inflicted. The exercise was intended to restore the offender to a right relationship with the Lord and in consequence to church communion.

Furthermore, the procedure was negative, an act of avoidance (1 Cor. 5:11,13; cf. 2 Thess. 3:14). The man would have been shunned, excluded from the Lord's Table and debarred from active membership of the church. And there was more than excommunication. According to 1 Corinthians 5:5, the individual had to be handed over to Satan for the destruction of the flesh, and 2:9 suggests that, understanding this, the church did not delay its obedience to Paul. But we are not told what, if anything, the procedure allowed the Evil One to do to the offender, even though he was perfectly capable of inflicting additional damage, as could be implied by 2:11: 'so that we might not be disadvantaged by Satan'. A veil is drawn over the affair.

In 2:6 Paul declares plainly that this disagreeable therapy has been **'sufficient'** to meet the need of **'such a person'**, someone whose sin was so appalling. 'Sufficient' would suggest intensity of misery rather than duration, and we recall that six or seven months at most elapsed between 1 and 2 Corinthians. There can be little doubt that the apostle received intelligence, perhaps from Titus, about the signal effect of the rebuke: the transgressor, now reduced to godly sorrow, was ashamed of himself rather than being grieved by the unhappy consequences of his sin (cf. 7:9-11). Because the church's action had been successful, severity must end. Paul was more discerning and more lenient than his readers.

Perhaps discipline had not been a policy endorsed by all. In that **'the many'** were in favour, it is implied that a minority were against it. Yet this lack of accord is relatively unimportant for the apostle, even though he intimates that the opposition still tries to be unhelpful. Be this as it may, the church must **'forgive'** (Greek: *charisesthai*, meaning to be [undeservedly] kind), and afford **'comfort'**, standing by the man as friends and fellow-worshippers (2:7). After all, he is a Christian — Paul never doubts this, and excessive discipline might lead him to suppose that if the congregation does not want him, nor will the Lord. He has given heed to the church and should not, so to speak, be treated as a tax-gatherer (Matt. 18:17). **'Such a person'** — that is, a demonstrably penitent believer and not now 'such a one' (1 Cor. 5:5) or 'that wicked person' (1 Cor. 5:13) — could be swallowed up by grief.[37]

Therefore the church must encourage the brother by ratifying a love which has been there all along (2:8). Perhaps Paul is telling the Corinthians to stir themselves to exploit their potential: because the root of the matter is in them, they are to let it produce fruit, and in this way honour their high calling (cf. Lev. 19:18; John 15:12; Rom. 13:10). **'Affirm'** reflects the sense of the background Greek word *kyrōsai*, 'to arrive at a favourable decision'.[38] It is not impossible that, even as an earlier church meeting may have resolved to remove the man from communion, Paul is hinting broadly that another meeting ought to be convened to welcome him back.

In sum, the apostle is saddened because when the Corinthians knew that their brother had sinned he was allowed to remain in communicant membership. This was because not a few concluded that his offence was unworthy of discipline (1 Cor. 5:1-2). To make matters worse, when the church applied Paul's therapy (1 Cor. 5:5-7), they did not know when to stop. This is why we have 2:6-8. The people were oscillating between an evil toleration of sin and an undiscerning application of the most severe form of discipline available to any church. Patently, all the way through this sorry matter there had been a breakdown of pastoral oversight. If the leaders within the church knew what to do both prior to and after the man's repentance, they failed to give sensitive direction. Conversely, if they did not have a grasp of the matter they must have come across, both to Paul and to others who saw what was happening, as incompetent. It is a measure of the apostle's consummate wisdom in dealing with a difficult situation that he refuses to cast aspersions on those who were particularly responsible, no doubt praying that his exhortations would bring them to their senses. But the leaders were not the church, and the wooden-headed manner in which the Corinthians as a whole

had handled this problem illuminates their immaturity. The apostle ignores the local hierarchy and
addresses all and sundry in the most plaintive terms.

2:9. And for this reason also I wrote to you, that I might know
the proof of you, whether you are obedient in all things.

Paul has disclosed that one reason for sending
1 Corinthians was his reluctance both to inflict and
to suffer grief through the exercise of discipline when
he was next with the church (2:3). Here he reveals
that the epistle **'also'** was dispatched to test them:
put on probation, were they prepared to be obedient
to his instructions, particularly in dealing with an
offender? It is interesting that the apostle did not say
as much in 1 Corinthians, although the call for
obedience was explicit.[39] Having received good news
from Titus (7:6-7), he now opens his heart.[40]

As in 2:3, **'I wrote'** is not a so-called 'epistolary
aorist' (= 'I am writing'), but signifies 1 Corinthians in
its entirety.[41] In the event, the Corinthians have
shown themselves to be **'obedient in all things'**. The
apostle needs to know this before expounding the
issues which divide the pseudo-apostles at Corinth
and himself: he refuses to offer spiritual meat to
carnal Christians (cf. 1 Cor. 3:1-3). With regard to
the erstwhile sinner, the church's disobedience to
apostolic authority would have been a sure sign of
gross unspirituality. Equally, it is in the interests of
the Corinthians to submit to Paul because, unlike his
adversaries, he has been instituted by the Lord as an
apostle (12:12), and there is about him the hallmark
of God-given authority. Fairly interpreted, this verse
is not a slip of the pen showing Paul to be an egotist.
He does not exercise dominion over their faith (1:24).

Blood, it has been said, can occasionally be
thicker than truth in the ebb and flow of church life,
meaning that when there are problems some may

back up an erring member if he or she is a relative or a close friend. When he wrote 1 Corinthians Paul knew that if the people were willing to apply discipline in this sensitive issue they would follow him in all else. Obedience to an instruction, rather than assent to a credal statement, is now being metamorphosed as a litmus test of integrity.[42]

2:10. But to whom you forgive anything, I also. Now what I have forgiven — if I have forgiven anything — was because of you in the presence of Christ...

'Forgive', introduced in 2:7 and to be brought in again in 12:13, is subtle. As has been noted, the background Greek verb (here, *charizesthe*) can signify forgiveness, as in Colossians 2:13: 'having *forgiven* us all trespasses'. Even so, 'forgive' is rather a blunt, black-and-white expression, the more precise meaning being to grant a favour. It may be that because sin has been involved, undeserved pardon is implied. Yet the word can have other nuances, as in Acts 27:24, when the angel tells Paul that 'God has *granted* you all those who sail with you.' The basic idea is that of accommodation to a need, yet without any prior obligation.

The Corinthian church is being summoned to give itself to the former offender. This is why Paul employs the present tense, **'you forgive'** [= 'are forgiving']. When the man has been received back he is to be treated as if he had never given offence.

There is more. The onus is on the church rather than on the apostle: **'... to whom you forgive anything, I also [forgive]'**. It seems clear that Paul refuses to detract from the prerogatives of the gathered congregation; he trusts them to do the right thing. Because discipline is their matter, not his, all that he wants to do is to support them when they apply his instruction by showing the offender their Christian love (2:8).

It transpires that the apostle has in principle yielded to the longing of the sinner to be accepted: **'Now what I have forgiven — if I have forgiven anything — was because of you in the presence of Christ.'** Paul's mind has been made up and he would readily admit the man into fellowship were he a member of the Corinthian church. But because the apostle is not one of them he does no more than give an indicator, leaving the issue there. This explains the self-effacing and somewhat hypothetical, 'if I have forgiven anything'.

The fact is that the congregation comes first. If Paul embraces the offender, so to speak, it is 'because of you'. The people, rather than the apostle, have been hurt; they were on the spot and he far away from Corinth when the unnamed individual crashed. Friendships remain at risk and solidarity is being strained. Therefore it rests with the church to take a fresh initiative. Paul knows that there needs to be an end to the penitent's isolation, from which it follows that if there is no reconciliation the fellowship as well as the individual must suffer. The apostle reveals his mind in order to show the way.

And it is a most serious issue, which is why the verse closes with 'in the presence [literally, 'in the face of'] of Christ'.[43] The episode has been brought prayerfully to the Lord, and Paul declares himself, writing as if Jesus stands at his shoulder. It is probably not the case that the apostle is acting officially 'in the person of Christ', an interpretation which might be too authoritarian for the context. He implies but does not impose.[44]

2:11. ... so that we might not be disadvantaged by Satan. For we are not ignorant of his thoughts.

The offender needs to be readmitted both for his own sake and for that of the church. Not only has he suffered enough, but the Corinthians have to prove their obedience to the apostle. And a further incentive for charity is presented: if the people show hardness they might fall victim to the devil's wiles: **'… so that we might not be disadvantaged by Satan'**.

The Greek word behind 'disadvantage', *pleonektein*, carries the sense of defrauding or unfairly gaining something for nothing at another person's expense. Paul will employ the verb again in 7:2 and 12:17-18, where he protests that neither his colleagues nor he had ever attempted to take material advantage of the church.

In the Corinthian letters Paul refers uniformly to the Evil One as 'Satan' (= 'the opponent / adversary'), and never as 'the devil' (= 'the slanderer').[45] This might be because his readers lived in an idol-infested society, the apostle having shown in 1 Corinthians that behind the non-existent gods of Olympus were evil spirits who desired to tear believers away from their God (1 Cor. 10:20). Thus it is here: Satan will harm the fellowship in one way or another if the latter maintains a rigid, hard-hearted attitude.

Paul's counsel in 1 Corinthians 5:5 was that the offender should be delivered to Satan for the destruction of his flesh. There is no need to discuss what this means, except that the man was to be given over by both apostle and church to Satan's malevolent attention. The present verse assumes that this had happened. Paul indicates that the penitent sinner must be welcomed back, thus retrieving him from the adversary of souls. If the Corinthians fail here they might find that Satan will rob them of one of their own, inflicting further damage upon a remorseful Christian left out in the cold. Further, the split between the minority who stand alongside the man and a somewhat callous majority who have

followed Paul thus far (2:6) might develop into a
chasm. This has to be prevented.

That Satan is capable of exploiting too harsh
church discipline is recognized by Paul: **'We are not
ignorant of his thoughts.'** Looking back, there was
nothing in which the adversary would have taken
more delight than in swallowing up a disciple of
Christ. Could he have succeeded, though, given that
even *this* man was presumably among those sealed
by the Spirit and assured of final salvation?
(1:21-22). Although the answer is negative, the
impossibility would not have inhibited a satanic
attempt. At Corinth, the devil, never a respecter of
sovereign grace, appreciated that havoc would be
spread along the way until his devices were eventually frustrated by a higher authority. It is about this
that Paul is mindful.

In his employment of the first person plural ('*We*
are not ignorant...'), Paul almost certainly refers to
himself, as in 3:1: 'Are *we* beginning to commend
ourselves again?' When he wishes to address the
church the apostle employs the second person plural,
'you' (as in 2:10 — 'to whom *you* forgive'), and when
he refers to the Corinthians and to himself he writes
'we all' (3:18; 5:10; cf. 1 Cor. 12:13). It follows that in
2:11, if he mentions the possibility of being de-
frauded by Satan, Paul is probably giving the church
a gentle hint that they should follow his lead in order
to avoid loss.

Application

The episode of the penitent sinner shows that churches need
pastoral oversight combining discernment, courage and gentleness. Such are the vagaries of human nature that without careful
shepherds the sheep will soon enough go astray. By God's

grace, Paul was deeply involved with the Corinthians, and led them wisely.

Another truth is that Christians who do not maintain their relationship with the Lord will probably not attend to the needs of others. It was precisely because the Corinthians were slipping spiritually that they failed to provide the care which the offender needed so much. If we do not keep our lamps burning, how can we show the way?

Sexual sin within a church is abhorrent, and those who are seen to fail may forfeit for ever any opportunity for service among the Lord's people. In the case of the Corinthian brother, we cannot assume anything except that when it was all over he must have been allowed to return to the fellowship. In this may lie an indicator. No church can be sure that Satan is not plotting its destruction. In truth, the reverse is always the case. We need both the whole armour of God and the wisdom behind 2 Corinthians. Loving discipline is a mark of obedience both to apostolic teaching and to the mind of Christ.

3. The ministry of the new covenant

2 Corinthians 2:12 – 4:6

Troas: opportunity and anxiety (2 Corinthians 2:12-13)

These two verses conclude Paul's explanation of why he did not travel directly to Corinth, and lead gently into his exposition of the superiority of the new covenant, as exemplified by the Lord's blessing upon his work at Troas.

2:12-13. But when I came to Troas for the gospel of Christ, and a door having been opened to me in the Lord, I did not have rest in my spirit in that I did not find Titus my brother: but having taken my leave of them, I went away to Macedonia.

When the apostle left Ephesus to travel to Troas (Acts 20:1), a Roman colony with a population of between thirty and forty thousand,[1] he must have known that at Corinth some were complaining that he had no true concern for the church. It was not so, and here Paul discloses that when he put into effect the changed travel plan and arrived at Troas he could not find rest of **'spirit'**, by which is meant his innermost being, such was his concern for the Corinthians.[2]

Much was at stake. Paul had expected Titus, who was travelling north to Macedonia from Corinth with important news, but failed to meet him. This was a serious disappointment because the two men must have arranged a time and place for a rendezvous, knowing that if they were inexact they could easily sail by each other when crossing the channel between Asia and Europe. Determined to find Titus, his own **'brother'**, by which is indicated a relationship between two colleagues who would not willingly leave each other in the dark, Paul advanced into Macedonia. As it turned out, on both sides of the Hellespont there were many opportunities. In Troas a **'door'**, an effective sphere of service, was opened for the apostle, although we do not know just how long he stayed there, while the expression **'went away'** may hint that the decision to leave Troas was not an easy one. At any rate, after sailing to Macedonia he encouraged the newly founded churches (Acts 20:2), not allowing concerns about Corinth to hinder him from ministering locally to both saints and sinners. The fruitfulness of the work in Troas is indicated by the words, **'... having taken my leave of them'**, in that Paul would not have taken leave of others than converts. That a church came into being is shown also by Acts 20:6-12, which recounts how Paul returned to Troas and was involved in the restoration of Eutychus. Note that the apostle is careful with words: he travelled to Troas **'for the gospel of Christ'**, suggesting that it had long been a minor ambition to work there.

Perhaps the picture of an open door was one of Paul's favourites. God had opened a door of faith for non-Jews (Acts 14:27), and a 'great' door of opportunity was open for the apostle at Ephesus (1 Cor. 16:9). Later, in Rome, the apostle covets prayer that a door might be opened for his words (Col. 4:3). The metaphor implies divine sovereignty: it is the Lord alone who opens gospel doors, and we never read about either the apostles or other Christians doing so: 'I have set before you an open door' (Rev. 3:8; cf. Isa. 45:1). Ultimately it is God who brings good news to men and men to good news. This is why preaching and heart-reception greeted each other: where the Lord opened geographical doors so that Paul could speak, he also opened hearts to accept the word. At Troas the door remained open.[3]

The New Testament does not tell us too much about Titus. He was a non-Jew (Gal. 2:3), although we do not know his place of origin. Undoubtedly, he was brought to Christ through Paul's ministry (Titus 1:4). If Galatians 2:1 refers to the apostle's journey to Jerusalem to be present at the Council recorded in Acts 15:2, Titus was at that early time, between the first and second missionary journeys, a colleague upon whom Paul could depend. Nor did he suffer from a swollen head (7:14-15; 8:16). To judge by his appointment to superintend matters in the congregations of an island as large as Crete (Titus 1:5), he must have been endowed with considerable diplomatic and theological abilities. His work there may not have been his last, in that 2 Timothy 4:10 reveals that by the time of Paul's last imprisonment in Rome Titus had travelled to Dalmatia, by necessary inference on the Lord's business. In 2:13 Titus appears as an essential link in the apostle's often turbulent relationship with the Corinthian church (8:6; 12:18). The fact that he was sent to prepare the way for Paul suggests that he was robust: such a task was not for the faint-hearted.

Application

Unconsciously though it may have been, Paul has shown that he was a master of objectivity. In turmoil because of what might have been happening at Corinth, he ministered at Troas as if all were well elsewhere. His problems were deposited in separate boxes, and the apostle had the capacity to open one box at a time while keeping the rest shut tight. It must have been difficult for him to prepare sermons for the congregation at Troas when worrying about why Titus had not put in an appearance, but he managed it. May the Lord help us to concentrate upon each task as it comes.

The triumphal procession
(2 Corinthians 2:14-17)

Throughout this letter the apostle makes much of the theme of strength in weakness. He has stated that God the Father 'is raising the dead' (1:9), and this principle surfaces as the letter leads into an exposition of the glory of the new covenant. The shift in emphasis is nicely placed because a full reply has now been given to the awkward question of why Paul did not travel directly to Corinth from Ephesus. But he maintains his guard, and in so doing is gently polemic: he suffers, he triumphs, he sees sinners coming to faith, he is aware that others reject Christ, everywhere he diffuses the fragrance of the gospel, and in everything he is strictly honest because God is watching him. In all this the apostle remains unlike 'the many, peddling the word of God' (2:17). Who, then, may they be? The Corinthians, he assumes, are able to name names.

2:14. But thanks be to God, who in Christ is always leading us in triumph and through us makes apparent the fragrance of his knowledge in every place...

Here Paul implies that he has met Titus in Macedonia. This leads him to anticipate 7:5-7 and his brief note of the encounter by bursting into praise for news from his friend that removed a massive burden from his mind. Not only should we be thankful for the apostle's planned digressions, of which 2:14 – 7:4

is an example, we need also to recall the issues immediately at stake. Although the problems at Corinth were internal, as, for example, the necessity for discipline, such was the strategic location of the church and such the gravity of the opposition being mounted against Paul that nothing less than the integrity of his message was being challenged. Had Corinth succumbed to the Judaizers, about whom the apostle has much more to write in this letter, Gentile Christianity at large would have been in peril. There are times when, from a human point of view, the Lord's work seems on the edge of collapse. Then God's people have to agonize in prayer, all the while enduring emotional conflict because the pressures appear to be too much. It had been so for Paul before he met Titus.

Even then, after Titus brought good tidings, the conflict was not ended, and this in spite of the fact that the apostle knew that on the whole the church was with him and that in principle he had won the battle for their hearts: it would only be a matter of time before the false emissaries vanished from the scene. This is why we have chapters 10-13, which serve warning against those of the opposition who still refuse to lay down their arms. When 2 Corinthians has been sent on its way Paul can proceed to Corinth with almost complete confidence about the church and about his ministry there. In anticipation, he triumphs. He will tell the congregation that, if necessary, he is prepared to wield the stick (13:2,10), but here he anticipates that such drastic action will be unnecessary.

The apostle thanks the God who has raised him (**'us'**) to the status of a senior military commander. Tested in combat, he has never lost a battle, and never will. His war is virtually a triumphal procession.[4] In practical terms, this means that from the time of his conversion near Damascus until his martyrdom, presumably in Rome, Paul has known victory after victory, his face never clouded with the shame of defeat. As the apostle writes 2 Corinthians he is joyfully aware that Corinth has given its name to yet another battle honour. Compare this verse with Colossians 2:15, where the defeated forces of evil are said to be led in humiliation within Christ's triumphal procession. Putting the two texts together, we infer that Christ leads his exultant servants at the head of his victorious train, simultaneously dragging vanquished enemies far behind both him and them.[5]

In 2:14 Paul indicates that although he has had to commit every human resource to the conflict, the outcome reflects upon the goodness of God and not upon the prowess of an illustrious servant of the gospel. In his letters common sense as well as humility always prevent the apostle from advertising how much he has done for the Lord, unless it is to magnify his office. No man was ever allowed to downgrade *this*: 'But by the grace of God I am what I am' (1 Cor. 15:10). Moreover, the Christ proclaimed **'in every place'** has caused the good news to triumph, and the arm of the Lord has stretched out to secure his own interests (2:14a). It follows that each conflict brings victory. Everywhere there is a manifestation of the **'fragrance'** of the knowledge of the Christ heralded by Paul. The present tenses show that, as the apostle sees matters, this is how it is at all times (2:14b).

In the New Testament the underlying Greek word for 'fragrance' *(osmē)* denotes a pleasant smell, with the exception of 2:16, 'a smell from death to death'.[6] There, Paul does not concede that the gospel *is* a bad odour, but that it is made out to be so by unbelievers who remain antagonistic. It is likely that 2:14 alludes to the practice of burning spices and incense and scattering flowers in the streets when a Roman general was afforded a triumphal procession. Paul, a leader, parades in triumph, and all have seen it — even if some are resentful.

And there might be rather more to the picture than this. In the Septuagint *osmē* usually occurs within a compound expression, a *'pleasing* aroma', in connection with the smoke that arises from an altar sacrifice. The Lord smelled the aroma that ascended from Noah's offering and promised that he would never again curse the ground (Gen. 8:21). Here, the knowledge of Christ, by which the apostle would mean the revelation of the good news of Jesus, is a fragrance to God (2:14). Heaven rejoices when truth is manifest.

2:15. ... because we are the sweet aroma of Christ to God among those who are being saved and among those who are perishing...

Another Greek word, *euōdia*, meaning a sweet smell, is employed, Paul applying the metaphor to his colleagues and himself: '**... because we are the sweet aroma of Christ to God**'.

Imagine an expensive perfume poured upon someone's garments or body (as in the anointing of Jesus by Mary — John 12:3). The individual will exude fragrance, and those who are near will be aware of it. The apostle claims that an infinitely precious perfume, the Christ whom he preaches, has been diffused upon his person, that the ever-present Lord detects it, and that God is pleased with his ministry. It is impossible to believe that Paul is not thinking about Levitical sacrifices, his ministry resembling a burnt offering from which a sweet smell ascends.[7] The emphasis of 2:14b is repeated.

Not only so, but because the apostle moves in the world of men, some of whom are believers and others not, all those with whom he comes into contact sense the aroma. Although it is true that believers are saved already (2 Tim. 1:9; Titus 3:5) and that unbelievers are condemned already (Rom. 8:1; cf. John 3:18), salvation and condemnation are depicted as processes: **'those who *are* being saved ... those who *are* perishing'**. The meaning is that those who live for the gospel will inevitably be recognized for what they are: the aroma they give off cannot be suppressed. Or, to switch from the apostle's metaphor, the light cannot be concealed (Matt. 5:14). Perhaps Paul has in mind 1:21, where he tells the Corinthians that they are being confirmed in Christ. As the days go by, the saints love the Lord more dearly and intelligently, and unbelievers become more established in their unbelief. Both groups react in their distinctive ways, the former with a developing appreciation of gospel fragrance, and the latter with a growing sense of nausea.

2:16. ... to the latter a smell from death to death, and to the former a smell from life to life. And for these things who is sufficient?

The twofold principle is developed. It needs to be said that the twin expressions, **'from death to death'** and **'from life to life'**, are not the easiest to interpret. Perhaps they derive from a Hebrew turn of phrase in which emphasis is given by repetition. Hence, 'from death to death' would mean 'really, utterly and totally dead'. Compare with the expression 'from faith to faith' (Rom. 1:17) and the English idioms, 'going from bad to worse' and 'from strength to strength'.

But there could be another approach. As far as the elect are concerned, the gospel and its ministers reflect life and therefore exude the fragrance of reality. That is, objective truth and divine power generate a heart renewal. This might be the meaning of 'from life [the gospel as conveyed by the apostles] to life [for the convert]'. With regard to those who are perishing and who back away from the living God, Christ and all to do with him exude the stench of corruption. Hence, 'from death [the gospel, again as conveyed by the apostles] to death [for the unbeliever]'.[8] The issue is stark: life or death (cf. John 3:36).

Either way, Paul introduces a rhetorical question. Because standing in the centre ground, between the living and the dying, is a mammoth task, the apostle asks, in effect, 'Who can cope? Who is able to present life to those who might remain dead and simultaneously be a guide to those who have found life but who tend to stumble in the faith, as is manifestly the case at Corinth?' The apostle assumes the answer to be that his colleagues and he *are* competent because (to go back to 2:14) God leads them in triumph. He will say as much in 3:5: 'Our sufficiency is from God.' These statements are part of the overall attack on the pseudo-apostles who have been operating in Corinth. Whereas Paul has a God-given ministry which he is able to sustain, they have no ministry and are grossly inadequate.

2:17. For we are not like the many, peddling the word of God, but as from God we speak before God in Christ.

The offensive continues, the apostle affirming that he is unlike **'the many'** who are in the business of **'peddling the word of God'**. Note the suggestive present tense: this is happening even as Paul writes. 'Peddling', found only here in the New Testament, suggests a small-time tradesman, a huckster, someone out for quick and dishonest profit. Josephus uses the related noun when describing the Phoenicians, constitutional entrepreneurs gripped by the love of money.[9] The false teachers at Corinth and elsewhere are men of this calibre with 'many' adherents, all of whom appreciate that if mishandled with skill the gospel can be lucrative.

Paul is not such a person. Rather, he speaks from a platform of sincerity.[10] Not only has his message been granted to him **'from God'**, a dangerous statement were the apostle a liar, but when he does speak he is sensitive to the fact that he has among his auditors Almighty God as revealed by Christ: **'We speak before God in Christ'** (cf. 'in the sight of God', 4:2). For this reason he is always ultra-careful. And, unlike many, he does not labour for personal financial reward.

Application

Paul was unique and his life's work unrepeatable. None the less, time-honoured principles remain, and in these verses there is counsel for those who labour in the gospel and who sometimes find the going hard.

Remember that the apostle had surmounted immense difficulties at Ephesus and that Troas and the subsequent journey to Macedonia were not easy (7:5). Corinth must have weighed heavily upon Paul because of troubles within the church. He knew that disagreement among believers is always bad enough (as, for instance, when Barnabas and he fell out over the business of John Mark — Acts 15:39), but when vitriol was hurled in his face the apostle must have plumbed the depths.

In the event he kept control because of his keen faith and acute understanding of the gospel: 'Thanks be to God, who in Christ is always leading us in triumph' (2:14). When pressures are intolerable we call upon the Lord and turn to the ultimate book. We find grace to help in time of need. We fight on. We overcome.

It is also true that if a man is honest with God he will be able to face the people, even those (and especially those) who are less than helpful. Paul knew that the Almighty was his constant hearer and that his sincerity would be vindicated. On the other hand, hypocrisy never helps.

Personal commendations
(2 Corinthians 3:1-3)

Paul, having impugned his opponents' integrity by asserting that 'many' have been making merchandise of God's holy Word (2:17), advances steadily. Aware that these people are Judaizers who have striven to bring the church under the yoke of Moses[11] and that 'some' of them (3:1) came to Corinth bearing impressive letters of commendation, the apostle declares that they, the Corinthians, are his credentials and that he needs none other. The implication is that the interlopers have failed conspicuously in this all-important matter: where are the churches established through their efforts? But it is evident to all who have eyes to see that Paul's ministry is from the Lord.

The apostle does not major on the patent misinterpretation of Moses served up by the latter's misguided disciples. Rather, he advances to the heart of the matter by showing that Sinai, when rightly understood, has given way comprehensively and permanently to Christ.

3:1. Are we beginning to commend ourselves again? Or do we need — as some do — commendatory letters to you or from you?

The apostle accepts that when a Christian moves from one church to another he might be unknown by the receiving fellowship. Therefore the sending church would be wise to issue a letter of recommendation to ensure his welcome. Apollos is commended by the Ephesians to the Corinthians (Acts 18:27), and in 1 Corinthians 16:10-11 Paul writes on behalf of Timothy. 2 Corinthians as a whole could be interpreted loosely as a letter of commendation for Titus and his colleagues who were on the point of journeying to Corinth (8:22-24). Phoebe is commended to the Romans (Rom. 16:1), and Mark is to be accepted by the Colossians if and when he comes to them (Col. 4:10). Early on, Paul himself had been commended in the letter sent by the Jerusalem Council to the Gentile churches (Acts 15:25).

Time has passed, and by now the apostle is in need of no document to validate his ministry; emerging congregations in Asia and Europe speak for him. His comments in 3:1 are acidic. First, he has taken pains in the first two chapters to show that his attitude to the church has always been pure and remains above legitimate suspicion. He loves these people, and if he has altered his travel plans it is for their benefit. But Paul is shrewdly sensitive to the machinations of the gospel tradesmen to whom he alludes in 2:17. Further, he is aware that what he has written thus far will inevitably be interpreted by his detractors as his letter of recommendation. Because no man of standing would lower himself to write on Paul's behalf, they will claim, the apostle has had the gall to ingratiate himself with the naïve majority at Corinth.

Penetrating the devious minds of his opponents, the apostle accepts that when the letter is read out critics in the church will mutter that its author is slippery: 'Just take a look at this. The man is beginning to commend himself, and not for the first time. But hold on, we understand his motive. Paul knows that he has to have money when he comes here, and will require us to back him up when he moves on from Corinth. But although he depends upon us, we do not need him.'

Not so, anticipates the apostle. We can paraphrase his riposte: **'Are we** [= 'I'] **beginning to commend ourselves** [= 'myself'] **again? Or do we** [= 'I'] **need — as some** [i.e. anonymous trespassers at Corinth] **do — commendatory letters to you or from you?'** (as would be the demand of some).

The first of the two questions contains neither the Greek *mē*, which would presuppose a negative answer, nor the negative *ou*, which would anticipate a positive reply. Paul gives no hint, and leaves it to his readers to work the matter out. The second question does incorporate *mē*, implying a negative response: 'We don't need such letters, do we?' We are being regaled with sanctified sarcasm. Without naming names — the Corinthians understood who the troublemakers were —[12] the apostle has learned that the latter introduced themselves by making a show of impressive credentials and that these documents had been accepted with due admiration (cf. 11:4: 'You put up with it well'). Who issued these letters, and what were their specific contents, is unrevealed. Paul's barbed point is that although the sham apostles realized that they had to proffer evidence of their standing, on pain of rejection, he has no requirement for such paperwork. It remains obvious that he is a servant through whom the church has believed (1 Cor. 3:5,10). His work in Achaia and elsewhere speaks for itself, fruitful evangelism remaining a commendation more than adequate to ensure his acceptance when he travels again to the city and when at a later date it is time for pastures new. 'For it is not he who commends himself who is approved, but he whom the Lord commends' (10:18).

3:2. You are our letter, having been engraved in our hearts, being recognized and being read by all men...

If there appears to be sarcasm in 3:1, in 3:2 the apostle employs irony, a somewhat different weapon. He neither requires a written reference to bring to the church, nor needs them to provide a certificate which he can take on his way; he bears with him at all times a letter of reference — the Corinthian church! The meaning, as implied by the previous verse but made plain here, is that the evident blessing of God upon Paul's labours at Corinth is sufficient testimony both to the genuineness of his mission and to the integrity of his person. Hence he can write with supreme assurance that **'You are our letter.'**

There is more. The church, considered as a letter of commendation, has been **'engraved in our hearts'**,[13] this visa being etched by the Lord upon the apostle's self-consciousness. The Greek verb *eggegrammenē* behind 'engraved' means something inscribed so deeply that it cannot be erased in any circumstances.[14] The word occurs with a similar sense in Luke 10:20: 'Your names *are written* in heaven.' Because the Corinthians remain the Lord's, they will stand for all time as Paul's letter of commendation. Wherever he may go, he has this internal witness from God, and his confidence remains unshakeable: no man can deprive him of the happy awareness that the Lord has employed him in bringing in part of the harvest. What is written upon the heart cannot be misunderstood.[15] Even if others dispute his call, he treasures his conviction and retains a letter to read at leisure. It follows that if God has not found him wanting, what does the judgement of others matter? As he had written earlier, 'But for me it is a very small thing that I should be judged by you' (1 Cor. 4:3).

Although the establishment of the Corinthian church has confirmed Paul in his vocation, it also serves as a timely reminder to others. Hence the rider, **'being recognized and being read by all**

men'. The congregation, by no means obscure, cannot be overlooked, being perceived as the direct result of the apostle's labours; it has not been augmented by stray Christians coming in from elsewhere, and had Paul not visited the city the latter might still be without any Christian church. To make his point, the apostle utilizes a play on the somewhat similar Greek terms behind 'recognized' and 'read', although an English translation is difficult.[16] The sense is that the church remains a living document 'recognized' as God's public validation of his servant. The Corinthians can be 'read' by all who take note, acknowledging that such is the calibre of these people — notwithstanding inner tensions — that they are the seal of Paul's apostleship (1 Cor. 9:2). It follows that when he arrives at Corinth the saints are under an obligation to receive him.

When a traveller finds himself far from home he will take good care not to lose his passport, a document vital for his security. If and when he is homesick he may glance at it to reassure himself about how he stands; it breeds confidence. This is how it is for Paul. Better still, he cannot lose his Corinthian visa because it is stamped upon his heart; wherever he may go, this church shows others and tells him that his status is incontestable.

3:3. ... making it apparent that you are a letter of Christ ministered by us, having been engraved not with ink but with the Spirit of the living God, not on tablets of stone but on tablets that are hearts of flesh.

An endearing blend of dogmatic theology and pastoral gentleness is brought to bear. Paul begins — but only just — to open up the one issue which has threatened to destroy the Corinthian church and, for that matter, the Gentile mission spearheaded by the apostle: is salvation by alleged meritorious works, or through faith in a risen Saviour? Because for the first time in 2 Corinthians the tension between law and gospel, between a gross yet all-too-common misinterpretation of Moses' ministry *vis-à-vis* that of Christ, is broached, this and the following verses should not be considered solely on their own merits or in isolation from the heresy that was then rocking the churches.

Nor would it be an exaggeration to say that the issue confronting the first readers of Paul's letter remains the greatest possible challenge to the truth of the whole Bible. Which do we prefer — humble trust in a perfect and welcoming Saviour, or an exhibition of our supposed merits for the benefit and pleasure of Almighty God, works denounced by the apostolic umbrella term 'the elements of the world'? (Gal. 4:3,9; Col. 2:8,20). Among Paul's writings, his treatment of this collision of forces is particularly emphatic in the Galatian, Colossian and Roman epistles, as well as in 2 Corinthians. The conflict was never absent from his mind.

In more detail, the false apostles at Corinth were, as has already been said, Judaizers (11:22-23). Knowing this, and having rebutted his critics by explaining the reason for the change in his itinerary, Paul opens his doctrinal attack. Skirmishing finished, the main engagement commences. In spite of the deliberations of the Jerusalem Council, an assembly which sent a definitive message on the subject to the Gentiles (Acts 15), the heresy that functioning Judaism was essential for the well-being of the churches was still being promulgated. Nor was Corinth immune to the virus. If we take this into account we can interpret with some precision. To judge by Paul's apparent silence on the matter in 1 Corinthians, the · controversy flared up locally within the six-month interval between the writing of that letter and 2 Corinthians.[17]

According to 3:2, the Lord has engraved the Corinthians on the apostle's heart.[18] A remarkable metaphor,
it prompts us to ask how these men and women at
Corinth have come to mean so much to Paul? The
answer is that there has also been another, prior
printing, if it may be so expressed, in that the Lord
engraved, or stamped, Christ upon the hearts of the
Corinthians. This is the force of the word **'engraved'**
in 3:3 (Greek, *eggegrammenē*, as in 3:2): the people
show plainly that they are a letter of, or from, Christ,
ministered, it is true, by Paul but inscribed nevertheless by the Holy Spirit sent from God the Father.

The expression **'making it apparent'** (a present
participle, *phaneroumenoi*),[19] standing at the beginning of the Greek text of the verse, is emphatic: the
Corinthians display themselves to the world. Thanks
to God, they cannot be hidden (compare Matt. 5:14).
The Lord has set up a monument to his grace — and
Paul was involved (1 Cor. 3:10). The establishment of
the church was **'ministered'** (an aorist, *diakonē-
theisa*, pointing to a *fait accompli*) by a loyal minister,
and the pseudo-apostles had nothing to do with it.
More importantly, Moses' ministry, in all its erstwhile
splendour, could not have done this thing.

Now comes an important double contrast. First,
this engraving was not accomplished by men with
'ink', but rather from on high, **'with the Spirit of
the living God'**. The language is emphatic, meaning
that the Corinthians were transformed spiritually by
the Lord. Second, the letter was inscribed, **'not on
tablets of stone but on tablets that are hearts of
flesh'**.[20] There is an obvious allusion here to Exodus
24:12, where God promises Moses that when he
ascends Sinai he will be given stone slabs upon
which Yahweh will write his law.[21] Jeremiah 31:31-34
is also recalled, a passage which promises that when
the era of the 'new covenant' dawns, God's law will be

written by Yahweh upon the hearts of all the covenant members.[22]

The overarching message of 3:3 is that, whereas
characters set down in ink on papyrus or parchment
can be obliterated or written over, the Holy Spirit has
recorded God's righteous demands upon the heart of
each believer. This means that the 'writing' can never
fade, can never be effaced and cannot have anything
superimposed on it. It is indelible and internal. In
effect, a spiritual document incapable of destruction
has been brought into being. Both the writing and
the materials endure for ever.

But what is the point of the contrast? Throughout
his exposition Paul takes for granted a fundamental
principle, which is that men will only do what they
want to do. Because we are sinful by birth, by instinct and by behaviour, we may gaze at God's moral
law (which for the Jews was centred on the Ten
Commandments), but invariably walk away from it.
The demands imposed, by whatever means, upon the
unrepentant by the Almighty irritate them, remain
unattractive and are powerless to compel inveterate
sinners. The problem with the Judaizers was that
they did not understand the depths of human sinfulness, reckoning that they were sufficiently righteous
for God and that they showed this by offering what
they deemed satisfactory obedience to his commandments. Compare this attitude with Luke 11:39:
'Now you Pharisees make the outside of the cup and
dish clean, but your inward part is full of greed and
wickedness.' Paul knew better, as Romans 7:23 and
the surrounding context demonstrate. And he
grasped that what sinners never achieve, God has
performed. Because they have been renewed by the
Spirit, believers want to serve the Lord (2:9).

This clash between Moses misinterpreted and the
gospel was not late in manifesting itself at Corinth.
Although Gallio, the Roman proconsul, was not, it

seems, aware of a distinction between the Jews and the newly emerging church (Acts 18:12-16), tensions were in place already, to judge by the apostle's abandonment of the local synagogue and his employment of premises elsewhere in the city (Acts 18:7); at a very early period geographical separation became inevitable.

Paul bases his case upon an awareness that there can be no compromise between Sinai and the gospel, even though others — such as Peter and Barnabas on one notorious occasion (Gal. 2:11-14) — failed to see things with his clarity.[23] Obedience to God is impossible without the work of the Spirit, and the Spirit is given to induce us to turn to the Saviour. Moses' administration never provided this facility (as, Paul will disclose, Moses knew well), and the apostle makes it clear, first, that because of the triumph of Christ there is neither justification nor sanctification for the devotee of Sinai at the expense of the gospel, and that, second, in the Lord these are the fruits of a work far more splendid than anything offered by the old dispensation. Paul is showing that his proclamation has a standing far higher than Moses' ministry. Therefore, the false apostles, who do not appreciate what Moses *really* taught, are in gross error.

Application

'He who wins souls is wise' (Prov. 11:30), and the man who is blessed by the Lord to the conversion of others is conscious that it was not his doing. Moreover, he has food to eat of which some know nothing (John 4:32), an awareness that will render him proof against incoming missiles. If you are feeling depressed, tell someone about your Lord and back it up with a prayer for that person's conversion. If your petition is heard, stay humble.

Confidence and the 'new covenant' (2 Corinthians 3:4-6)

The Judaizers who came to Corinth were self-assured. Paul responds by asserting that he also is confident, but in another way. Although he does not commend himself (3:1), and although he acknowledges that he lacks sufficient personal resources for his work (3:5), he is sure of himself in that God has instituted him as a servant of what he terms 'the new covenant' (3:6); the fact that numerous churches have come into being through his ministry remains a stunning confirmation of the ministry given to the apostle. Conversely, in that Paul's critics have promulgated obedience to Moses' law, they deal out death to all who listen to them (3:6).

But there is a danger. Such are the dimensions of what he has written that the apostle must protect himself again from a charge of megalomania. Aware that the opposition is eagerly seeking any excuse by which to bring him down, Paul anticipates that any apparent boastfulness will be seized upon instantly. These verses are, therefore, something of a personal defence.

3:4. Such confidence we have through Christ towards God.

The apostle exercises **'such confidence'** in the truthfulness and the outcome of his mission. Because he is involved in a work the grandeur of which eludes comprehension, Paul applies a Greek word *(toiautē)* meaning 'such' or 'of this sort'. It is as if for a moment he stands back in wonder to exult in the design, beauty and vastness of a temple of which he has become one of the principal architects. At the same time he accepts gladly that there is a higher perspective: the unceasing triumphs of the gospel are all of God. The architect is not the proprietor, and certainly not the object of veneration within the temple. Paul is explicit: he retains his confidence **'through Christ'**, meaning that his work has been given to him by none other than the Saviour. Furthermore, he rejoices in this not only when he writes letters to Christians, in this case the Corinthians, but also in his private contemplations, meditations directed **'towards God'**. In his heart Paul blesses the Lord that he is certain of his ministry. All is of God, and the apostle does not aspire to anything else. Let certain difficult Corinthians, as haughty as they are antagonistic, take this into account. Would they be as eager to bless God for their high station, supposing that they had been granted such eminence? The suppressed question and its negative answer are obvious: pride kills gratitude.

3:5. Not that from ourselves we are adequate to reckon anything as from ourselves, but our adequacy is from God...

The principle opens out. A major theme of this epistle is that the Lord only uses those who are humble and weak; self-confidence is anathema to heaven. This conviction underlies, for example, 4:7-8; 6:4; 7:5-6; 11:30; 12:9-10. In 3:5 the language is careful and two-edged. Negatively, it is not the case that the apostle is **'adequate'** in himself even to suspect that his work derives from anything that flows **'from'** him:[24] it is beyond him even to think like this. Paul does not glow with magnanimity, a benign lord distributing pennies to the poor. Positively, he is sufficient for the task. **'But'**, a strong Greek word *(alla)* carrying overtones of the English idiom 'on the other hand', is brought in to reinforce the emphasis: with God all things are possible, and in the apostle's case this adequacy flows from within the Godhead.[25]

3:6. ... who has made us adequate as ministers of the new covenant: not of the letter but of the Spirit. For the letter kills, but the Spirit gives life.

We approach the heart of the letter: Paul's teaching about the **'new covenant'**, of which he is a **'minister'** (Greek, *diakonos*). This theme has been anticipated by 3:3, where a contrast is drawn between the inscribed tables of stone given to Moses and the tablet of the human heart engraved by the Spirit of God. In 2 Corinthians the word 'covenant' occurs only in this chapter (3:6,14 — with reference to the 'new' and 'old' covenants respectively), although it occurs also in 1 Corinthians 11:25 in connection with teaching about communion.

Because of the importance of the idea of 'covenant' we need to spend time with this verse.

1. Covenant

In the New Testament, as in the Septuagint, the Greek word for 'covenant', *diathēkē*, implies a unilateral decision, an arrangement originating from and established by a single individual or party rather than a joint declaration by two or more sides. Among Greek-speaking peoples in those days the word often stood for a man's last will or testament, an instruction for the disposition of his assets after death.[26] This is its undoubted meaning in Galatians 3:15 and Hebrews 9:16-17. The person who draws up his testament is in no way controlled by the wishes of others. Although he may take their views into account, ultimately he acts according to his free will.

2. God, men and covenants

In the Hebrew Scriptures the word which translates into English as 'covenant', *b'rit*, is employed very often with regard to contracts between God and men. Sometimes these arrangements are based on consent, when Yahweh presents terms to selected individuals who are required to accept them. At other times administrations are defined and brought into being by the Lord without prior consultation and with no demand for reciprocity. Perhaps the most outstanding example is the covenant signified by the rainbow: Yahweh informs Noah unilaterally that he will never allow a second worldwide flood (Gen. 9:12-17). In brief, in the Old Testament a covenant is either a declared will in which the testator is active and the other party purely a recipient, or it can be a conditional promise, the fulfilment of which depends upon the co-operation of the second party with the testator. But (to repeat) when God is involved, the common element shared by these two variant forms of covenant is that the Lord alone dictates the terms.[27] It is never the case that men propose a plan to Yahweh upon the basis of which he might enter into relationship with them, or is obliged to do so. He alone stipulates the conditions.

3. The Greek Old Testament

The notion of sovereignty is without doubt the main reason why the Jewish scholars who gave their Greek-speaking fellow-Hebrews the Septuagint version selected the word which can be transliterated as *diathēkē* to render the Hebrew *b'rit*. It is true that this translation word is slightly 'dynamic', not being a precise equivalent (are there ever precise equivalents?), but it possesses the merit of conveying the vital idea of God's initiative. There was, it is true, another Greek word, transliterated as *synthēkē*, meaning a bilateral settlement (compare the derived English 'synthesis', a placing together of at least two elements). The Septuagint translators could have requisitioned this for service but chose otherwise, almost certainly because although *synthēkē* is found occasionally in the Greek Old Testament, as in Isaiah 28:15, lamenting that a sinful people have made a 'covenant', or mutual agreement, with death, it suggests a two-way decision about the terms of an arrangement. This nuance would have been inappropriate with respect to divine covenants.[28]

4. The 'new covenant'

The term 'new covenant' occurs in 1 Corinthians 11:25,[29] and it may be assumed that the first readers, well taught by Paul, were not unaware of its importance by the time they received 2 Corinthians. Pointing to the relationship experienced by the Christian believer with his God, this covenant is deemed to be 'new' because it has replaced the obsolescent 'old covenant' (3:14) between Yahweh and Israel as mediated by Moses at Sinai.[30]

Or so Paul assumes. This is the heart of the controversy with false apostles who refuse to countenance the idea that the Sinai dispensation has ended. The apostle disagrees: because this 'new' arrangement has not only displaced the 'old', its inherent perfection means that it will never be superseded by anything better. There *can* be nothing superior, the Greek word behind 'new' *(kainē)* suggesting freshness, something that does not wear out. It may be new in time, but it possesses an undying relevance.

5. Justification and sanctification

There is one tremendous difference (at least) between
the presentation of the 'new covenant' in
1 Corinthians 11:25 and here in 3:6. In the former
passage Paul brought to the fore the fact that Christ
died for our sins. Although in 2 Corinthians we find
allusions to Exodus 24 and Jeremiah 31 — the latter
passage predicting that Israel under the 'new covenant' will *want* to honour God's law — 1 Corinthians
11:25 is concerned with a sinner's legal justification
rather than with the inner work of the Spirit.[31] Compare with Matthew 26:28, which tells that at the Last
Supper our Lord stressed that his blood, the 'blood of
the covenant', will secure the forgiveness of sins.
Although the outworking of the new covenant
achieves considerably more than this, because
1 Corinthians considers Christ's offering as the
fulfilment of Passover, justification has priority (cf.
1 Cor. 5:7: 'Christ, our Passover, was sacrificed for
us').

But whereas this truth is assumed in 3:6 and its
immediate context, it is not advertised. Paul con-
tends with adversaries who remain tragically optimistic about their innate capacity to obey the laws of
God. Although this was not a major concern in his
previous letter, developing problems in the church
compel him in 2 Corinthians to opt for a contrast
between the letter of the law and the work of the
Spirit: it is Jesus as proclaimed by Paul who grants
the Spirit, and it is the Spirit who renews the heart.[32]
Renewal was no part of Moses' ministry any more
than was justification. The apostle is aware that
when the two appear, they always do so in tandem.

6. 'The letter'

By **'letter'** is meant the law of Moses rather than a letter written by Paul or anyone else.[33] In context the apostle insists that the ministry granted to him is not an external ministry of demand, condemnation, or even of predictive promise, all recorded in inscribed characters. Rather, it leads directly to fellowship with God.

These words are pointed. Paul assumes that Moses' law presented Israel with a body of commands addressed through the eyes to the mind and heart. In the event the people were unwilling to honour it in spite of the fact that they had committed themselves to obedience (Exod. 19:8; 24:3,7). Because they defaulted they were condemned. Further, because the Lord was as gracious as he was realistic, and in the knowledge that Israel would remain disobedient, the delineation and then the institution of the book of the covenant are followed immediately by detailed prescriptions for a form of worship centred around the tabernacle. It is significant that Exodus 20-24 leads at once to Exodus 25-31, a block of righteous demands being succeeded by a routine which sketches the theoretical basis for reconciliation. The sequence shows that both components of the law (moral and civil-ceremonial) were intended to stretch Israelite minds. As many must have recognized throughout the era of the old covenant, this elaborate system was a blueprint for the person and work of Christ.

Otherwise expressed, the tabernacle arrangement was an inseparable part of the law given to Israel as the basis of what would be for the foreseeable future a conditional covenant.[34] The Lord stipulated that Israel would remain as his people and he as their God in the event of their obedience to his requirements, his fidelity being assumed. But not only was this an impossibility, given the pernicious sinfulness of the family of Jacob, the sacrificial system made no provision for *actually* justifying and renewing sinners when they fell, as Israel did continuously. This is why, historically, the covenant collapsed, albeit through no inherent design fault: 'You could not be justified in the law of Moses' (Acts 13:39). In short, the elements of Moses' legislation (popularly known to Jews as 'Torah', meaning 'teaching' or 'law') are like so many segments of an indivisible web, a web which can only deal out death to those who prefer to stick to what they misconceive to be God's final self-revelation.

7. 'The Spirit'

Paul indicates that his ministry is not of 'the letter' but, now, **'of the Spirit'**. Like the terms of the old covenant, those of the new administration have been laid down by God. Unlike Sinai, they are not dependent upon man's obedience even though the latter is a necessary duty.

At this point we need to be careful. Although belief in what the Bible says about Christ and reliance upon him are obligations incumbent upon all who hear the gospel (cf. Rom. 1:5: 'through whom [Christ] we have received grace and apostleship for *obedience* to the faith among all nations for his name'), they are neither merit-earning exercises nor do they lie within the ability of unregenerate men. Remember Ephesians 2:8, which tells us that although our faith is a condition of our salvation, it remains a sovereign gift of God, or 2 Peter 1:1, which opens a letter addressed 'to those who have *obtained* like precious faith'. What God requires he sometimes grants, among other blessings graciously providing an atonement for sin and also the faith that men must exercise when they approach the Saviour. This means that the new covenant is put into effect unilaterally by the God who bends the hearts of sinners, in consequence of which they want to honour him. Born again, they exercise 'freed will' (to coin a term) rather than 'free will', the latter being a mind-set which, if left to its own devices, will always deviate from things divine. Because of what the Lord does there is life in place of death, holiness in place of open sin, and mercy in place of condemnation.

This does not mean, let it be said, that converted Christians are slave robots, automatically responding to signals fed in by an external controller. They turn to the Lord because as rational beings they now desire to do so. To be impelled by the Spirit is not the same as being compelled.

8. The challenge

There is a sting at the end of 3:6 in that '**... the letter kills, but the Spirit gives life'**. The present tenses are luminous: sinners who ignore the gospel in favour of Moses, should they have basked in his light, are in the process of being consigned to death by Sinai, whereas those who follow the good news are being made alive. Which, then, will it be: law or gospel, the false apostles or Paul?[35]

9. A summary of 3:6

1. Although God has constituted Paul as a servant or minister of the new covenant, the apostle remains unworthy of such an honour. Yet he has been enabled to fulfil his responsibilities. **'Who'** (that is, God), commencing the verse, is powerful: **'who has made us adequate'**.

2. Unlike his opponents, the apostle can recall a time when God had definitely appointed him to office ('who *has made* us ...'). What of them?

3. The new covenant must be interpreted in terms of the Old Testament concept of covenant — a contract proposed by God.

4. The new covenant is unilateral and unconditional, its terms and its application deriving from God alone.

5. It involves the gift of the Holy Spirit, who grants life, transforming sinners so that they seek to do the will of God.

6. The new covenant is opposed to and replaces the conditional Sinai covenant, that of 'the letter', which, consisting largely but not solely of demands, failed deliberately and comprehensively to renew those to whom it was directed.

7. The former 'old' covenant (3:14) mediates condemnation and death to those who perversely misinterpret it as their route to fellowship with God.

There are other differences between the two covenants, and the New Testament takes pains elsewhere to point these out. This summary tries to bring into focus the agenda of 3:6, Paul being selective both in what he wishes to say and in what he prefers not to mention.

Application

In the work of evangelism, although the Lord uses his servants, it is not because there is anything in them that would be sufficient to lead others to Christ. Prayerfulness, personal integrity, understanding of the Bible and clear proclamation of the truth are essential, but none of these, even in the aggregate, can ever save a soul. A true conversion finds its dynamic within the Godhead and is a fruit of sovereign grace. Mercifully, the Lord employed others to bring us to faith, and he may even have used us in a similar fashion. Let us be grateful and diligent, and give him the praise.

Not only is the Bible uniquely a divinely inspired book, it is the only volume which reveals the doctrine of justification by faith. All other religions, ancient and modern, proffer death to their adherents because they prescribe salvation by works, a ladder made of sand which cannot deliver from hell and lead to heaven. We need to go to God's Word and stay there. This was Paul's burden as a minister of the 'new covenant'.

Two glorious ministries placed in contrast (2 Corinthians 3:7-11)

In these verses 'glory' occurs, both in noun and verb form, no less than ten times. The apostle contrasts the arrangement administered at Sinai with that centred upon Jesus Christ, of which he is an appointed servant. Paul concedes that the former dispensation was glorious, but asserts that the latter is infinitely more so, to the extent that in its light Moses' ministry appears inglorious. If the old system was, by universal consent, so marvellous, what, then, of the new?

The presentation is almost certainly a development of the attack upon the Judaizers. Their motivation has been called into question (2:17 and, by implication, 3:1), and Paul digs deeper: they have promulgated something which by design can never meet man's innermost needs and which is now redundant. It follows that the blind are leading the blind.

3:7. But if the ministry of death inscribed in letters on stone came in glory, so that the sons of Israel were not able to look at the face of Moses because of the discontinuing glory of his face...

Thus far in the letter the apostle has twice raised the theme of ministry: the Corinthians are said to be a letter of Christ 'ministered' by Paul (3:3), he personally being a 'minister' of the new covenant (3:6).[36] A contrast is now presented between the old and new

arrangements, the two opposed to each other both in
design and effect. The word **'ministry'** (Greek, *dia-
konia*) signifies an administration which dispenses
the provisions of its controlling covenant: Moses'
ministry fulfils itself, and so does that of the new
covenant.

Although this and the surrounding verses are
deeply doctrinal, the last thing that Paul offers is
doctrine unrelated to real life. The apostle indicates
that his avenue of service is far superior to that of
Moses, by which it is not implied that he is a better
man than was Moses; the issue is strictly impersonal. But Paul senses that he risks being castigated
as someone who holds in contempt those laws by
which ethnic Israel was required to live and worship.
This challenge was anticipated in 1 Corinthians 9:21,
where the apostle insists that, whereas he is not
controlled by Moses' law either in whole or in part, he
is subject to the law of Christ.[37] By this he means
that our Lord's teaching and his example are two
components (at least) of the moral imperative incumbent on believers. Now, he takes the matter further.

First, Paul assumes that his readers will be aware
of the book of Exodus, which is why he points to
chapters 20 and 34, the present verse opening up a
developed contrast between Moses' work and that of
the apostle. The former was glorious in that, among
other matters, it specified the sanctions of the laws of
God and dealt out death to transgressors. Condemnation as the just consequence of sin was its splendid, if melancholy, business. This **'ministry of
death'**, encapsulated in the Ten Commandments,
was **'inscribed'** (transliterated from Greek, something like 'entyped') on two stone tablets because it
was meant to be operative for the foreseeable future.[38] And it was none other than God who chiselled
it out. Moses understood the sombre implications
because he knew what was in the heart of man, and

Paul stands with him in this: 'For Moses writes about the righteousness which is of the law, "The man who does these things shall live by them"' (Rom. 10:5; cf. Gal. 3:12). But what of the man who does not do 'these things'? In themselves the commandments were immaculate and the joy of God's true people, even though Sinai asked for more than the tribes of Jacob would want to give. 'The law of the Lord is perfect' (Ps. 19:7). The problem was that ethnic Israel was distinctly imperfect. A collision was inevitable, and it soon came when Aaron led the people into gross idolatry (Exod. 32).

When Moses descended from Sinai his face shone supernaturally to such an extent that the children of Israel were — observes Paul — **'not able'** to look at him, but not because of any repellent tendency in Moses; sinful people were terrified by the majestic presence of God. The apostle is aware that prior to Moses there had been nothing like this and that at that time his ministry was as indispensable as it was unique. It came into being **'in glory'**, a magnificent thing because it originated with the God of Israel and exhibited his righteousness in relation to sinners. Paul claims elsewhere that it remains holy, righteous, good and spiritual (Rom. 7:12,14).

But — and it is a huge 'but' — when contrasted with the good news of Jesus, this ministry is seen to have had fundamental limitations. They were there all the time, but in the clear light of the gospel day they have become patently obvious. Paul realizes that there is a need for exposition.

First, Moses' dispensation was strictly *negative*: it was the herald and instrumental cause of death, and life is far better than death. Because the people were law-breakers, Moses' legislation presumed their just condemnation.

Second, it was an *external* ministry. The demands of the law were engraved on stone rather than upon human hearts, 'heart' meaning personality, a man's true ego. Tablets of stone could be, and in the event were, smashed (Exod. 32:19), whereas an inscription on the heart becomes, so to speak, the permanent expression of its bias. At Sinai the people's affections were unmoved by the letter of the external law presented to them, their instinctive resistance to the Lord remaining undiminished. When Moses brought God's commands to Israel there was a confrontation: holy demand was met by perverse refusal. The ensuing explosion became a leading motif within the Old Testament dispensation.

Third, Moses' ministry was designed to be *temporary*, although not in the short term. The fading sheen on the legislator's face was emblematic of the fading lustre of his work (Exod. 34:29-35), implying — as Paul sees the matter — that in time there would be another, superior ministry. Moses passes from the scene in deference to the Victor over the grave. The apostle employs a Greek verb, *katargeō*, translated here as **'discontinuing'**, to signify ineffectiveness, exhaustion or even termination. For example, according to 1 Corinthians 2:6, the rulers of this world are fading away, the same word being used.[39] In 3:7 Paul assumes and interprets.

Although Exodus 34 does not state that the radiance on Moses' face passed away, the apostle takes it for granted that Moses veiled his face so that Israel could not gaze upon the disappearance of this glory, his vanishing facial splendour representing Moses' temporary ministry (3:13).[40] The apostle builds upon the fact that Exodus 34:33 reveals that when Moses had finished speaking to Israel with an uncovered face, he *then* donned the veil until such time as he went to speak with the Lord. To repeat, according to the apostle, Moses had no objection to the people seeing his glory, but he denied them the spectacle of

a vanished glory. Why this was so is discussed by
3:13.

Fourth, when Moses came down from Sinai his
face shone with such an intensity that *all who saw
him were afraid* to come too close (Exod. 34:30),
preferring to witness the radiance safely from a
distance. As noted earlier, they averted their gaze.

At this point Paul advances, his four negatives
ushering in a number of positive inferences, 3:7
flowing into 3:8 as one sentence.

3:8. ... how, rather, will not the ministry of the Spirit be in
glory?

First, the new covenant is in no sense an instrumental cause of death. On the contrary, Christ
crucified, risen and glorified is *the source of life*
through the Holy Spirit. This is why Paul refers to the
covenant as **'the ministry of the Spirit'**, developing
the thought of 3:6 ('the new covenant ... of the
Spirit').

Second, this ministry of, or from, the Spirit grants
renewal. Sinners are transformed into willing saints.
Moses' legislation was an external ministry incapable
of changing attitudes. Now, in Christ, the Holy Spirit
generates reversed preferences: with their hearts
liberated from the dominion of sinful desire, men
turn to the Lord.

Third, the ministry of the Spirit *will never be
rendered obsolescent.* Perhaps the operative words in
3:8 are **'will ... be in glory'**, the future tense being a
magnificent understatement. Looking back, we know
that whereas the old covenant came relatively late in
time, perhaps about seven centuries after Abraham,
and functioned for one and a half millennia until
being retired in favour of the new covenant, the latter
was inaugurated in the first century A.D. in what

Hodge finely terms 'the certain sequence'.[41] Having arrived, it exercises itself permanently. The blossom bears fruit, and much of it.

Fourth, *there is no fear*. Whereas disobedient Israelites at Sinai had reason to be terrified by the sight of Moses' glorious face, the Christian believer is in direct relationship with God. Compare with 3:18: 'But we all with a face that has been unveiled, and beholding the mirrored glory of the Lord, are being transformed into the same likeness from glory to glory.'

Sanctified logic supervenes in the form of a rhetorical question: **'How, rather, will not the ministry of the Spirit be in glory?'** If the old and negative was unquestionably splendid, the ever-new and positive is immeasurably more glorious. In that the polarities are opposed, the relationship is that of infinite contrast, a magnificent juxtaposition. The reader is expected to draw his own conclusion and to grant his eager assent to the proposition.[42]

3:9. For if by the ministry of condemnation there was glory, how much more does the ministry of righteousness abound in glory!

Paul has depicted his ministry as that of 'the new covenant', implying an old covenant, and has shown that the former is the fountain of life rather than death in that it involves the activity of the Holy Spirit (3:6,8). Now an additional contrast is laid down between the old and the new arrangements. When it had no superior rival to humble it, the divinely appointed instrument of death was incomparably wonderful. However, the new covenant shows itself to be far more glorious in that it administers what Paul terms **'righteousness'**. The consuming fire of Sinai's mountain has given place to the radiance of Christ,

and the gospel is said to **'abound in glory'**. Unlike
the rhetorical question of 3:8, we are given a flat
statement;[43] this is how it is.

We need to step carefully. In a sense Moses' administration *did* exhibit the righteousness of God in
defining, detecting and condemning evil (as well as
anticipating Christ). Paul divulges in Romans 7:7
that 'I would not have known sin except through the
law.' For this reason it would not be inaccurate to
consider Sinai as in its own fashion a ministry of
righteousness. God is always right in his dealings
with men and angels, both holy and wicked, because
he can be no other, his righteousness being the
outward reflex of his essential holiness. Moreover,
since 'righteousness' is a relational term, the triune
God is righteous within himself.[44]

With regard to those personalities whom God has
created for his pleasure, the Bible shows that if they
are sinful and do not obtain mercy, they remain the
just objects of condemnation. This is one species of
righteousness, as in Psalm 51:4: 'You are justified
[= righteous] when you speak, and blameless when
you judge.' Yahweh's denunciation of David's sin was
acknowledged by the erring king as righteous, and in
Romans 3:4 Paul alludes to this, giving the principle
a universal application: 'Let God be true but every
man a liar.'

Yet there is another, grander, manifestation of
divine righteousness, and it is to this that 3:9 refers.
The emphasis, just for the moment, turns away from
the theme of inner renewal and sanctification to that
of forensic justification, the declaration by God that a
believing sinner is deemed legally guiltless because of
Calvary. God's rightness, so to speak, gratuitously,
but not improperly, sent Jesus to suffer and properly
upholds all who repent and commit themselves to the
Saviour. He who was inherently righteous died for
the inherently unrighteous as their sin-bearer (5:21;

1 Peter 3:18). Because of the perfections of the Lord Jesus and his reception in heaven by the Father, all who turn to Christ *must* find acceptance at the throne of God; it would be unjust for the Father to turn away any who attach themselves to the Son by faith. 'If we confess our sins, he [the Father] is faithful and just [= righteous] to forgive us our sins and to cleanse us from all unrighteousness' (1 John 1:9). The New Testament is specific: 'The [saving] righteousness of God is revealed' in the gospel (Rom. 1:17).

Whereas Sinai knew nothing about this, the gospel knows nothing other than this. This is the message of 3:9. Moses was given a glorious work, but Paul was the steward of a ministry immeasurably more magnificent than Sinai, gracious justification because of Christ displaying a glory far exceeding the splendour of righteous condemnation. The implication is that because they profess to look to Moses, the pseudo-apostles and their acolytes do not understand. Although Paul at this point does not say as much, he implies that justification because of Christ remains the only way forward. He anticipates that his readers will accept that this is the case.

3:10. Also, that which has been glorified has not been glorified in this respect — on account of the surpassing glory.

The apostle raises the temperature to boiling point, beginning by stating the obvious — that the theophany at Sinai was sublime. We can only attempt to imagine the spectacle confronting Israel at that place and time: a shaking mountain, flame, cloud and the sound of a supernatural trumpet. The angels of God were there.[45] Above all, the voice of Yahweh addressed some two million souls. Later, when Israel begged for Moses to be their mediator, his face shone.

Paul sums this up brilliantly by enlisting a Greek term (a neuter perfect passive participle, *to dedoxasmenon*) meaning **'that which has been glorified'** (by God). This points back to the superseded glory of the previous revelation. It is as if the apostle indicates that the Lord made certain that the giving of the law would be accompanied by a degree of glory never to be forgotten. But, remarks Paul, such is the wonder of the new covenant that it has the effect of making the old administration appear virtually ignominious. The latter **'has not been glorified in this respect — on account of the surpassing glory'**.[46] In its time, Moses' dispensation radiated a God-given splendour, and in its way that splendour persists. This is accepted gladly. But because the Lord has brought in an infinitely superior system there can only be contrast rather than comparison.[47] Viewed in the surpassing light of its successor, Sinai is dark and gloomy, standing in deep shade. On the Mount of Transfiguration Moses and Elijah appeared in glory, but the splendour of the Son of Man exceeded that of both (Luke 9:28-36). Although Mosaic law remains an object of admiration and instruction for the new-covenant believer (cf. Rom. 7:9; Gal. 3:24), in this all-important matter, at least, it has been abased.

This verse must have caused the false apostles and their adherents intense pain. It was certainly meant to bring them to their senses. Busily retreating from Christ, allegedly to serve a system that had been dismissed, they forgot (if they ever knew) that it is the ultimate glory of God to forgive undeserving sinners. Calvary towers above Sinai. Glory is given to God in the highest because a Saviour has been born (Luke 2:11-14).

3:11. For if that [which is] being discontinued was through glory, how much more is that which remains in glory!

Sanctified reason is called for by the apostle, who assumes that something which fades away is by definition inferior to that which abides in undiminished splendour. The ministry of death (3:7), alias that of condemnation (3:9), is said here to be moving to its predetermined end. The Greek verbal noun *to katargoumenon*, standing for the old dispensation, **'that** [which is] **being discontinued'**, is cast into the present tense and is either passive, meaning that God is winding up the Sinai administration even as Paul writes, or is perhaps set in what is termed the 'middle voice', suggesting that Moses' arrangement is in the process of bowing out gracefully because it accepts that its work is done and that the gospel must supervene. Either way, this assertion is comparable with Hebrews 8:13: 'What is becoming obsolete and growing old is ready to vanish away.' Further, the Greek term behind **'that which remains'**, *to menon*, is both active and couched in the present tense, declaring that the new system has come into operation and is immune to redundancy.

There is more. This thing being brought to nothing was originally introduced **'through'**, or 'by means of', **'glory'**.[48] At its inception it was accredited by the manifest glory of the Lord, glory being the medium through which it was seen by the people. It is otherwise with the new covenant, the thing which remains. It has been revealed **'in glory'**, which means that the gospel is impregnated with splendour. Whereas the first covenant was validated by an outburst of glory, its successor *is* glory.[49] Yet again, the clear implication is that Paul's antagonists are backward-looking, with little or no appreciation of the marvel of redemption. As far as the apostle is concerned, they appear not to know God.

It is true that in many of his letters, notably Galatians and Colossians, the apostle grapples with Judaizers, professing Christians of Hebrew extraction who were circulating within the churches. What, then, is different about 2 Corinthians? At Corinth Paul's message and authority were being undermined to an extent that is not so obvious elsewhere. There is in this letter a much more personal slant because the apostle has to demonstrate the folly of those who usurp leadership at his expense. Paul defends both the gospel and his office because they are inseparable.

Application

Christianity has been operative for two millennia, albeit in a variety of forms; sects and denominations have proliferated. Neither it nor they are about to vanish. Happily, there is a twin-track procedure by which we can estimate the integrity or otherwise of any particular expression of the faith. First, we need to look carefully at the manner of life of its proponents: 'By their fruits you shall know them' (Matt. 7:20). Second, we must examine the system in question and try to see how it functions. This is how Paul handled the pseudo-apostles, showing that their theology was grossly inadequate and its logical outcome tragedy in the making. By no means all that glittered at Corinth was gold. Scrutinize heterodox teaching and ponder where it would lead you. Test every fragment of strange doctrine against the Bible and ask if it can really be from God.

Nor is this an academic exercise. Sinai's administration was God-given, but in Paul's day it was passing away in favour of the gospel. What, then, of all other religions which by definition never came down from heaven? They must vanish, and their adherents can never inherit the earth. This is why we must look to the Jesus promised by the Old Testament and presented by the New.

The people of the old covenant and those of the new
(2 Corinthians 3:12-18)

The gulf between Moses' ministry and that entrusted to Paul is elaborated by an examination of Exodus 34:29-35 concerning Moses' descent from Sinai. Aware that the supernatural glow of his face was fading and that a diminishing facial radiance represented an inherently obsolete covenant, he veiled himself so that Israel would not comprehend the symbol and from that deduce the reality (3:12-15). On the other hand, Paul and his colleagues have no such reluctance, being assured that the new covenant can never be outdated and that the believer's likeness to Christ must be enhanced as time goes by (3:17-18).

The apostle also throws out a promise: if and when anyone turns to the Lord (which, he assumes, most Israelites, unlike Moses, never do), that person will behold his glory (3:16).

3:12-13. Having, therefore, such a hope, we employ much boldness, and not as Moses who used to place a veil over his face so that the sons of Israel should not look at the end of that [which was] being discontinued.

The apostle personalizes the tension between the two covenants, drawing a contrast between Moses and himself in terms of their respective ministries. It is almost as if Paul reveals the mind of Moses at the time when the prophet ascended Sinai some one and a half millennia earlier. This is in 3:13, following 3:12, where the apostle gives expression to his own immense confidence.

'**Therefore**', because of the enduring glory of the ministry that has been entrusted to him, the apostle retains **'such a hope'** (3:12). Paul has no doubts about the prosperity of the new covenant of which he is a minister: it cannot fail to achieve the grand object for which it has been designed. Christ, through the Holy Spirit, will grant life, communicate the verdict of justification and renew sinful hearts. It will operate until the end of the age. The apostle retains an assured hope that it will indeed be so. Absolute and ultimate truth parades itself openly and unashamedly, concealing nothing and triumphing in its gift of life.

For this reason Paul is bold when he speaks. There is no reticence because no hypothetical and as yet undisclosed revelation from the Lord will ever supplant his ministry. In the apostle's day **'boldness'** (Greek, *parrēsia*) was a privilege of the free man, one who was entitled to speak confidently and without restraint about any matter. Paul enjoyed such freedom, whereas Moses, lacking a life-giving ministry, acted under a conscious constraint.[50] It is the chief glory of God to save rather than to condemn, which means that because the good news tells of salvation it will never be superseded. Its service will never grow old as did Moses' preparatory administration.

The apostle's comprehension of Moses' self-awareness is astonishing if it is recalled that Exodus 34:33-35, which tells about the prophet covering his face, does not disclose the motive for this unusual act even though it might be implied. Nor is light shed on the matter elsewhere in the Old Testament. It follows that, were we to remain with Exodus, a veil would lie over the whole affair. Negatively, the Exodus passage does not suggest that Moses, alarmed by the people's retreat from him, covered his face in order to restore contact. As Paul perceives the matter, there was a more profound reason, and it is only through studying 3:12-13 that we begin to understand. Questions arise.

1. How *does Paul know why Moses wore a veil?*

We need to remember this word 'veil' (Greek, *kalymma*, something which conceals) because it will be important when trying to interpret 3:16. It is improbable that the apostle bases his theology upon an unsupported inference, which suggests that the only way in which he grasps why Moses covered his face must be by means of a direct revelation: the Lord must have informed the apostle about the lawgiver's undeclared reason for concealment.[51] If this was not so then Paul is indulging in rash speculation at best and fantasy at worst.

But the apostle is not fantasizing. Nor is he rash. Nor is he dabbling in a make-believe of Jewish myth to bolster his ministry (cf. Titus 1:14: '... not giving heed to Jewish fables and commandments of men who turn from the truth'). He comprehends why Moses was so reticent, and why he himself does not share that reticence. And he tells all.

2. Why *did Moses wear a veil?*

The apostle goes further than the Old Testament, revealing that Moses habitually covered his face so that the children of Israel would be unable to stare at the **'end'** (Greek, *telos*, meaning a cessation or terminus) of his facial glory.[52] So far, so good. But it is not far enough. Why did Moses do this? Why was it deemed necessary that Israelite eyes should not gaze upon the culmination of the fading process?[53] Had they noticed it they would surely have peered intently, for which reason Moses denied them the opportunity. At this point Paul does not give us a clear answer. Nevertheless, in the light of 3:14 we can safely draw an inference.[54]

Notice that it was not the fading process as such that was screened. To repeat, what Moses (as interpreted by Paul) did not want the congregation to see was the 'end' of **'that** [which is] **being discontinued'**. He did not intend them to behold a formerly shining face which after a space of time (just how long is not known) reverted to its normal appearance.

Overall, the entity that was passing away was undoubtedly 'the old covenant' (3:14), corresponding to the fading glory on Moses' face (3:7). The prophet's vanishing radiance represented the temporary nature of his ministry: 'The law was given by Moses but grace and truth came through Jesus Christ' (John 1:17). In effect, the facial appearance of the prophet symbolized the quality of the ministry that had been entrusted to him as the faithful senior servant in God's house (Num. 12:7). In denying Israel the spectacle of a cancelled glory, Moses prevented them from appreciating that the Sinai covenant would in due course come to an end. There was, so to speak, a cover-up both of the prophet's face and the governing principle.

3. Why was Israel kept in ignorance that the covenant between Yahweh and themselves was strictly temporary and by implication preparatory?[55]

Part, though not the whole, of the answer to this question lies in the sad fact that most Israelites were unregenerate. When Moses was away from them for the first forty-day session upon Sinai they apostatized and displayed their perversity by worshipping a golden calf (Exod. 32:1-9). If we take into account the glory of the theophany seen by this sinful people we may conclude that a further revelation at that time and at that place would have been an intolerable burden. They were granted as much as they were able to digest, but no more. Such was their spiritual and moral inertia that they would have been unwilling to plumb the more remote mysteries of God had they been revealed. Ultimate truth cannot be appreciated by carnal, unregenerate men (1 Cor. 3:1). Paul is terse: 'Their thoughts were hardened' (3:14).

Although at Sinai the children of Israel asserted no less than three times that they would be obedient to the terms of the covenant (Exod. 19:8; 24:3,7), the golden-calf incident showed otherwise. Nevertheless, if considered as an isolated event, this tragedy might not have afforded final proof of the ingrained, sinful bias of the people; time was needed to show that the commandments would never renew evil hearts. In its own fashion, the period from the settlement in Canaan until the coming of the Saviour was rather like a lengthy laboratory experiment in which the quality of Israelite piety was tested to destruction by continuous exposure to divine law. Would they, could they, obey if denied the grace of God? In the event, never. The fear of the Lord was seen to be absent from the overwhelming majority of Jacob's children, those who were not included among the elect remnant, the ideal seven thousand of the time of Elijah (1 Kings 19:18; Rom. 11:4). This long-term experiment was severe, involving, among other matters, the chastisement of the Babylonian exile. In short, the virulence of original sin was established as a firm principle admitting of no exceptions. Only later, centuries after Sinai, would there be a revelation of the greater glory of God in Christ. Then the old system would be displaced by the new covenant to which it had always pointed. Guidelines had to be laid down prior to the institution of the final arrangement:

'For Christ is the end of the law for righteousness to every one who believes' (Rom. 10:4). But none of this was on the immediate agenda at Sinai.

It follows that at the mountain the multitudes might well have supposed that the prophet's radiance, just like the covenant between them and Yahweh, was permanent. They would not have been able to imagine anything else. If so, when he covered his face Moses did not disillusion them. Nor did he perpetrate a lie; because they did not have a heart for the whole truth, it was not the time for a perfect revelation. Hence the veil. The people were left as they were found, in their hardened condition.[56] It was with them as with so many in later years who heard our Lord, who remarked to his disciples that 'To you it has been given to know the mystery of the kingdom of God; but to those who are outside, all things come in parables, so that "seeing they may see and not perceive, and hearing they may hear and not understand, lest they should turn and their sins be forgiven them"' (Mark 4:11-12).

Look at it in this way. Because young children in a primary school are unable to appreciate complicated mathematics they are denied algebra. They will probably not be aware that there is such a discipline. Yet if they are keen their appetite for knowledge will expand steadily and their time will come. On the other hand, if in their earliest years they are dull they may not want to know more, and should someone talk about the concept of learning algebra they might react negatively. As time passes children of this ilk fall behind other youngsters, at best content with a few half-understood morsels of elementary instruction. Even their multiplication tables remain a problem. At Sinai the Lord gave a primary lesson through his servant Moses, and that was enough for the time being: Israel would not have been able to advance. To make matters worse, even then the twelve tribes were dull, and had Moses divulged news about a future covenant the nation would have been contemptuous. Tragically, succeeding generations failed to sense that their lawgiver had provided a foundation, and that there was more — very much more — to the syllabus. Indeed, Moses prepared for redundancy before he died, telling Israel, albeit guardedly, that there would be another, greater, Prophet.[57] But the passing of the centuries showed that they did not want to know.

3:14. But their thoughts were hardened. For until this very day the same veil remains over the reading of the old covenant, it not being lifted away — because in Christ it is being discontinued.

The apostle vaults across a time-gap of one and a half thousand years, from Sinai to his own century: **'But their thoughts were hardened. For until this very day the same veil remains.'** Important issues are introduced.

1. Hardened minds

The verse opens with the strong 'but' (Greek, *alla*): '*But* their thoughts were hardened.' Because 'hardened' is passive, implying an external hardening agent (God),[58] the meaning is that it was not granted to unbelieving Israel to see the eclipse of Moses' radiance. There was nothing to be gained. Had they seen the vanishing vision their sinful hearts would have remained adamant. 'What of it?' might have been their rejoinder. Or, worse, they would possibly have taken this as yet another reason to reject Moses, a resentment to which they were addicted.[59] Why should *they* follow a fading administration?

In the New Testament 'harden' has a harsh connotation: the hearts of the disciples are so hard that

they do not understand spiritual truth (Mark 6:52;
8:17-18, the latter alluding to Isa. 6:9-10 and Jer.
5:21), and the Jewish crowds are unable to discern
the soon-to-suffer Messiah among them (John 12:40,
citing Isa. 6:10). A majority within Israel do not
accept the way of faith because their hearts have
been made hard (Rom.11:7-8, citing Deut. 29:4 and
Isa. 29:10).

In sum, not only does hardness of mind and heart
mean a gross unwillingness to heed the truth of God,
it is also a condition for which the sinner is solely
responsible, yet which God sometimes allows, even
ordains, but which God alone can heal. Deuteronomy
29:4 brings out the last truth powerfully: 'Yet to this
day Yahweh has not given you a heart to perceive
and eyes to see and ears to hear.' In 3:14 the apostle
is saying that at Sinai most of the sons of Israel were
left in their sins, and that in Paul's own day an
identical situation pertains.

The Greek *noēma* behind 'thoughts' occurs elsewhere in the New Testament (2:11; 4:4; 10:5; 11:3;
Phil. 4:7), and seems to have been a favoured word of
Paul, standing for a mind-set, or even purpose or
design, as is definitely the case in 2:11: 'We are not
ignorant of his [Satan's] *thoughts.*' At Sinai, throughout the settlement and now in their synagogues, the
Hebrews had, and have, no intention of giving serious thought to the Word of God. The family intention
was determined long ago.

2. The reading of the 'old covenant'

Because the expression **'old covenant'** occurs nowhere else in the New Testament it must have a
pointed meaning.[60] The apostle asserts that whenever
excerpts from the Law of Moses are read out in the
Jewish synagogue (each individual portion standing
for the five books of Moses, Genesis to Deuteronomy

inclusive), it is as if Moses were there in person. As at Sinai, when the veil concealed the prophet's diminishing radiance and when Israel was unable to discern the temporary nature of the God-given covenant, so it still is among the Jews. Like their forefathers they are debarred from appreciating that Moses' ministry had always been destined to fade.[61] Obdurate, they profess that they can justify themselves by what they calculate is an adequate obedience to the law and by rendering compensation in the event of transgression.[62] When the rabbi stands to read from the inspired Torah his words are, so to speak, covered.[63] The attentive congregation is impervious to the built-in inadequacies of the Sinai arrangement.

We need to observe that there is a delicate and unobtrusive equilibrium in 3:14 between divine sovereignty and man's responsibility. Although the Lord could have opened the hearts of the people at Sinai, he did not. Even so, their blindness was their sin. Similarly, the fact that he has not unlocked the hearts of many of Paul's Jewish contemporaries in no way mitigates their perversity. Not only will they not turn to Christ that they might have life, it is also the case that they are permitted to continue to misinterpret Moses (compare John 5:40,46-47), an inertia for which they alone are answerable. In his day Moses told Israel that they had seen with their eyes yet refused to take to heart all that the Lord had done for them (Deut. 29:1-4). Paul's point is that the tragedy persists.

3. Moses and Christ

The apostle is aware that he has been positioned at the turn of the ages: the old covenant is, even as he writes, **'being discontinued'** (3:14). The truth is conveyed vividly by a Greek verb, *katargeitai*, which has appeared in 3:7,11,13. As in those verses, it occurs here in the present tense and (probably) the passive voice, giving emphasis to what was happening in the first Christian century to an outdated system. And the Lord was achieving this displacement **'in Christ'**. The old was being replaced by the new, promise by reality, the demands and the anticipations of the earlier covenant by gospel provision, and shadow by substance.

But none of this has been revealed to the majority of the Jewish people. It is likely that Paul employs a play on words to bring out the force of such an important statement. A loose translation shows the sense: **'The same *cover* [= veil] ... remains, it not being *uncovered* that in Christ it** [that is, the old covenant] **is being discontinued.'**[64] God was in control, and although the Jews ought to have known what was happening, they did not — and the Lord allowed them to remain cloaked in spiritual darkness. Even though the truth about the Saviour did not lurk in a corner (Acts 26:26), it was screened from Israel. Had the Jews been looking to Jesus they would have beheld the glory of their Messiah and in that light would have recognized Moses' ministry for what it once was.

3:15-16. But until this very day whenever Moses is read, a veil lies over their heart, though whenever someone turns to the Lord, the veil is removed.

Paul employs repetition for the sake of emphasis. At the inception of the Sinai covenant a veil dropped gently but certainly upon the reading of the law (3:14). The same veil currently blankets the heart of every unbelieving hearer in the synagogue (3:15). The earlier phenomenon has given rise to the latter, and the latter is an intensification of the former. **'Their heart'** stands for the collective will of the people of

Israel who do not wish to appreciate the inner meaning of the law. This dullness has continued, laments the apostle, **'until this very day'** and is manifest **'whenever Moses is read'**. A thick darkness covers the ancestral people of God.

But there is good news: **'Whenever someone turns to the Lord, the veil is removed'** (3:16). There is more to this statement than meets the eye.

1. The apostle generalizes

The promise is for every Jew (although the Gentile is by no means excluded). And this good news is valid at any time. Hence the absence of the third person pronoun in the underlying Greek, as if to emphasize the blessedness which results 'whenever' anybody turns.[65]

2. Turning to the Lord means repentance and faith

'Turns' translates a Greek verb, *epistrephō*, which occurs, for example, in Acts 3:19: 'Repent therefore and be *converted*, that your sins may be blotted out'; and in 1 Thessalonians 1:9: 'For they themselves declare ... how you *turned* to God from idols to serve the living and true God.' There are many other examples in the New Testament. The implication of 3:16 is that Israel's basic failing is that of unspirituality: self-alienated from their God, they do not desire him.

3. 'Lord' points to Christ and implies that he is God

To turn to the one is to turn to the other. The Greek word rendered 'Lord' is the Septuagint's *Kyrios*, the only word used to translate 'Yahweh', and Paul provides a deliberate parallel.

4. The verb 'removed' is significant

Again, we have to consult the background Greek, in this case *periaireō*, which means 'to remove or strip away a cover that is wrapped around something else'.[66] Fairly common in the Septuagint, where it usually translates a Hebrew verb meaning 'to cause to turn or to unwind',[67] it is found in Exodus 34:34: 'But whenever Moses went in before Yahweh to speak with him, he [Moses] would *take the veil off* until he came out.'

There can be little doubt that 3:16 alludes to the Septuagint of Exodus 34:34, picking up the words for 'removal' and 'veil', and that it does so for two reasons: first, to declare the promise of the gospel; and, second, to draw an unfavourable contrast between Moses and the non-Christian Jews who profess to obey him.[68]

Moses sought the Lord. When he did so he necessarily turned away from the people: 'Then Moses returned to Yahweh, and said, "Oh, these people have sinned a great sin, and have made for themselves a god of gold!"' (Exod. 32:31). It was then that he would remove the veil. This is the explicit testimony of Exodus 34:34.[69] The apostle implies that those who imitate the prophet, who turn from apostate Judaism and who seek the Lord (that is, Jesus Christ) discover that the veil drops from their eyes. Not only do they comprehend the glory of the Messiah, they understand the role of Moses and of the law within the overall scheme of salvation. This is the promise.

Negatively, the fact was that in Paul's day (as since) most Jews neither turned to the Lord nor imitated the faith of Moses. They did not save themselves from a perverse generation (Acts 2:40). They could not be considered as Moses' disciples because they did not do as he did. Having elected not to comprehend the one whom he served, they remained insensitive to the inner meaning of Moses' Christ-orientated ministry. Compare with our Lord's statement that 'He [Moses] wrote about me' (John 5:46). Their blindfold remained.

In passing, we ought to observe that Paul's interpretation of Scripture is that of an inspired genius. He understood that, according to Exodus 34:33-34, Moses at Sinai backed away from his apostate people prior to turning to the Lord. Have the false apostles perceived this?

3:17. For the Lord is the Spirit, and where the Spirit is — freedom!

This verse develops 3:16, the emphasis falling upon the final word, **'freedom'**, as if Paul rejoices in the awareness that when a Jew turns to the Saviour the veil of misunderstanding about Moses is stripped away and release from the nightmare of self-justification becomes a real experience. The apostle recapitulates from 3:6: 'The letter kills but the Spirit gives life.'

It could be put like this: Moses was the lawgiver; we are law-breakers — and Christ has shown himself the law-keeper on behalf of his people. But that is not all. Risen from the dead and the Lord of all, our Saviour is also the life-giver through the bestowal of the Holy Spirit. 'The last man Adam became a life-giving spirit' (1 Cor. 15:45).

Some commentators take 3:17 almost as a proof text for the doctrine of the Trinity, teaching that the Holy Spirit and Christ are distinct and yet, together with the Father, are one within the Godhead.[70] Although the doctrine is true, surely it is not Paul's purpose here to provide an exposition of the relationship between the Second and Third Persons of the Trinity. His concern is to display the extreme contrast

between the old and the new covenants, the risen
Messiah achieving what was never in Moses' gift. In
Christ the believer has received the spirit of adoption
(Rom. 8:15). Nevertheless, there is an implicit refer-
ence to the Holy Spirit in that the Spirit of God is the
Spirit of Christ (cf. Rom. 8:9; Gal. 4:6).

One question remains: what is 'freedom'? This is a
rich word with a variety of connotations. In addition
to what has been suggested, it would signify, first,
that the believer is released from condemnation by
the law (3:9); second, that he is freed from the dominion of sinful impulses, the Lord being his delight
(as in 3:18); third, that, if a Jew, he is released from
any obligation to consider the law of Moses in any of
its parts as his rule of life (3:11);[71] and, fourth, that
there is liberation from the corruption of the body (cf.
4:14; 5:1-5). But freedom does not mean moral
licence. We are not allowed to sin so that the grace of
God may be given opportunity to parade itself (cf.
Rom. 6:1). Nor does the true believer want to live like
this.

In short, we have here an echo of the words of the
Saviour when confronted by unbelieving Jews:
'Therefore if the Son shall make you free, you shall
be free indeed' (John 8:36).

3:18. But we all with a face that has been unveiled, and
beholding the mirrored glory of the Lord, are being transformed into the same likeness from glory to glory, even as
from the Lord, the Spirit.

The principles laid down in 3:17 are applied in 3:18.
Following an outline of the major points of this verse,
the commentary gives a more detailed exposition.

Paul generalizes. **'We all'** refers to Christians, to
all Christians and to none but Christians (cf. 5:10;
1 Cor. 12:13). Standing apart from those Jews who
profess to be followers of Moses, those who convert to

Christ are participants in a transforming experience. In one sense all believers stand where Moses stood. Turning away from Israel to meet the Lord, the prophet removed his veil. In the presence of the glory of God his face became glorious. Similarly, the collective **'face'**, as it were, of the saints is unveiled and they behold the splendour of the Lord. They, too, become glorious.

Notwithstanding the parallel, there are two differences between the corporate experience of believers and that of Moses: whereas the radiance upon his face faded, Christians become increasingly glorious. Further, the intensification of *their* glory is spiritual, not facial and physical, their inner man **'being transformed'** into the **'likeness'** or image (Greek, *eikōn*, whence the English 'icon'/'ikon') of Christ. This comes about through the work of **'the Lord, the Spirit'** who operates in the hearts of his people.

Paul pens these words to show that, notwithstanding the claims of the Judaizers, who misunderstand Moses, the lives of the Corinthians and many others have been metamorphosed by the Messiah as preached by the apostle. Legalism has been put to shame.

In detail, 3:18 states that all Christians behold the **'mirrored glory'** of the Lord, seeing their God, as it were, by reflection, *via* the image of God, the Lord Jesus Christ.[72] 'He who has seen me,' our Lord taught, 'has seen the Father' (John 14:9), implying both unity and distinction, the only way by which they can 'see' the Son being, of course, by faith. To the believer Christ becomes 'the image of God' (4:4; cf. Col. 1:15; Heb. 1:3), and in the Saviour's face (that is, in his person) the disciple's heart perceives the glory of that God (4:6).

Second, the veil has been lifted from the faces, or personalities, of the saints, and, unlike Moses' veil, will never be replaced. Christians are not at Sinai and do not have to minister to the twelve unbelieving tribes. This is the certain meaning of the adjective **'unveiled'**.[73] When by faith we turn to Christ, the mirror-image of God, we become increasingly like him. Whereas the physical glory of Moses' face diminished to vanishing point, the inner, spiritual radiance of the Christian who keeps in touch with his Lord intensifies as time goes by.

Third, the heavenly glory by which and into which Christians are being transformed is not unlike that of the Lord (cf. the transfiguration: Matt. 17:2; Mark 9:2). The Greek verb behind 'we are being transformed', *metamorphoumetha*, includes the root *morph* (as in 'morphology', the study of the forms of things). The idea is that our essential being escalates from one degree of glory to the next, and so on, so that ultimately we shall be identical to Christ with respect to his humanity.[74] Paul's language is as strong as could be. Elsewhere, too, he indicates that this process is happening now: 'The new man ... is being renewed ... according to the image of him who created him' (Col. 3:10; cf. Rom. 12:2).

It is possible that 'beholding the mirrored glory' means something like 'reflecting glory as would a mirror'.[75] If so, the believer sees Christ, the complete expression of the glory of God, and becomes a secondary mirror of that radiance. It is with their unveiled faces, that is, by their transparently guileless personalities, that the saints mirror his splendour and manifest their new state. Parallel, 'You are the light of the world' (Matt. 5:14) against, 'I am the light of the world' (John 8:12).

Be this as it may, it seems that the primary contrast drawn by Paul is between those who do and who do not believe. Delivered from allegiance to the law, the former have been introduced to the presence of Christ and behold his glory (cf. John 1:14). The emphasis would appear to be upon what Christians 'see', although, with characteristic subtlety, it would not be beyond Paul to entertain a double meaning:[76] we reflect what we observe.

Finally, 3:18 is no more explicitly trinitarian than its predecessor. Although the personality of the Holy Spirit is assumed, the sense is probably that when 'the Lord [who is] the Spirit' exercises his sovereign power there must be renewal,[77] as indicated by Paul's employment of the Greek *kathaper*, **'even as'**. It is to be expected.

Application

This passage is invaluable because of the light that it sheds upon the present standing of the Christian in this world and of his hopes for the future.

First, the apostle assumes that the believer is justified. He is in a right relationship with God, and his situation in this respect is perfect and permanent. When we have been with the Lord ten thousand years (as the hymn reminds us), our justification will be exactly as it is now, and as it was when we turned to Christ.

Second, Paul takes for granted that the Christian is, in a sense, perfectly sanctified. (Don't be alarmed by this statement. Read on!) The apostle has indicated that the believer is a 'saint' and that he is a letter written, so to speak, by the indelible ink of the Holy Spirit (1:1; 3:3). God has detached him completely, permanently and irreversibly from the world of unbelief, and he is nothing less than 'a new creation' (5:17).

Consistent with, and complementary to, these grand truths, the apostle teaches that there is such a thing as gradual or developing sanctification within the heart of each child of God. As time goes by we become more and more like our Saviour. Born-again believers grow (John 3:6). The process is analogous to the birth of a baby and its development to adulthood. Subjectively, we are not what we were, and we are not what we must be.

It was from this awareness that Paul derived his considerable patience with and love for the Corinthian church. He was always ready to imagine them as potentially in the glory (see, for example, 4:14). This is why we also have to exercise God-given patience with the saints when they fumble and fall. Think about them as they will be a millisecond after the final resurrection. And let's contemplate what we shall be like (for example, no more bad temper or perverse thoughts!). If we can stir ourselves to think like this we shall be better church members and better friends. In short, our eschatology ought to define and refine our relationships.

'This ministry'
(2 Corinthians 4:1-6)

The apologia for the new covenant is expanded, attention being given to those who do not respond positively to apostolic preaching. It is probable that we need to read between the lines, inferring further criticisms aimed against Paul: he gives up easily when problems arise (4:1); he is dishonest, possibly in money matters (4:2); he distorts the true meaning of God's Word (4:2); sensible people dismiss his message (4:3); and it is his manner to say more about himself than about Jesus, striving to expand his empire (4:5).

If this background to 4:1-6 is correct, what we read here is a series of succinct replies complemented by what amounts to an affidavit concerning Paul's integrity, all this backed up by an analysis of the state of those who reject his ministry. This climaxes with a powerful and extraordinarily apt exposition of the principle that it is the Lord both of creation and re-creation who illumines the hearts of those who believe.

4:1-2. On account of this, having this ministry, even as we have received mercy, we do not become discouraged. Rather, we have renounced the hidden things of shame, neither walking in trickery nor falsifying the word of God, but by the manifestation of the truth commending ourselves to every man's conscience before God.

The apostle outlines the spirit in which he discharges his duties as a servant of the new covenant. Just about everything we read here is two-edged. First, Paul tells how he responded to the call he received. We rejoice. But in Corinth, in the sixth decade of the first century, there were enemies who would not have been happy when they heard these things, recognizing that what we term 'chapter 4', no less than other parts of the letter, was directed against them. We know that the false teachers did not appreciate Paul's gospel and did not conduct themselves in the way that he did. It is not unlikely that they did not know Paul's Saviour. In short, were there no false leaders at Corinth, the apostle might not have felt led to dictate these words. Unless this is taken into account the subtlety of the passage will pass us by.

'On account of this, having this ministry, even as we have received mercy, we do not become discouraged' contains a duplication, one or other of two elements being capable of omission. Had the apostle written, 'On account of this, even as we have received mercy, we do not become discouraged,' or, 'Having this ministry, even as we have received mercy, we do not become discouraged,' the reader would have understood. But Paul is emphatic, drawing attention to the majesty of the work committed to him. Attacking his inflated opposition, he admits that he is unworthy of such a commission but is conscious that God has set his hand upon him. The opening 'on account of this' — 'this' being the transforming power of the Spirit — points vividly to the apostle's conversion and his call to the ministry,[78] and 'even as we have received mercy' highlights the driving force behind his commitment to the gospel:[79] both what it is and what it has done for Paul make him a never-flagging steward, even though he does not deny that at times he has been tempted to give up. Because theology and experience join forces to inhibit fainting fits he does not grow weary, will not lose heart and mocks despair.[80] There is neither desire nor need for such follies. Does not the apostle march with Christ in the royal triumphal procession? (2:14). Certainly. Have the false apostles such a ministry? No — because they neither sought nor found God's grace. Paul challenges the Corinthians to think.

In 4:2 the apostle looks back again to his conversion and call. Even then, in the earliest days, he knew that bad religion could yield rich pickings. Knowing himself to have been an object of mercy, at that time he made a conscious decision, almost a vow, to discard (aorist, **'rather, we have renounced'**) what he depicts as **'the hidden things of shame'**. What these hidden things might be is suggested by 2:17, which alludes to the financial motive. In the present verses two other facets of religious quackery are unmasked.

First, the purveyors of error are **'walking in trickery'**, the Greek for 'trickery' implying a cynical readiness to do anything. The transliteration is 'panergon', 'all work', being amenable to any species of hoax. The apostle describes himself ironically in this way in 12:16 in that, being sly, he has preferred to minister free of charge in order to deflect accusations of money-grabbing. There and also here he insinuates that, whereas his routine has never been sinful, certain unnamed operators are crafty because they are inherently covetous. If 4:1-2 is paralleled with 11:3, where the serpent, the devil, is said to have exercised cunning, Paul might be making another subtle implication, to be unfolded later — namely, that his adversaries serve the Evil One.

Nor does the apostle falsify or adulterate **'the word of God'** — either the Old Testament or (better) the inspired gospel message busily being misapplied by the pseudo-apostles in order to bolster their

Judaizing tendencies. **'Rather'** (*alla*, a strong Greek word meaning 'on the other hand' or 'nevertheless'), he is concerned solely to be an effective communicator of what is of God, and does so **'by the manifestation of the truth'**. And his experience tells him that this way of doing things is not unfruitful: **'... commending ourselves to every man's conscience before God'**. Conducting his preaching ministry as if God the Judge is present in each congregation (cf. 2:17; 7:12; 12:19), the apostle has been careful to be accurate, relevant and truthful. To a point, the medium has become the message in that the preacher remains his own best sermon illustration. In consequence, Paul's hearers, whether or not they convert to Christ, are impressed because they discern that this man is not crooked. True as he is to the Lord, his transparency has become his principal recommendation, acknowledged without exception by all. Because truth is an immensely powerful weapon, and because the false apostles are ignorant of this, they have employed letters of commendation (3:1).

A preacher who honestly proclaims Christ will be accepted by his society as a man of worth, even if in God's strange providence there are not many conversions.

4:3-4. And even if our gospel has been veiled, it has been veiled among those who are perishing, among whom the god of this age has blinded the thoughts of unbelievers so that the illumination of the gospel of the glory of Christ, who is the likeness of God, should not shine.

Qualifying what he has just said, the apostle concedes that not all who hear come to faith; there **'even'** remain some who turn away.[81] As in 2:15, they are defined as **'those who are perishing'**, which means that they are being progressively stripped of all that they have and must end up with nothing.

They do not appreciate the legitimate claims of the gospel because **'it has been veiled'**.[82] Even as the old covenant when read out usually has a cloaked, undecipherable meaning (3:14), and just as the hearts of most Jewish unbelievers are veiled when they hear Moses' law (3:15) — two sides of the same coin — so, now, the good news is not always accepted for its true worth. As Hughes remarks, 'The unveiled gospel, openly proclaimed, has been veiled *to* them because it is veiled *in* them.'[83] In essence, the apostle reflects the words of our Lord in John 5:46-47: Jews who do not understand the true meaning of Moses' ministry will never come to terms with the revealed Saviour.

To recapitulate, within the boundaries of the former dispensation the true office of the law has been veiled, most Israelites failing to perceive that it was never designed to be an end in itself. Their hearts remain immune to invasive truth, and they are unable to appreciate reality. Although the law anticipated its own redundancy in favour of Christ (e.g., Deut. 18:18-19), they do not want to understand. They prefer obscurity.

If, then, there are still some who maintain that Moses' law is the final revelation of the will of God for ethnic Israel, it is inevitable that they remain blind to the glories of the gospel. Dazzled by Moses, they have eyes for none else, least of all for Jesus, the alleged Christ, whose cross is an utter scandal. Further, beyond the confines of Israel there are multitudes so charmed by the world that the good news of salvation is screened off. For them, baptism in the name of a Jewish 'Christ' would be a folly, and remains out of the question (1 Cor. 1:23). There is no beauty in him that they should desire him (Isa. 53:2). The apostle proffers his readers a universal diagnosis.

Why, then, this blanket of darkness? In 4:4 an insight is granted into the mysterious ways of God,

Paul revealing that **'the god of this age'** is at work, 'age' being the world order which endures until the end.[84] The figure of the veil in 4:3 is developed into that of blindness: it is not the case that some men wish to behold Christ but have a veil arbitrarily thrust upon them so that, sadly, they cannot see. Those who do not perceive are unbelievers, working out their lives with their **'thoughts'** deliberately closed to the good news.[85] The devil has accomplished this so that salvation might not shine in their hearts. In this respect they acquiesce, albeit unwittingly.

The apostle introduces a striking word sequence: **'... so that the illumination of the gospel of the glory of Christ, who is the likeness of God, should not shine** [upon them]'.[86] The contrast is vivid. On the one hand, we are to imagine a brilliant light, that of Christ, the exact likeness (again, the Greek *eikōn*) of God as proclaimed in the good news. On the other, we are to visualize rational men who voluntarily sustain a spiritual disability so profound that all they see is blackness. It is as if a man happily deprived of sight were to turn his eyes towards the sun.

Several details must be taken into account. In 4:3 Paul describes his preaching as **'our'** good news.[87] His message has come by direct revelation (Gal. 1:11-16) and is in full accordance with the Old Testament (1 Cor. 15:1-4). Moreover, it agrees with the good news proclaimed by other apostles (1 Cor. 15:11). Not only is there no taint of arrogance in defining the gospel in this fashion, but it would be hard for Paul to delineate his message in any other way.

The devil is described as 'the god of this age', and for each of three background reasons. First, because he seeks to establish himself as God (even, as we are told elsewhere, having offered Jesus inducements to worship him);[88] second, because he is the remote object of the worship of all unbelievers;[89] and third, because he exercises a temporary, non-absolute authority in the world at large.[90] Behind both atheism and every world religion there stands the prince of darkness. This is the case even though men are unaware of the matter.

But Satan remains subordinate to the true, living God. The qualifier 'this age' implies the reality of a different age, or world, the realm of light and holiness where the Lord has his throne. God alone is 'the King of the ages' (1 Tim. 1:17, Greek text). Further, the spiritual disability inflicted by the devil upon many has been Satan's sin *and* their sin. Although the man healed by our Lord was blind through no fault of his own (John 9:3), it is otherwise with unbelievers who refuse to see (John 9:41). Their sin remains. To 'blind' the mind is a metaphor for the mysterious influence of Satan over men, operating in such a way that in their infatuation they are none the less responsible agents.

The assertion that the Evil One **'has blinded the thoughts of unbelievers'** does not suggest an obvious sequence. Perhaps we are being told that diabolical blinding occurs *prior to* unbelief and is the instrumental cause of the latter. Or is Paul indicating here that those who resist the truth are *then* given over to blindness and to a reprobate mind? (Rom. 1:28). The first view is better because the apostle indicates that the gospel is hidden to those who are perishing (that is, who do not believe), and this because they have been deprived of spiritual sight. Nevertheless, when unbelievers were made blind is almost irrelevant. The fact that they were blinded at some stage and therefore do not believe is the point being made.

To evade the Christ of the gospel is to run from God. In those times, as now, a 'likeness' or 'icon' was understood as an exact representation of its principal,[91] from which it follows that people who worship two- or three-dimensional idols accept in theory that the fulness of the originals resides in their representations. Having stated in 3:18 that believers are being metamorphosed into images of Christ (with respect to his humanity), the apostle asserts that the way to God is through Jesus Christ, who alone is the authentic icon of deity.[92]

Finally, the devil is said to operate among all who hear the gospel. Paul does not comment about those who through no fault of their own have not been evangelized, his immediate point being that the enemy of souls is permitted to harm permanently some to whom the message comes. In the apostle's mind there are, so to speak, three concentric circles: first, an outer circle, the totality of the human race; second, a middle circle, all who hear the gospel; and, third, a centre circle, those who are enabled by the Lord to see the light. The band between the circumferences of the inner and centre circles represents those blinded by Satan.

4:5. For we do not proclaim ourselves, but Jesus Christ the Lord — and ourselves your servants because of Jesus.

Paul has made a remarkable claim in 4:3 by referring to 'our gospel'. It is not hard to see that a statement like this would be seized by the false apostles and their adherents: 'Here', they would claim, 'is a man who enthrones himself by preaching untruth and who, try as he might, cannot prevent his motives from slipping out. He is preoccupied with his synthetic message for his own selfish purposes.'

We know that Paul was sensitive to this kind of charge, which is why in 3:1 he is careful to affirm that, unlike others, he does not need letters of commendation and why he never offers himself as a self-appointed leader. He is accountable: 'We must all appear before the judgement seat of Christ' (5:10). At

most, he has become a servant of the gospel, albeit of
a senior rank, elevated to his station by someone
greater than he: 'Who then is Paul, and who is Apollos, but ministers through whom you believed?'
(1 Cor. 3:5).

At this juncture the apostle anticipates the calumnies which the reference to 'our gospel' will probably
evoke. Negatively, he has never sought the adulation
or the money of the gullible. Positively, he is a herald
whose task it is to announce the just claims of **'Jesus Christ the Lord'**.[93] Here, 'Lord' is a predicate,
meaning that the Saviour ('Jesus') *is* the divine
Messiah ('Christ'), the incarnate Yahweh.[94] In view of
the dignity of the person of our Lord and because
Paul's ministry is irrefutably Christ-centred, how is it
possible for his adversaries to criticize the apostle as
a mini-dictator? Conceivably, others, particularly the
false teachers, might be of this ilk (cf. 1 Peter 5:3: '...
not being as lords over those entrusted to you'), but
not Paul. Because he is determined to know nothing
apart from Christ crucified (1 Cor. 2:2), let the
church ponder the calumnies of those who would
unseat him.

There is more. Paul concedes that he does, in a
sense, proclaim himself: **'... [we preach] Jesus
Christ the Lord — and ourselves your servants
because of Jesus'**. There has always been a close
relationship between the preacher and the people,
and the apostle would not dream of denying it. But
the association is diametrically opposed to the perception being put about by some. Paul appreciates
that as a servant of the Lord it is essential to dedicate
himself to the churches.

This needs consideration. It is not the case that
the Corinthians are his masters by right, and the
apostle their bond-servant (cf. 1 Cor. 7:23: 'Do not
become the slaves of men'). Rather, although he does
not allude to the parable, Paul is in the position of

the faithful servant of Matthew 24:45-47 who was placed by the master over the household and whose responsibility was to give timely nourishment. Or, as 1:24 has it, the apostle labours for joyfulness among the believers. This is why 4:5 adds the qualification: 'because of Jesus'. And Paul has to operate in this way; were he unwilling to place himself at the disposal of all he would win none. As it is, 'I have made myself a servant to all, that I might win the more' (1 Cor. 9:19). This is discerning and intelligent humility.

At the end of the verse the Lord is presented in stark simplicity as 'Jesus', the one who became the human servant of God and thereby the Redeemer (Phil. 2:6-8). Paul has followed in the steps of the Master 'because' of whom he is eager to give his all for the churches of Christ.

4:6. For it is God who said, 'Light will shine out of darkness,' who has shone in our hearts for the illumination of the knowledge of the glory of God in the face of Christ.

The reason why the apostle is content to remain a steward and why he has no intention of indulging in self-aggrandizement is explained: God has performed a work in Paul's heart of such a magnitude that it could not have been the deed of any man, however capable. And because it is the apostle's task to communicate the good news of Christ, through whom God can and does repeat this unique transformation time and again, it would be folly, not to mention blasphemy, should Paul aspire to be the head of the Christian constituency. To recapitulate from 2:11, when the apostle employs the unadorned pronouns 'we', 'us' and 'our' he almost always points to himself, and it may well be so here in the reference to 'our hearts'.[95] The rationale is that Paul's conversion has defined his ongoing ministry. Because of the radical change in his disposition (4:6), he has treasure to disburse (4:7).

On the Damascus road the Lord illumined the understanding of Saul of Tarsus. Such was the sinful blindness of the man that he would never in a million years have thought seriously about a crucified and resurrected Christ. Therefore, had the Lord not done this thing it would not have happened. In detail, it is true that at the time of his conversion the apostle saw a great light and subsequently lost his sight.[96] But here he reveals that in addition to the external, blinding radiance there was an internal illumination (Greek, *elampsen*: 'He shone in our hearts'). Whereas the former struck him down, the latter made a new man of him in that he realized that Jesus is the Messiah. This is virtually conceded in Galatians 1, where he writes, 'The gospel ... came through the revelation of Jesus Christ,' and, 'God ... called me through his grace, to reveal his Son *in* me' (notice 'in', not 'to', Gal. 1:11-12,15-16).[97] Acts 26:16-18 tells us that the glorified Jesus announced that he would employ Saul as a medium of spiritual light, and it is to this wide-ranging commission that he alludes here (Greek, *pros phōtismon*: 'for the illumination of the knowledge'). It follows that if Christ did this for the apostle, Paul cannot be an autocrat. Conversely, what manner of men were the pseudo-emissaries at Corinth?

The sovereignty of God in renewal is given a magnificent illustration, that of the formation of light on the first day of the creation week: 'God said, "Let there be light," and there was light' (Gen. 1:3). Paul elects to apply this verse rather than to quote exactly from the Greek Septuagint. Nor does he give a pedantic translation of the Hebrew when he explains: **'For it is God who said, "Light will shine out of darkness," who has shone in our hearts for the**

illumination of the knowledge of the glory of God in the face of Christ.'[98]

Whereas Genesis reveals all that God did in the beginning, the apostle focuses upon the divine intention *after* the formation of the unlit Earth (Gen. 1:1-2), when the Creator decreed that light must shine. The point being made is that the magnitude of what happened to Paul on the road to Damascus can be evaluated *only* by measuring it against the event of day one. Even as an obscure and barren Earth was illumined by a primary act of God, so this same God has brought about an effulgence of spiritual light in the Pharisee's heart. To repeat, the apostle denies in effect that he would, or could, ever be in a position to usurp the lordship of Christ in the life of the church. Others have made the attempt; he never has. The Lord gives light, not Paul.

The exposition of spiritual illumination is telling. The apostle accepts that, by analogy with our planet prior to the creation of light, he was in profound darkness before conversion. His faith sprang from a God-given spiritual renewal, the 'heart' standing for the complete personality. Light radiated within him and the apostle came to recognize the 'glory of God', a glory which he qualifies most carefully as visible only **'in the face of Christ'**.[99] 'Face' probably stands for person, meaning that at the point of conversion Paul set his mental gaze upon the person of our Lord, perceiving in him the glory of the living God.[100] **'Knowledge'** is possibly introduced to counter the claims of the pseudo-apostles: it is not that Paul has within him undifferentiated light, an undefined awareness of the Almighty. Rather, in Christ he has come to possess the 'illumination of the knowledge of the glory of God', the term 'glory' encompassing the plan of redemption centred around our Lord; the general revelation of God offered by creation has been consummated by special revelation in Christ.

In summary, the system of religion publicized by the heterodox visitors is formless, void and obscure. At creation God shattered darkness with light, Paul assuming that the world in which Adam and Eve found their habitat came into being during the six days of creation. In common with the Old Testament and those documents which in his century were being assembled as our 'New Testament', the apostle declines to interpret spiritual experience in terms of notional sacred myth or metaphorical Hebrew poetry.[101] And there is an elegant logic behind the recall: given the darkness of Judaism and the tensions at Corinth, the only adequate parallel to renewal by Christ in this particular exposition can be the historic creation of light. The analogy expands what Paul has written concerning Moses' provisional, fading dispensation and, by contrast, Christ's redeeming work, the principal glory of God.

Let the Judaizers and others take careful note. Which is better — the shrinking glow of Sinai or the dazzling, creative light of the new covenant administration?

Application

The metaphorical light which shone in Paul's heart on the road to Damascus became the sum and substance of his ministry. The criteria remain the same for every servant of the gospel even though he does not perform miracles, has not yet seen the glorified Lord and is not an author of Holy Writ. Today's minister must seek strength from God so that he will not give up when the work is difficult. He does not consider his vocation as a money-spinner, and takes care so that his manner of life has an impact on the consciences of those who know him.

The man of God must not be dismayed when some reject his message, knowing that others came to Christ through his work and that the grace of God is discriminatory. Second to the Lord, the church is all-important and he will be its intelligent slave (Greek, *doulos*; 4:5). Given the influence of neo-Darwinism, he will want to read any useful book concerning modern science and the book of Genesis, never forgetting that Christ and his apostles entertained a particular interpretation of the first three chapters of the Bible.

4. Earthly and heavenly homes

2 Corinthians 4:7 – 5:10

Life through death
(2 Corinthians 4:7-15)

It is possible that Paul's Jewish critics drew attention to the anomaly between the apostle's manner of life, which tended to be inglorious, and his assertion that the 'new covenant', of which he was allegedly a senior steward, is far more glorious than Moses' administration. If we assume that Paul did not hammer out his theology of the differences between the two covenants from the start in this letter, we can imagine the Judaizers trying to persuade the church that whereas the apostle's poverty and change of travel plans (among other matters) showed that his doctrine was seriously flawed, they suffered from no such disadvantages. From which it followed that the people should attend to their benefactors when the latter magnified the glories of Sinai.

If this was so, Paul's intention is to demonstrate yet again that his apostolic career is nothing other than a visual representation of the principle that there must be death before there is resurrection, and that the grave is the appointed cradle of life. He remarked earlier that God delivers those who place their lives in jeopardy for the sake of the gospel (1:9), and here he develops the theme.

A twofold rationale is evident. First, Paul's repeated escape from near-death situations testifies to the life-giving power of the crucified and risen Jesus, in order that the Corinthians might look, learn and grow in grace (4:11-12). They would have been eager to know what was happening to him, and the information that came their way must have been an education. Second, when the Corinthians gaze at Paul, they will sense that the false emissaries are not what they claim to be. Life out of death has become a sifting mechanism.

4:7. But we have this treasure in earthen jars, so that the surpassing greatness of the power may be of God and not out of us.

At the time of your conversion you came to Christ because the Lord summoned you. Were it not so and had your 'conversion' been no more than a passing phase — the product of, say, emotional pressure, or a need to find relief from temporary difficulties — you would not have endured in the faith. Now, in retrospect, you give your 'Amen' to the verse which declares:

> What a wonderful change in my life has been wrought
>   Since Jesus came into my heart!
> I have light in my soul for which long I had sought,
>   Since Jesus came into my heart.

In practical terms, at that precious time you heard what was told you by someone sent by the Lord — and you believed what was said. Although you remain thankful for whoever was involved in your conversion, details now tend to fade. It was all of God, to whom be the glory.

The situation in which the first churches found themselves was much the same. Had, say, Damaris and Dionysius at Athens been attracted by some dazzling but deviant Jewish philosophy put on show by Paul (Acts 17:21,34), or had the Corinthians been as gullible as the Samaritans when influenced by Simon Magus (Acts 8:9), the apostolic mission would soon have foundered. Paul's 'gospel' would have attracted the anathema pronounced by Gamaliel against all that is not of God (Acts 5:38-39). Nor would Christ have received his just glory. The apostle was a sent man (which is what 'apostle' — Greek, *apostolos* — means), and the Lord gave the increase.

But, unlike us, the earliest churches had, so to speak, little time to wait and see. The Corinthians had no local evangelical tradition upon which to lean. Nor did they possess the complete New Testament as we know it. Furthermore, there were numerous Jewish synagogues bitterly opposed to the scandal of a crucified Messiah, and Paul was thought to be a troublemaker wherever he went (see, for example, Acts 17:7; 19:26). And among the churches there were those who could not tear themselves away from the idea that Moses' law, per se, had an abiding relevance for Christians. Who, then, was right? Validation of the God-given authenticity of the message was needed urgently.

For this reason the man who spearheaded the Gentile mission had to be seen to be a mere man for all that, devoid of innate strength and lacking the resources and adulation which the world would afford temporarily to the great and the good. The immediate conclusion would be that if someone like Paul had become the human agent responsible for numerous congregations of reborn, God-fearing and holy people dependent upon an invisible Saviour, then this work must have been God's work. None other could have done it. The almost infinite contrast between the patent frailty of the apostle and the astonishing effects of his labours inexorably leads to the conclusion that Christ was all that he was said to be. This is something of the rationale behind 4:7.

Paul defends his work by showing that, far from trying to lord it over the churches, he has been unassuming. Beset by troubles, were he to be denied the help of God he would not survive — let alone triumph — in a hostile world. The verse falls into three parts: the treasure, the earthen containers and why the Lord has seen fit to deposit the former in the latter.

1. 'This treasure'

There are three fairly similar interpretations. The first is that 'this' may refer back to 4:1, where Paul says that 'we have *this* ministry'; in other words, this form of service for the Lord is 'this treasure'. The second is that 'this' points to the apostle's subjective knowledge of the revealed glory of God, a knowledge which is irrepressible and which compels him to commit his life to proclaiming 'Christ Jesus the Lord' (4:5). Third, 4:7 may take into account 4:1-6 if taken as a block, 'this treasure' being 'this ministry' (4:1), but expounded in 4:2-6 both in terms of apostolic honesty in a malignant world and by analogy with the creation of light. The treasure, then, is labour spent in disseminating 'the light of the knowledge of the glory of God'. The last approach seems preferable, whence it follows that ministers disburse wealth in the exercise of their ministry.

If so, the work of the gospel is infinitely valuable. Christ is incomparable and the blessings he grants to fallen sinners are beyond estimation. Here we have a fine example of the emphasis of apostolic understatement: because no man can compute the preciousness of the good news, Paul describes it simply as 'this treasure'. The dynamic of these two words is breathtaking.

2. 'Earthen jars'

In ancient times, as now, items of value were reserved in expensive containers. The golden sarcophagus of Tutankhamun of Egypt (c. 1361–1352 B.C.), discovered early in the twentieth century, comes to mind, as also the golden chest in which were deposited the remains of Philip of Macedon (c. 382–336 B.C.), father of Alexander the Great, unearthed in 1977 near Thessalonica. The gospel is a treasure of incalculable value, more lustrous than the brightest star and capable of achieving infinite good, yet carried about, so to speak, in the most inexpensive and common of all man-made containers — a fragile, unglazed and unadorned earthenware vase or pot.[1] The paradox is extreme: 'In a great house there are not only gold and silver vessels, but also those of wood and earthenware, and some for honour, others for dishonour' (2 Tim. 2:20). The clay container, be it noted, occurs at the end of the list.

Such a receptacle was the apostle Paul. There was nothing about him that the world would value. Usually penniless and of no fixed abode, often in prison (though through no fault of his own), sometimes sick (Gal. 4:13-14), always at the mercy of malevolent Jews and hostile Gentiles, an allegedly academic stick-in-the-mud too clever for his own good (Acts 26:24), and a turncoat from his ancestral religion, here was a man whom decent society would have been wise to ignore. There were some at Corinth who despised him as an individual without presence

(10:10) and devoid of social credibility. Death was his daily companion (4:12).

3. 'The surpassing greatness of the power'

The single Greek word behind 'surpassing greatness', *hyperbolē*, means something that stretches beyond conventional boundaries and is virtually limitless. It and two related words are, it is true, found elsewhere in the New Testament, yet only in Paul's writings.[2] The apostle rejoices in the immense potential of the gospel entrusted to his care.

The meaning is that the power of God, as manifested through Paul's evangelism, does far more than override the weakness of the apostle, a weakness which might be thought by some to prejudice his endeavours. The meanness of the vessel fades into oblivion in the light of a glory which pervades the hearts of the many converts who flock to Christ. Because the Lord refuses to allow the suspicion that Paul's accomplishments are the work of an unaided man, he sees to it that his servant suffers indescribable frailties. The apostle acquiesces gladly — and the churches grow in their assurance that all has been **'of God'**.

In one way this verse does relate to all believers who concern themselves with the propagation of the gospel, and we are thankful. In another way, 4:7 and the verses that follow may apply to none of us. If Paul suffered as none other has suffered, with the exception of the Lord, we have here a historic statement.

4:8-10. In everything we are being afflicted — but not hard pressed; are perplexed — but not in despair; are being pursued — but not abandoned; are being struck down — but not destroyed; always carrying about in the body the deadness of Jesus so that in the body the life of Jesus might be made apparent.

Apostolic tribulations are splashed colourfully and liberally on a broad canvas, Paul beckoning to us to ponder his brush strokes. In 4:8-9 there are four positive statements, each followed by a negative. Because God is in charge of all things, 4:10 explains the divine strategy. The adversative **'but'** (Greek, *alla*) occurs in each of the four contrasts, as if to show that against all proper expectations Paul is constantly delivered from the final extremity.

'In everything we are being afflicted' means that the apostle is being bruised continuously and from all directions. Compare with Mark 3:9, which records that our Lord requisitioned a boat 'lest they should *crush* him'. Wherever Paul operates there are pressures which tend to squeeze the life out of him. Notice the present tenses, indicating that affliction is ongoing although never lethal: **'but'** he is **'not hard pressed'**. It is likely that the qualifier 'in everything' governs each of the four assertions:[3] being afflicted, being perplexed, being pursued and being struck down. There is no situation which fails to push the Lord's servant to the limits of toleration.

'Perplexed — but not in despair' reveals that there are always matters which cause the apostle deep disquiet. Frequently he does not know what to do and cannot predict the outcome of the immediate problem. Yet he never gives up hope, and in order to remind the Corinthians about this he brings in a virtually untranslatable word-play, meaning something like 'uncertain but not completely uncertain' (Greek, *aporoumenoi all' ouk exaporoumenoi*). A superficial contradiction with 1:8, where Paul tells his readers that when he was in Asia 'we despaired even of life', is unreal. Although from the human perspective there was no escape from the perils in Asia, the apostle never surrendered the conviction that the Lord would stand by him. In 4:8 he writes in absolute terms: God has never deserted him, and never will.

'Pursued — but not abandoned' shows that whenever Paul pauses to look behind him there are enemies growling at his heels. Because he is, so to speak, a warrior being hunted down by superior forces, survival seems doubtful.[4] Yet he never runs alone because there is always someone at his side. Demas and others may abandon him, but the Lord Jesus will never do so (2 Tim. 4:10,16). Each day yields a fresh discovery of the truth of Hebrews 13:5: 'I will never leave you nor forsake you.'

'Struck down' in 4:9 reveals that the apostle experiences again and again the trauma of being overthrown by an adversary to find himself prostrate awaiting the final stroke of the sword. Marvellously, the blow has never fallen, nor will it: '... **but not destroyed'**.

Why these things are so is disclosed in 4:10. Negatively, Paul is not granted a series of merciful deliverances from God in consideration of his loyal service. Positively, the divine tactic exploits the fact that men generally pay more attention to what they see than to what they hear. The apostle proclaims that Jesus suffered at the hands of men but was raised by God from the dead. Very well, let the world behold a process of mini-resurrections reoccurring in the experience of Christ's senior servant. He carries about in his body the **'deadness of Jesus'**, meaning that he, like the Lord in his time, is destined to be rejected by men.[5] The reference in 4:10 would be to the apostle's external trials rather than to his internal anxieties. The apparent hopelessness of Jesus during his earthly ministry is reflected, albeit dimly, by that of Paul: as good as dead, he has no prospect save that of rejection and ultimately the grave. This is how it is on almost a daily basis[6] — but for a purpose. Even as Jesus triumphed over disaster, so too the apostle has been delivered from, as Hodge puts it, 'an uninterrupted succession of indignities and suffering',[7] in consequence of which men suspect that the resurrection of which Paul has so much to say might not be a fallacy: '... **so that in the body the life of Jesus** [in addition to the Lord's deadness] **might be made apparent'**. 'Made apparent' (Greek, *phanerōthē*) is significant, occurring more often in 2 Corinthians than in Paul's other letters.[8] Unseen realities eventually make their presence felt, whereas the superficial gloss of the false apostles and their minions is without substance.

The world watches us Christians, particularly when we are called upon to suffer. It is precisely then that the testimony that 'Christ lives in me' (Gal. 2:20) can score.

4:11. For we, the living, are constantly delivered to death because of Jesus so that the life of Jesus might be made apparent in our mortal flesh.

The theme of 4:10 is developed, Paul acknowledging the strange providence of God which decrees that he, the honoured apostle, should be constantly delivered to the final extremity. **'Constantly'** may mean 'from the beginning onwards',[9] as perhaps in the statement that 'Cretans are *always* liars' (Titus 1:12) — in other words, deceit never ceased to flow through their veins.[10] The apostle is saying that past experience has become an inevitable precedent for the future.

But, by God's grace, the mission has continued: '... **we, the living'**. Thus far the world and the Evil One have not succeeded in destroying this minister — nor will they. His survival is due to an intelligence higher than that of Satan which deems it wise to deliver Paul repeatedly to **'death'**, then to rescue him. Although the apostle does not allude to Job, an obvious parallel would be with the patriarch (Job

1:12; 2:6). But, unlike the latter, who lived beyond the ambit of the dispensation anticipated by Moses, there is a reason for this: **'because of Jesus'**.

Notice that in 4:10,11 the Lord is referred to four times as 'Jesus', the emphasis falling upon the earthly ministry of the man of Nazareth. By implication there is a species of continuity between the human Master and his servant: in order to broadcast the truth that God vindicated Jesus, Paul too is handed over to situations which, were they to run their course, would leave him dead (cf. 1 Cor. 11:23, referring to Christ's being delivered to the executioners). Suffering has become an integral aspect of the apostle's ministry for the Lord.

Outward trials are matched by personal frailty. Because of Paul's lack of bodily strength, death appears the only reasonable certainty, the divine purpose being **'so that the life of Jesus may be made apparent'** in the apostle's body (4:10), described in a near-repetition as his **'mortal flesh'**. The probability of death from outside plus internal weakness clamour for one outcome, but it never transpires. The apostle returns to continue the fight, and the world wants to know what manner of man he is. Paul retorts, 'It is obvious, isn't it? The risen Christ is manifestly within me. Because he cannot die and because I am his, I live.'[11]

Here is evangelism with teeth. Paul was the original pioneer missionary to regions beyond (10:16), a man who must have had a remarkably strong relationship with his Lord to allow himself to submit to such a lifestyle. And his nerves had to be of iron; in adversity and frailty he could not allow himself to snap. As Alford remarks, the apostle had learned that 'God exhibits *death* in the *living* that he may also exhibit *life* in the *dying*.'[12]

4:12. So, death is at work in us — but life in you.

The apostle expounds in further detail the underlying
rationale for his sufferings. There is a twist in that,
strangely, they guide the Corinthians, as others, in
the direction of life. A mysterious equilibrium operates between two equal but opposing forces: **'So,
death is at work** [or, 'is energetic'; Greek, *energeitai*]
in us — but life in you.'

Sarcasm is absent, unlike 1 Corinthians 4:8-10,
where Paul contrasts his difficulties and poverty with
the comfort enjoyed by many in the church. The 'life'
mentioned here is not so much Paul's 'survivability'
but, rather, the resurrection life of Jesus experienced
by the Corinthians thanks to God and the tenacity of
the apostle. Strangely, death, a strictly negative
entity, is at work, the meaning being that the apostle
is ready to endure any hardship if he knows that
there will be fruit for his labours. He maintains his
resolution through thick and thin.

For all that, there may be a subtle hint of irony.
Do fraudulent apostles suffer as Paul suffers? No.
Has their 'ministry' conveyed the life of Christ to the
Corinthians? No. Should not these bewildered saints
give their close attention to Paul as he refutes the
dishonest criticisms being brought against him? Of
course they should.

*4:13-14. But having the same spirit of faith, in accordance
with what has been written, 'I believed, wherefore I spoke,'
we, too, believe and therefore speak, knowing that he who
raised the Lord Jesus will raise us also with Jesus and will
present us with you.*

The apostle directs his readers to Psalm 116:10
(Septuagint, Ps. 115:1), and in 4:13 he quotes exactly
from the Greek version. Can there be any doubt that
he expects his readers to be acquainted with Psalm

116, and by implication with the whole of the Old Testament? Paul's **'what has been written'** (Greek, *to gegrammenon*, a perfect participle) sums up his high view of the inspiration of the Old Testament: a Hebrew in ancient time may have penned this psalm, but the emphasis on *written* Scripture implies divine activity. What God caused to be set down has been taken into account by Paul. Let the Corinthians follow his lead.[13]

The quotation is important because of its context, the psalm being a song of thanksgiving to God for deliverance, possibly from severe illness or even from wicked men. The remainder of the verse and the following one (Ps. 116:10b-11) flow together as an antithesis, meaning that there was a time when the psalmist thought that God, just like men, did not care what happened to him: 'I was in great trouble. I said in my alarm, "All men are liars [or, 'failures']."' In the event, faith prevailed. Giving himself to worship, the writer discovered that his afflictions mattered to Yahweh. Even if the world remained aloof, God was at hand.

In more detail, the Hebrew text of Psalm 116:10 translates literally with something like: 'I believed *because* I spoke.' The probable sense is that the psalmist's words were the outcome of his faith. To paraphrase, 'It is obvious that I believed because I spoke out. Equally, I would have remained dumb had I not trusted.' Paul may employ the Greek version because it reflects this approach.[14]

In that the psalmist called upon the Lord, the only one who could deliver him, the apostle has often found himself in a similar position. He is making the double point that difficulties have driven him to place his trust in the Lord and that God has never failed. He can identify with the Old Testament writer because he shares **'the same spirit of faith'**. When the apostle suffers he leans upon his God and then gives utterance. Notice that he speaks *when* he is in distress rather than later, so confident is he of imminent divine aid. This is faith!

There may be two reasons for the citation of Psalm 116:10. First, the context requires us to interpret the whole psalm as a typical anticipation of Paul's suffering, faith and survival. For the moment his approach is to allow the anonymous Old Testament saint to exemplify the apostolic lifestyle rather than to saturate the church with a catalogue of his own miseries. He anticipates that the latter ploy, 'a little folly', will arise, as proves to be the case (11:1,16-33), but now is not the moment. Second, in that the apostle identifies so easily with an inspired writer of the old order, he implies that he belongs to the Israel of God. Here is a subtle criticism of the false apostles that would not have been missed.

'Spirit' in the expression 'spirit of faith' is possibly not the Holy Spirit, although the Spirit of God does grant faith. The apostle discloses that, like the psalmist, he too has a trusting spirit.[15]

The next verse, 4:14, has an immense sweep. The reason for Paul's conviction that the Lord will deliver him from present evils is that he believes in the ultimate resurrection, lesser mercies being tokens and anticipations of the ultimate.[16] Simultaneously he suffers, he believes and he speaks. Paul's **'knowing'** is a perfect participle (Greek, *eidotes*), meaning that this sense of assurance has come to stay. Consequently, the Corinthians ought to understand that the Father, who raised **'the Lord Jesus'** from the dead, thereby proclaiming him the Lord of all (cf. Rom. 1:4), will **'raise us'** (Paul) to present him along with the church before his throne in glory.[17] How can the church, then, abandon Paul in deference to these *arriviste* apostles?

'With' occurs twice — 'with Jesus' and 'with' the readers. The underlying principle is that, although the death of Jesus happened at a particular point in time and the deaths of Paul and the Christian readers of 2 Corinthians will occur at other times, yet the Lord and his followers belong together; because Christ is the first-fruits and the church the main harvest[18] the community cannot be divided. In the light of the plan of God for his people, even the day of death matters relatively little; all are one in the Lord.

Is there another deft touch of irony here? Some at Corinth have been busily depreciating Paul and his life's work. No matter. When the Corinthians rise from the dust they will recognize their apostle because he will stand with them. He is no charlatan, and they should know it.

In that Paul refers to the resurrection of his body, he might have expected that he would die before Christ's return. But does this not contradict passages such as, 'We shall not all sleep,' and 'We who are alive and remain until the coming of the Lord will by no means precede those who have fallen asleep'? (1 Cor. 15:51; 1 Thess. 4:15). The explanation is that although the apostle knew that he might die, he accepted also that he might survive to witness the advent of the Lord. Because both alternatives were possibilities he could write from each perspective as occasion demanded. The interpreter must take this into account.

4:15. For all things are because of you so that grace, having flourished through the many, may cause thankfulness to abound for the glory of God.

The apostle sums up: **'For all things are because of you.'** There is a solidarity between Christ and his people: if Paul endures so much 'because of Jesus' (4:11), his sufferings are equally 'because of you'.[19] Considered as belonging to Christ, the Corinthians provide the immediate motivation for the apostle's labours as those for whom perils are to be borne.

The second part is a little more complicated: '... **so that grace, having flourished through the many, may cause thankfulness to abound for the glory of God**'. There seem to be two principal interpretations.

First he may be recalling 1:11: '... you also helping together on our behalf in prayer, that thanks may be given by many people on our behalf for the gracious bestowal to us through many' (cf. Phil. 1:19). When the Lord delivers the apostle from the next round of affliction, the prayers of increasing numbers (not merely a wooden 'many') will be answered,[20] the saints will be thankful and God will be praised. The primary emphasis, then, is upon Paul's motivation for service, upon God's mercy to him and upon the importance of prayer on his behalf. Although praise shown by many is desirable, it is not the dominant theme.

In the second interpretation, although 1:11 again comes to mind, gratitude comes under the spotlight. Paul's sufferings and subsequent rescues, always acts of grace, are planned for the sake of many Christians, both at Corinth and elsewhere. The intention is that the beneficiaries of the apostle's ministry might glorify God by giving thanks: 'All things are because of you, so that grace [manifest in the conversions of many], having flourished through many, thankfulness [for Paul's message and for salvation experienced through it] might abound for the glory of God.'

This commentary prefers the latter approach. In 1:11 the apostle writes about the 'gift' (Greek, *charisma*), but here about 'grace' (Greek, *charis*), the frames of reference possibly being slightly different. Accordingly, the apostle is more concerned that increasing numbers of Christians thank God for their

conversion rather than that they should be grateful
that he is still alive and well.

Application

The average minister of the gospel is always under scrutiny:
whereas true friends care for him and remember him in their
prayers, others are curious as to whether he works on Sundays
and plays golf or goes fishing during the other six days of the
week. What is he paid, they want to know, and why did he
become a minister? Everybody — whether saint or sinner —
looks at how he reacts when under pressure. If he crashes there
is the inferno of disgusted comment.

Wise to this sort of thing, the apostle was careful both to
protect himself and to be an encouragement for the saints. His
main point in 4:7-15 is that he has to remain a living witness to
the truth of the resurrection. If men see for themselves that Paul
has a resilience inexplicable apart from divine grace, then they
might consider applying to Paul's God. In this respect the apostle
is hopeful, knowing that holiness is a force for good (4:15).

What applied to Paul then is not less true for others now. For
example, the pastor ought not to be considered as the official
church soul-winner. The world looks at those who sit in the pews
with a gaze almost as intense as that directed towards the man
in the pulpit, which means that all of us need to mount our
personal defence of the faith. One day, when apostles, pastors
and congregations worship in the glory, evangelism and witness
will be no more. Until then the churches cannot afford to rest.

Things that are seen — and things that are not seen (2 Corinthians 4:16-18)

These three verses are a self-contained explanation for Paul's eagerness to surmount the many difficulties which come his way. Having stated that he does not lose heart (4:1) and that his inner self is being renewed by the living Christ (4:7,10-12), the apostle develops the strength-in-weakness theme so prominent in this letter. This anticipates his exposition of the Christian's hope for the future, both post-mortem and when the Lord returns (5:1-5).

4:16. Wherefore we do not become discouraged. Yet if our outward man is wasting away, our inner self is, rather, being renewed day by day.

'**Wherefore,**' asserts Paul, '**we do not become discouraged**' (4:16). In the previous section the motive for the apostle's dogged perseverance was that he had been appointed a steward of 'this ministry' (4:1), a service far superior to that granted to Moses. Now, from 4:16 onwards, Paul majors upon the blessed hope. Notwithstanding a decaying body, he does not give up. There are two associated reasons for this: first, a daily renewal process in the heart which promises relocation in an ultimate heavenly home (5:1-2); second, immediately after Paul leaves this world, should he die, he will be with Christ spiritually (5:8-9).

Perhaps it would not be an exaggeration to suggest that the section 4:16 – 5:10 is unique in Paul's writings with respect to its concise exposition of the three stages in the overall experience of the believer: first, our Christian pilgrimage in this world; then, second, the intermediate period, should death supervene, extending to the moment when Christ comes; and, third, the resurrection state.

The **'outward man'**, man's physical being, is decaying. The background Greek verb for **'wasting away'** *(diaphtheiretai)* occurs, for example, in Luke 12:33: '... nor moth destroys'. The principle is that the first sin in Eden, where Adam and his posterity apostatized (Rom. 5:12,19), has triggered the degradation of creation. The sun burns out, clocks run down, leaves fall and the body is dying (Gen. 3; Rom. 8:20). Note the apostolic present tense: Paul admits that this process of disintegration activates itself within him even as he dictates the letter, and that one day, unless Christ returns soon, his physical system must collapse.

The words **'yet'** and **'rather'** — **'*yet* if our outward man is wasting away, our inner self is, *rather*, being renewed day by day'** — bring out the contrast between two theatres of experience: the outward and physical, that failing vehicle belonging to a passing world, and the inward and spiritual self.[21] Paul the Christian is being renewed 'day by day'.[22] The New Testament, be it noted, never speaks about the outer and inner aspects of the unbelieving, non-Christian man, the focus invariably falling upon what is happening to the child of God. At this point the apostle discusses his steady, uninterrupted progress towards the glory of another world.

'Day by day' indicates that inner renewal advances on a twenty-four-hour basis. Perhaps it is observable as each day passes. Yet what is meant by 'being renewed'? Colossians 3:10 exhorts believers to

'put on the new man who is being renewed in knowledge in accordance with the image of him who created him,' and Romans 12:2 demands that the saints
'be transformed by the renewing of your mind'.[23] We
can infer that renewal means both knowing more
about Jesus and becoming more like him, This way
of looking at the verse is virtually confirmed by 3:18:
'We all ... are being transformed into the same likeness.' Paul experiences a developing Christlikeness,
and all this while his physical constitution becomes
progressively weaker. Even so, it is not a question of
balance, as if the positive compensates nicely for the
negative. An inner God-given strength far outstrips
bodily decay, the proportions being staggeringly
different. It might also be that the Judaizers carp
that an alleged apostle of Christ should exhibit more
glory than did Moses, thereby justifying the alleged
superiority of the 'new covenant'. 'True enough,'
responds Paul. 'It is so, but not in the way you
imagine.'[24]

In brief, the apostle's testimony is, so to speak, a
fuller development of Psalm 68:19: 'Blessed be the
Lord, who daily loads us with benefits.' Almost dis-
passionately Paul observes the wearing down of his
bodily system — yet there are no wistful memories of
earlier times. He looks ahead. Currently there is
spiritual development plus the supply of every need,
and at death (should the apostle taste it) Paul will be
with Christ to anticipate the resurrection.

4:17. For the current lightness of our trouble is producing for
us an excessively excessive eternal weight of glory...

'**For**', with which 4:17 begins, connects with the
preceding verse, which asserts paradoxically that
fatigue and continual sufferings are much more than
offset by spiritual benefits. The reasoning develops:

physical decay is pressed into service by God as a stepping stone towards the glory that will be.

Perhaps the operative word here is **'producing'** (Greek, *katergazetai*), meaning to bring something — in this case, glory — into being. This is a favourite expression of Paul's, to judge by the number of occasions he employs it.[25]

The contrasts are stark: 'lightness' and 'weight'; 'current' and 'eternal'; 'trouble' and 'glory'. There is a magnificent imbalance in that the experience of weakness and suffering generates something that is beyond measure, utterly, or in an extraordinary degree, beyond comprehension. Together with its relatives, the Greek translated here by **'excessively excessive'** is employed by no writer other than Paul in the New Testament,[26] one possible reason being that he takes delight in expounding the extremes of sorrow and joy inherent in his own Christian experience. Here he coins an expression, possibly a typically Hebrew duplication, in an attempt to sketch the effect produced by troubles which have their place in the scheme of things, but which, with heaven in view, are temporary, have insignificant substance and are as nothing when contrasted with the final blessedness. He also employs the vivid present tense, 'producing', as an analogue to 'day by day' in 4:16, the intended implication being that the anticipation of glory intensifies as time goes by.

It is likely that the apostle brings in a further duplication. In the Septuagint the background Greek terms employed in 4:17 for 'weight' and 'glory' usually translate a single Hebrew word *(kabōd)* which can bear each of these meanings, as, for example, in Psalm 19:1: 'The heavens declare the *glory* [or "weight"] of God' — meaning that the skies proclaim the significance of one who is not to be ignored.[27] Perhaps Paul takes up the parallel to emphasize his teaching about the blessed hope.[28] Here is a paraphrase of 4:17 which might help to bring out the apostle's play on words: 'For the immediate lightness of our trouble produces for us *in excess to excess* an eternal *glorious glory.*'

The writer does not suffer stoically with an uncomprehending endurance of what blind fate brings upon him, any more than he believes that his troubles enhance an imaginary credit account with God; the matter is far more subtle. Although Paul has been saved by the sufferings of Jesus alone, and rejoices that it is so, he is aware that his many sorrows usher him into a far better world, the two scenes bearing no comparison. The cross is the necessary precursor to the crown.

4:18. ... we not noticing the things that are seen but those that are not seen. Things seen are transitory; those not seen are eternal.

This verse continues the sentence beginning at 4:17. Speaking for himself and on behalf of all believers (**'we'**),[29] the apostle confesses that he is **'not noticing the things that are seen'**, by which is meant the visible world and all in it, **'but'** (again, the powerful Greek *alla*, 'but on the contrary') prefers to fix his sight on what are **'not seen'**, by which he means Christ and all things to do with him: the latter alone merit special attention. 'Noticing' translates the Greek *skopountōn*, the root of which occurs in our 'tele*scope*' or 'micro*scope*', suggesting a mark at which to point. Not being insensate, Paul is genuinely affected by the unhappy world in which he lives and might die. Nevertheless, he is in the same situation as Abraham and his family, who 'saw' the promises (Heb. 11:13), and Moses, who saw 'him who is unseen' (Heb. 11:27; cf. 11:1). The apostle might, if he had so desired, give prior attention to worldly issues, but chooses otherwise: he sets his mind on things

above (Col. 3:2). That this is a persistent discipline is
demonstrated by the present tense inherent in 'noticing'.[30] Concerning the reality of unseen things
above, Paul entertains no doubts.

Actually, 4:17 is a bridge which connects 4:16 to
4:18. In 4:16 Paul informs us about his renewal of
spirit, and in 4:17 he voices his sublime confidence
that present calamities plus inherent weakness
generate eternal glory. This is because he is in the
habit of gazing upon heavenly realities (4:18). Discipline nurtures hope, and hope enhances resilience
and fortitude.

And the theme continues. Notice the linkage
between this verse and its predecessor, 4:17, and its
successor, 5:1:[31]

4:17	4:18	5:1
transitory light suffering	→ things that are seen	→ our earthly tent house
an eternal weight of glory for us	→ things that are not seen	→ a house / building from God

Whereas invisible realities are for ever, this world
is for a season, although it is not denied here (or
anywhere else in the Bible, for that matter) that time
will exist in the eternal state.[32]

Application

Marcus Aurelius, a Roman emperor who died in A.D. 180, was a
Stoic, a guardian and servant of his people, and (it was said) a
gentle man. Never a Christian, he must have had the church
often in his thoughts, to judge by remarks he lets fall in his

celebrated *Meditations*. Almost certainly pointing to the followers of Jesus, he writes about 'those who do their deeds behind closed doors' as people 'who can live out their lives in the utmost peace of mind, even though all the world cries out against them what they choose, and the beasts tear limb from limb'.[33] If there is such an allusion, it would point out that the Christians were observed by the circus crowds to be at peace when faced with a horrendous death. Like Paul a century earlier, they did not flinch in the teeth of adversity. Should we? May God give us grace.

Groaning
(2 Corinthians 5:1-5)

Thus far in the letter the apostle has referred occasionally to physical death. Severe problems in Asia
(1:8-10) and the ageing process (4:16) remind him
that he will not remain in this world for long. One
way or the other, he must depart. But death, should
it occur, is not the end, and here Paul gives a detailed exposition of the Christian hope, implied in
1:22 and alluded to in 4:14. He comments about one
aspect of our hope while we are here, about the
intermediate period following death and about the
eternal state following the second advent and the
resurrection of the body.

**5:1. For we know that if our earthly tent-house is dismantled,
we have a building from God, a house not made with hands,
eternal in the heavens.**

Before we examine this verse reference ought to be
made to the interpretation given by Hodge in his
commentary on 2 Corinthians. He argues that Paul's
**'house not made with hands, eternal in the heav-
ens'** is not the resurrection body but heaven itself,
the abode of the believer when he dies.[34] Although
this exposition will not examine his understanding in
detail, it would only be right to say that it disagrees,
preferring the view that here the apostle points us to
the end of the world and the resurrection body rather
than to the intermediate period. One difficulty with

Hodge's approach is that it damages the symmetry of
5:1, according to which our earthly house is contrasted with the house not made with hands, the two
houses obviously being entities of the same order: if
the former is a body, so too the latter. The contrast is
not between our immediate physical body and the
habitat provided by the heavenly sanctuary, even
though elsewhere in Scripture heaven is described as
a dwelling.[35] Present and ultimate physical states are
in mind. Read this verse and its context in parallel
with 1 Corinthians 15:53-54 and doubts will vanish.

The apostle begins with a certainty, **'For we know
...'**, developing the preceding verse: 'We [are] noticing
... the things ... that are not seen... For we know ...'
(4:18 – 5:1). The Greek word translated 'know', *oida-
men*, implies awareness springing from revelation
rather than common-sense recognition of what is
real: the Spirit within Paul has granted him the
conviction that if he dies and parts company with his
temporary body he will in due course be granted a
permanent bodily abode. And what he claims for
himself he claims for all believers.

The human body is described in somewhat elaborate terms, **'our earthly tent-house'**. A more literal
translation might be 'our earthly house of the tent',
meaning 'our tent-dwelling on earth', and possibly
echoing the Greek version of Job 4:19: '... those who
dwell in clay houses, of which we also are of the
same clay'. Compare with 1 Corinthians 15:40, where
the apostle refers to 'earthly bodies'. The idea is that
the Christian's physical being is like a fabric tent
functioning as a temporary residence. The apostle
manufactured tents when at Corinth (Acts 18:3), and
perhaps he had this in mind when he wrote, as well
as recalling the forty-year journey of Israel in the
wilderness following the departure from Egypt. The
Hebrews lived in tents, for the most part discarding
them when they settled in Canaan. Even though this

analogy does not surface, Paul's Greek verb *katalythē* (**'is dismantled'**) points to the possible disassembling of the 'tent', the body, by death at the end of the Christian's earthly pilgrimage.

So, the apostle, like other believers, may die. **'If'** shows that he does not assume that it must be so, the reason being that Paul remains uncertain about the timing of the second advent of Christ. It is not out of the question that he might survive to witness the descent of the Lord from heaven.[36]

Further, the application in 5:1 of the Greek verb *katalythē* behind 'dismantle' to physical death is rare, suggesting that Paul is alluding to the teaching of Jesus concerning his own death and resurrection. According to John 2:19-21, Jesus announces that if his adversaries destroy 'this temple', in three days he will raise it, his 'body', up. In Mark 14:58 (cf. Mark 15:29) false witnesses declare that 'We heard him say, "I will destroy this temple that is made with hands, and within three days I will build another made without hands."'[37] The allegations in Mark are close enough to the words of Christ in John to suggest that our Lord did predict that a new temple would be raised up, even though he did not say that he would destroy the existing structure. Strikingly, in 5:1 the apostle brings in exactly the same expression, 'not made with hands' (Greek, *acheiropoiēton*).[38] The parallel is too vivid to allow a happy coincidence, leading to the inference that here, as in 1 Corinthians 15:23,49, Paul links the resurrection of Jesus with that of the believer: even as Christ died and rose, so must the Christian.

If, then, the apostle dies, he nevertheless has **'a building'**, an edifice that will be **'eternal in the heavens'**, constructed according to a perfect specification and not by a local contractor with materials that degrade as time goes by. And it will last for ever within an environment immune to the depredations of sin — and all this because it is **'from God'**. **'We have'** is daring, and probably ought to be understood as expressing Paul's confidence in his ultimate resurrection. His future possession of a glorious body is so certain that he can refer to his occupancy of it as having in principle already commenced. He has been given the key to the door even though he has not yet unlocked it. The employment of a present tense to expound future reality is by no means uncommon, thus lending credibility to the view. 'We die,' in 1 Corinthians 15:32 and, 'I pass through Macedonia,' in 1 Corinthians 16:5 are two other examples in Paul's letters. The apostle knows that it will be so. Could language be more assertive, more hopeful, more relevant? What does it matter if in this world his work for the Lord deprives him of so many creature comforts? The need is to be addressed.

5:2. For in this we groan, longing to be clothed over with our dwelling which is from heaven...

This verse and its context might be read in parallel with Romans 8:18-30, where the apostle outlines the expectations of glory entertained respectively by the created world, the believer and the Holy Spirit. In verses 22, 23 and 26 of the passage in Romans the verb 'groan' and the related noun 'groaning' are deployed,[39] as if creation, the earthly church and the interceding Spirit within our hearts are impatient, sighing in glad but restless anticipation for what is not yet. Now, in 5:2, together with 'groan', the apostle employs **'longing'**, another emotive term, to amplify his exposition. Because he introduces the word elsewhere only with regard to meeting absent friends, it may be that he gives us a clue to his meaning here.[40] Painful expectation is not without pleasure.

The point to be made is that in 5:2 Paul asserts that **'In this we groan.'** 'In this' may refer to the bodily 'tent' in which we find ourselves: 'In this [tent] we groan.' Or, it may point forwards prospectively: 'In this [blessed hope] we groan.' Or, third, 'in this' may refer to the span of time which must elapse until final glorification: 'In this [waiting period] we groan.' Opinions vary, but one would opt for a link with 'habitation' in the centre of 5:2: **'In this** [habitation] **we groan, longing to be clothed over with our dwelling which is from heaven.'** The idea is that of continuity, the earthly making way for the heavenly. There is both comparison and contrast between the present body and that of the resurrection state.

'To be clothed over' is significant. In the New Testament the background Greek word occurs here and in 5:4 alone, although in John 21:7 the related noun means an upper or outer garment, as also in the Greek Old Testament and ancient literary usage.[41] In 5:1 Paul describes the resurrection body as a 'building' and a 'house'. Now, employing an extended metaphor, the apostle compares it to a 'habitation', a permanent home which, like an outer garment, is meant to be worn *over* other clothing.[42]

This forceful combination of ideas shows that the resurrection body is to be a development of our present frame. The eventual transformation will not be a transition into something unlike that with which we are clothed, but — to repeat — will involve continuity. The thought of 1 Corinthians 15:53 — 'For this corruptible [thing] must *put on* incorruption, and this mortal must *put on* immortality' — is intensified here by the use of a compound verb, a conventional word for 'put on' being prefixed by the Greek *ep'*, meaning 'upon'.[43]

Furthermore, notwithstanding the possibility of death, Paul desires to be alive when Christ returns. Compare with 1 Cor. 15:51: 'We shall not all sleep, but we shall all be changed.' It might be that the apostle will escalate from the earthly scene to the final glory in one step by omitting the intermediate state. Although the latter would be a blessed experience ('far better' in Philippians 1:23 comes to mind immediately), Paul prefers glorification as soon as possible without having to wait for it in company with the spirits in heaven. Verse 2 implies heavily that transfiguration by donning the over-garment is better than, as in verse 1, resurrection following death.

5:3-4. ... and if indeed we are disrobed we will not be found naked. For we who are in the tent groan, being burdened because we do not want to be disrobed but to be clothed over so that what is mortal might be swallowed up by life.

These verses are a continuation of 5:2, the apostle contemplating the possibility that Christ will return during his lifetime.

There are two textual issues that have to be addressed before an exposition is possible. First, the Greek behind **'and if indeed'**, opening 5:3 and meaning something like 'of course', might not be the original reading. There could have been a more powerful word, translated 'if after all' or 'since'.[44] Either way, the sense is that, should Christ come back during Paul's lifetime, thereby obviating the latter's decease, certain consequences must follow. Also, again in 5:3, the Received Text's 'having put on' is sometimes replaced, as in the United Bible Societies' edition, by its opposite, 'disrobed' or 'having put off'.[45] Again, the thrust of the passage is not disturbed: **'Indeed, having put on** [the heavenly body] **we will not be found naked'** means much the same as **'if indeed we are disrobed** [of the earthly tent] **we will not be found naked.'** Textual evidence probably inclines towards the first reading, but this commentary stays with the United Bible Societies' Greek text.

Paul declares that if he is alive when the Lord returns he will not survive as a naked spirit but be a whole man in possession of both body and soul. At the advent his heavenly body will materialize instantly as a species of top-garment superimposed upon the old, fraying tent. This, he discloses, must be immensely preferable to the shock of death when his spirit would journey to be with the Lord and the disembodied righteous.[46]

And immediate transformation is better because Paul writes as a Hebrew schooled in the Old Testament Scriptures. These show that physical death, a consequence of Adam's apostasy, is a disintegration of the two fundamental components of a man's being, his body and his soul (Gen. 3:19). From this it follows that the blessedness of being a spirit in paradise (cf. Luke 23:43) is incomplete, intermediate and temporary. Contrary to some Greek philosophers, neither Paul in particular nor the Bible in general regards the body as a prison-house, release from which would be a boon.[47]

If, then, the apostle can transfer directly from this earthly body to the ultimate glory, bypassing death and the intermediate state, he will avoid a situation which, however preferable to the pressure of living by faith, is nevertheless an ongoing disorganization of the whole man. This the apostle does not want. Because physical death is unnatural and loathsome even though its sting has been drawn (1 Cor. 15:56), Paul longs for the fulness of salvation as quickly as possible. Stretching out for it (Phil. 3:11-14), he is aware that the return of Jesus during his lifetime can provide the only linear route.

Notice that in 5:2 the apostle groans in anticipation of donning the habitation from heaven. Now, in 5:4, he confesses that he is burdened, groaning **'because'** he does not want to be disrobed,[48] thus becoming an ethereal spirit. Rather, he desires to

advance as soon as possible from this sin-laden state
by putting on the heavenly body. The former is described as **'what is mortal'**, our complete earthly
existence, and the latter as **'life'**, sin-free existence in
the age to come. Moreover, in that the first is to be
'swallowed up' by the second, there is a direct
parallel with 1 Corinthians 15:54 plus a recall of
Isaiah 25:8: 'He will swallow up death for ever, and
the Lord GOD will wipe away tears from all faces.'
This proves, if proof is needed, that the contrast in
these verses is between our earthly and resurrection
bodies. Paul contemplates the destiny of those who
are alive when Christ returns, the metaphor altering
yet again. First we were presented with the picture of
a change of dwelling, then with that of a change of
clothing. Now we are regaled with the prospect of life
gulping death down so that it disappears for ever.[49]

Looking back, we know that the Lord did not see
fit to grant Paul his desire to avoid the intermediate
state. After his death his spirit entered the abode of
the blessed to await the great day of resurrection. At
the time of writing of this commentary he is still
there, together with many others. We may or may not
join them, depending on the occasion of the day and
the hour (Matt. 24:36).

**5:5. He who has prepared us for this very thing is God, who
has given to us the deposit of the Spirit.**

In the previous verses the apostle has written about
the possibility of being alive to greet Christ in person.
Even so, the whole matter is in the hands of God,
and Paul spares no pains to make this clear: whether
dead or alive, saints will robe themselves when the
Lord provides their garments. A number of points
arise.

First, the apostle brings to bear one of his preferred action words, employing it in a past tense:

'prepared' *(katergasamenos)*. Because preparation is a *fait accompli*, believers are ready for the future.[50] The idea is that because the Almighty has put the scheme into motion it must reach its fulfilment: **'He who has prepared us for this very thing** [the investiture of the heavenly body directly or via the intermediate state] **is God.'** The emphasis is where it should be, upon God, the note of assurance reflecting the confidence of 'we have' in 5:1.

Barnett, in his important commentary on 2 Corinthians, takes a somewhat more refined approach, suggesting that 'this very thing' or 'this very purpose' (Greek, *eis auto touto*) points not only to the resurrection state but *also* to our groaning, our longing and our being burdened (5:2-4), all the work of the Holy Spirit.[51] But perhaps Barnett tends to overstate his presentation. Although divine preparation manifests itself in the believer's acute expectation, 'this very thing' seems to reflect its antecedent in 5:4, the swallowing up of death by resurrection.

Second, Paul, writing as an emissary of Christ, intends to comfort (or correct?) his readers. What we have here is a plain-to-read declaration that if we are believers we shall inherit eternal glory.

Finally, another channel of assurance is mentioned, the Holy Spirit given to us as **'the deposit'**,[52] a truth introduced in 1:22. The Lord has committed himself to his people in terms of a personal relationship, from which it follows that the plan of salvation must triumph. As Romans 8:11 tells, 'If the Spirit of him who raised Jesus from the dead dwells in you, he who raised Christ Jesus from the dead will also give life to your mortal bodies through his Spirit who dwells in you.'[53] When the Lord begins a matter, he finishes it. That the soul lives for ever is a metaphysical certainty, the awareness of which is never absent from the minds of all men. About this Paul has no concern, his message being that a precursor of glory is the presence of God in the hearts of his people.

Application

The question arises as to why Paul writes about the future. Although 5:1-5 focuses immediately upon the apostle's personal expectations, it is highly probable that he has pastoral concerns in mind. At Corinth, if some queried the resurrection of our Lord (1 Cor. 15:12), many must have entertained hazy views about heaven.

It may be that, like the Corinthians, not a few Christians today are uncertain about the afterlife. Furthermore, the vexed question of the so-called 'millennium' (Rev. 20:2-7) necessarily affects the interpretation of our progress towards resurrection glory. On this issue brethren can differ strongly. Perhaps the writer of this commentary ought to declare himself by stating that, in his opinion, the exposition of 5:1-10 offered here makes sense only if we adopt what is termed the 'amillennial' view. Turning the argument around, one would suspect that 5:1-10, if fairly interpreted, does no favours to the 'premillennial' approach.

Life in this passing world
(2 Corinthians 5:6-10)

The preceding section (5:1-5) emphasized Paul's aspirations for the resurrection state. Assuming that this would be better than anything else, the apostle now draws attention to his preference to be with the Lord in the intermediate period, should this be God's plan for him, rather than living down here by faith.

It is not impossible that Paul is responding in these verses to adversaries and shallow Christians at Corinth who regard discipleship as a primrose path and who sneer at the apostle as an ever-travelling, dubious fellow who usually finds himself in hot water within and beyond the churches. Be this as it may, he affirms that as a servant of the new covenant his ethical standards have been defined by the one who called him and who will one day hold him and all Christians to account. There is more: Paul's level of blessedness in the age to come depends upon the quality of his commitment to Christ in this brief span of time.

5:6-8. Therefore, always being courageous and knowing that being at home in the body we are away from home, away from the Lord — for we are walking by faith, not by sight. But we are courageous, and delight more to be away from home — from the body — and to be at home with the Lord.

Standing by itself, 5:1-5 would almost certainly be misconstrued. We might, not without some semblance of reason, suppose that a discontented apostle longs to be in a better place, implying for the benefit of his readers that those who are not like-minded are in some sense unspiritual, lacking an appreciation of what it is to exercise Christian hope. The present verses complement what has been written as a preventive to misunderstanding. In no sense does this man pine to be dispatched, perhaps as a martyr, into eternity.[54]

All this is sanctified realism. If in 5:1-5 the apostle reveals that he prefers translation to death, he is aware nevertheless that the latter might be his experience; he cannot be sure. Dropping the metaphor of the tent-dwelling, he writes plainly: 'being at home with' or 'away from home' indicate that it is a matter of 'either / or'. Should Paul die, his disembodied spirit will ascend to remain with Christ during the intermediate period: there and then he will be at home. Although less blessed than ultimate glory, it would be a vast improvement upon the present faith-relationship with the Lord who has made his home with him. The immediate point is that to be at home, albeit spiritually, with Christ and therefore to behold the object of worship must be superior to the tension of relying upon the unseen.

But this does not mean that living by faith is shameful, a matter for regret. Far from it. Paul insists that he is **'courageous'** (5:6,8) and that he is filled with hope — **'knowing'** (5:6); the present scene is no more than provisional, and the awareness cheers him. Indeed, were the apostle to deprecate the life of faith he would slight the Holy Spirit who, as the God-given precursor of final glory, indwells him during his earthly pilgrimage (1:22; 5:5).

Life with Christ runs, then, in three consecutive stages. The notes covering 4:16 have developed the point, but here is a recapitulation because the sequence is assumed in 5:1-8. The notions of being or

not being at home occur in more than one sense, and
to overlook this would lead to some confusion. What
we have here is an instance of Paul's subtlety. First,
there is the discipline of being at home (Greek, *endēmeō*) in this mortal body and walking by faith until
either death or the second advent supervenes.
Should death occur we shall be at home (again,
endēmeō) with Christ immediately and personally,
albeit in the nakedness of the spirit-world, and
absent (Greek, *ekdēmeō*) from the present bodily
home.[55] This second stage would be better than the
first. Hebrews 11:16, which describes the aspirations
of the saints *in heaven* 'now' provides a parallel.
Finally, the saints will be with Christ after he returns
and in possession of their heavenly bodies, each a
personal home, within the eternal habitat, which is
no less a home. This will be better than the second
stage, should it occur, and obviously superior to
living by faith. The verses immediately under consideration (5:6-8) do not, it is true, point to the glorified
state, but they presuppose it, as shown by the
'therefore' in 5:6, which builds upon the concept of
the gift of the Spirit as the 'deposit'.

In detail, **'courageous'**, occurring for emphasis at
the opening of 5:6 and again in 5:8 after a digression
in 5:7, is another of Paul's favourite words in this
letter,[56] suggesting fearless resolve in the prospect of
blessed yet unseen certainties. Elsewhere, a good
example occurs in Hebrews 13:5-6, where the writer
speaks confidently because the Lord never abandons
his people. Further, in the light of the glory to be, the
apostle is **'always'** enterprising even though —
because he cannot be in two places at once — being
at home in this world means not being at home in
heaven. There, he will enjoy an active relationship
'with the Lord', the Greek *pros*, 'with', indicating
positive communion.

Not that Paul is miserable: **'for we are walking by faith, not by sight,'** is added as a qualifier; 'faith' now must lead to 'sight' then (5:7). 'Sight' probably means what will be seen rather than the action of looking — as in, for example, 'Give me a *sight*, O Saviour, of thy wondrous love to me.'[57] The apostle wants to behold Christ. The present tense inherent in 'we are walking' means that he places his confidence in Christ as he moves about in the world at large, the opening 'for' in 5:7 leading to the assertion that being absent from the Lord does not mean that Paul is denied the Lord's presence. It is simply that for the moment the apostle cannot actually *see* his Master.

Furthermore, Paul takes delight in the knowledge that if he dies he will quit this earthly home (**'away ... from the body'**) to enter immediately into the presence of Christ. Of the two, this remains his decided preference.[58]

5:9. Wherefore we aspire, whether being at home or being away from home, to be acceptable to him.

The apostle sums up. His desire is to be with the Lord Jesus, preferably by the direct route of transfiguration, or, if a higher wisdom should decree, via the intermediate process of death and a disembodied state. These things being so (**'Wherefore'**), and because the apostle is currently **'at home'** in his dying body and therefore **'away from home'** with the Lord — two sides of the same coin (hence **'whether'**) — his ambition is, while he has some time left, to please his Saviour. He is saying that a habitat which is strictly interim and to that extent relatively unsatisfactory is not allowed to disaffect his work. Compare with 5:6, 'always being courageous'. It is doubtful that the apostle is alluding here to earthly ministry to be followed by service *after* the home-call, a view affirmed by some:[59] Paul's concern is with the here and now, leaving the final issue to God. The next verse (5:10), referring to deeds performed 'through the body', appears to confirm this.

The Greek verb *philotimoumetha*, translated as **'we aspire'**, means 'to love honour',[60] a desire to secure commendation from a superior. The apostle has striven to be granted the accolade of 'Well done, good and faithful servant,' when the Lord appears in glory (Matt. 25:21,23). 'And everyone who has this hope ... purifies himself' (1 John 3:3).

Floating before the apostle's eye is the spectre of certain unnamed individuals doing their utmost to tear his reputation to shreds. In context, this verse is a further protestation of his sincerity. Because it is Paul's great honour to serve Christ, his work can never be that of an empire-builder. The assurance of salvation has generated diligence and holiness.

5:10. For it is necessary for all of us to be revealed before the judgement seat of Christ so that each may receive back for himself those things which he did through the body, whether good or evil.

Future certainties are not the sole incentive for hard work: Christ will judge his people in the light of our stewardship here during our earthly pilgrimage. A cluster of observations arise.

First, the opening **'For'** develops the line of thought in the previous verses. The apostle does not know if he will be in his body or away from it when the Lord returns. Either way, Paul aspires to being honoured by Christ at the end of all things (5:9), knowing that he must give an account of himself. He has no fear.

The apostle writes on behalf of the whole church: **'all of us'** (cf. 'we all', 3:18). Neither the Corinthians nor any others can be exempted from scrutiny by

Christ. Moreover, this terminal evaluation of the pilgrims' progress will be distinct from the final judgement of a sinful world by our Lord.[61] Although Jesus, when he comes again, will appear as the Judge of all men, leading the redeemed into life eternal and dismissing the wicked to eternal punishment, it is not about the latter that 5:10 speaks. The verse concerns the sheep rather than the goats, those who inherit life. The judgement of the church is to occur, so to speak, within the gates of the heavenly Jerusalem and will not be punitive. There is no question of less fruitful Christians being turned out from heaven to face everlasting perdition.

Thus it is that we shall **'be revealed'** before the **'judgement seat of Christ'**. The Greek verb behind 'be revealed', *phanerōthēnai*, means 'to be exposed', to be stripped of every artificial covering. 1 Corinthians 3:13 — 'Each one's work will become *manifest'* — employs the same root to present the truth,[62] as does also 1 Corinthians 4:5: 'The Lord ... will both bring to light the hidden things of darkness and *reveal* the counsels of the hearts; and then each one's praise will come from God.' It can hardly be doubted that 5:10 parallels these two statements from the earlier letter, demonstrating that Paul is concerned with Christian accountability rather than with the judgement of the wicked. The Lord will examine us for what we are in this present world.

The Greek *bēma* behind **'judgement seat'** is never employed elsewhere in the New Testament with regard to our Lord, with the exception of Romans 14:10,[63] and this rarity lends vivacity to its occurrence here. Such a seat, usually standing on an elevated judicial platform, was occupied by someone empowered to adjudicate within the confines of an administration. Although they were not aware of what they were doing, Pontius Pilate in Jerusalem, Herod Agrippa I, grandson of Herod the Great, at

Caesarea, Gallio in Corinth, and Porcius Festus, again at Caesarea, had occasion to preside in judgement on matters not unconnected with the kingdom of God.[64] Christ, examining his people within the confines of the heavenly realm, will award praise or censure according to his estimation of our service.[65]

And there is a divine necessity about this matter: **'it is necessary'** for us all to be revealed. The believer is a servant as well as a disciple, and because he is a servant he must be confronted by his past activities and by Christ.[66] And, if we think about it, if this were not so there would surely be an inadequacy in the overall programme of salvation. Paul's meaning is that although our justification and eternal salvation are gracious gifts from God and are not to be revoked, the degree rather than the reality of our eternal blessedness is to be determined by Christ the King when he examines us. Moreover, the apostolic doctrine of salvation by grace through faith, proclaimed so manifestly elsewhere, is perfectly consistent with the teaching of 5:10 concerning reward or loss according to works. These two themes tie up exactly with the letter of James and so much else in the New Testament, true faith issuing in love (Gal. 5:6), and love generating good deeds. Where there are no deeds performed for Christ's sake there is probably no genuine faith.

Amazingly, this world is the arena where believers prepare for relative praise or rebuke when Christ comes back. Paul is specific: **'... so that each may receive back for himself those things which he did through the body, whether good or evil'**. What we Christians do in the brief span between conversion and either death or the advent of the Lord, whichever is the sooner, must determine our eternal status *in* heaven. We receive back as our own, are recompensed, either for useful service rendered or for wrongdoing.[67] The principle is that because we are servants there will be a precise allocation of praise or blame, or perhaps praise mingled with blame since saints are neither totally holy nor completely evil. This, let it be said, is realistic. Because all believers entertain godly ambitions as well as make mistakes, we need an incentive of this dimension to alert us.

The final words of the verse, '... whether good or evil', are significant. Coming after the plural 'the things which he did', 'good [thing]' and 'evil [thing]' are both singular. The principle seems to be that the totality of one's life is to be given scrutiny: in the aggregate was it worthy of the Lord or unworthy?[68] Will our lives have been an adequate response to the love of God in sending Christ to die and rise for us? Paul directs his shaft principally at those within the church who make mockery of their profession and who run the risk of being saved 'yet so as through fire' (1 Cor. 3:15). Assessment of both our overall utility and motivation within the kingdom of God is the issue here. 'And behold, I am coming quickly, and my reward is with me, to give to everyone according to his work' (Rev. 22:12).

Application

Although the general judgement and that of the church are distinct, evidence does not lead us to believe that they will be separated in time, as if one is to precede the other. This raises questions. In a discussion on the matter with my wife she remarked that a cynic might argue that because there are so many saints and sinners, and because it seems that each is to be interviewed on an individual basis, the process will be time-consuming (to say the least). The point was fair, and at the time I had no immediate answer. So, what can be said? Simply, that Paul evidently believed that the judgement will begin and end on 'that day', by definition a brief space of time (2 Tim. 1:18; 4:8). With this we let the matter rest and await events.

The final verse of the section, 5:10, also constitutes a warning against judging ourselves too severely or commending ourselves too generously, and against being hasty in our assessment of other believers. We ought not to deny Christ his prerogative. Paul reminds the Corinthians that 'With me it is a very small thing that I should be judged by you' (1 Cor. 4:3).

But what about the intermediate state, being 'at home' with the Lord, if it is assumed that we shall die before Christ returns and that there will be time in the afterlife? Must we not infer that although it will be blessedness, it will none the less be a waiting period, as when a justly confident student has sat an examination but has not been told the result? Paul, having finished his earthly course two millennia ago, still anticipates what the Lord will say to him.

We are currently seated at our desks in the school or university hall. Question papers have been placed before us, so to speak, and we write busily, striving hopefully for a superior grade (we *did* work hard!). All too soon our allotted time is gone. We close our file and lay down our pens, entering into the nervousness of life after examinations. If Christ does not return soon, in heaven our disembodied spirits will continue to await, perhaps with a degree of trepidation (who knows?), the comments of the great Examiner.

This being said, in the final age the joy of each saint will be complete. We need to guard against the fallacy that our happiness will be proportionate to what we may imagine we achieved here. The man who gained an extra two talents was invited to enter into the joy of his Lord *together with* the colleague who earned five (Matt. 25:21,23), even though their innate abilities and eventual profit margins were distinctly unequal. Paul's teaching is designed to generate confidence. Enthusiasm and commitment are all-important.[69]

Finally, it must not be assumed that we shall die: the Father alone knows when Christ will return (Matt. 24:36). Nor may we presume that he will appear during our lifetime. We allow for each eventuality and prepare for the final assessment.

5. The ministry of reconciliation

2 Corinthians 5:11-21

Motivation always commends itself (2 Corinthians 5:11-15)

Paul contrasts himself with lurking figures at Corinth who take pride in appearances (5:12). They are almost certainly the men who, he has alleged, are religious entrepreneurs peddling the Word of God, and who have resorted to letters of commendation to ingratiate themselves with a gullible church (2:17; 3:1). His point is that because he will give account to his Master, he has been zealous to fulfil his commission, knowing that his sincerity must impress all who have a care for truth. More importantly, at the outset of his Christian life Paul reinterpreted the death of Jesus upon the cross, assessing it as a vicarious sacrifice for others. His understanding of the love of Christ has gripped the ex-Pharisee to the extent that he knows that it would be wrong for him, as for all believers, to live for himself. All are debtors.

5:11. Therefore, knowing the fear of the Lord, we persuade men but have become evident to God — and, I hope, also to have become evident in your consciences.

This verse must be read in the light of the preceding section (5:6-10). Conscious that at the last day he will have to answer to his Master, Paul acknowledges a reverential fear of the Lord Jesus, whom to please is a duty as well as a consuming desire.[1] His ministry, which can only endure for a few more years at most, is controlled by an awareness of the final reckoning. Not fearful of condemnation, the apostle is nevertheless concerned lest he forfeits commendation. This is the burden of the first part of 5:11.

It is not that Paul has qualms about the outcome. In the heart of the verse he acknowledges that **'we'**, by which he means himself, **'have become evident to God'**; others may entertain perverse opinions about the apostle, **'but'** the Lord knows the truth. 'Evident' (Greek, *pephanerōmetha*, here in the perfect tense) is exactly as in 5:10 and carries the sense of having become, and remaining, apparent. Paul admits that long ago he was confronted by Christ in such a manner that he has never since played the hypocrite. Commencing his apostolic vocation with a conscience void of offence, he has kept it that way and there is nothing for which he needs to be ashamed. The apostle's carefulness has always been his preparation for the day of reckoning. Further, if his ministry works itself out in the fear of God, it is hardly likely that he is a charlatan.

Be this as it may, what God sees, the Corinthians perhaps do not. Paul declares that he is concerned to **'persuade men'**, the present tense (Greek, *peithomen*) stressing habitual action. But which men? It might be that, knowing that he has to report to his Lord, the apostle endeavours to convince his readers about his integrity as an apostle and evangelist. Woe to him if he does not preach the gospel! (1 Cor. 9:16). This interpretation makes sense because within the church at Corinth there were murmurs of discontent[2] and it was essential that 'men', Christians in general, not to mention unbelievers with whom Paul came into contact, should understand him. If his person were to be impugned successfully his message must fall to the ground, a disaster to be avoided at all costs. So the meaning may be that, yes, he will convince the saints about his honesty, the Lord seeing all the while that he is genuine. So much in 2 Corinthians serves this master-plan, and in 5:11 the apostle seems to give definition to the reason why he writes the letter. On the other hand, persuasion might mean evangelism — in other words, let certain Corinthians think what they will, the apostle pursues his calling.[3] The latter interpretation is the better one.

Nor is Paul without confidence that his relationship with the Corinthians has not been strained to breaking point: '... **and, I hope, also to have become evident in your consciences**', hope being considerably more than a vague and insubstantial wish, even though the apostle retains a slight uncertainty concerning what his readers think about him. None the less, 'to have become evident' is rendered again in the Greek perfect tense (*pephanerōsthai*): in time past the Corinthians came to accept that their apostle was the man he appeared to be, and this awareness has not completely evaporated. For the most part their consciences whisper that, contrary to what others say, there is no duplicity in him.[4] Paul suspects this to be the case.

5:12. We are not commending ourselves to you again, but are giving you an opportunity for boasting about us so that you may have something for those who boast in appearance and not in the heart.

The apostle is aware that his critics in the Corinthian church will seize upon 5:11 as evidence that he is a

'holier-than-thou' practitioner for whom truth is
unimportant. They credit to him their own motives,
acting (unwittingly, no doubt) on the principle that
all things are impure to the impure. This problem
has surfaced at 3:1, where Paul insists that, unlike
some, he has no use for letters of recommendation,
the church being an irrefutable proof of the blessing
of God upon his ministry. So why does he commit
himself to writing 5:11, with its massive claim that
he has a clear conscience before God and that one of
the main concerns of the epistle is to convince certain vacillating Christians of his integrity? The present verse explains.

The ploy is to provide ammunition for the apostle's
loyal friends at Corinth who know him to be true and
who have to contend with a powerful undercurrent
attempting to unseat him. Perhaps Paul was sensitive that some were not sure about who was right
and who was wrong, and were in danger of falling
prey to the opposition. In short, the Corinthian
church was in danger of being split by what appeared
to be a personality clash but, as we have seen, was in
fact a battle of ideologies: salvation by faith in a risen
Saviour or adherence to a bizarre species of Judaism.
Characteristically, the apostle refuses to name those
who are opposed to him, and he does not identify his
supporters. The former are **'those who boast in
appearance** [literally, 'face'] **and not in the heart'**,
and the latter are simply **'you'**, the majority element
within the church. It remains for the people to work
out on which side they stand.

The reinforcement that Paul conveys to the majority is his motivation as unfolded in the previous
verses. Not only has he never commended himself to
the church, he does not do so **'again'**. **'But'**, the
strong Greek adversative *alla* ('rather' or 'on the
contrary'), is brought in for emphasis: he is **'giving'**
his friends an **'opportunity for boasting'** on his

behalf in order to counter those whose judgement is superficial.[5] Does the apostle have in mind 1 Samuel 16:7, where Yahweh informs Samuel concerning Eliab: 'Do not look at his appearance or at the height of his stature, because I have rejected him; for God sees not as man sees, for man looks at the outward appearance, but Yahweh looks at the heart'? Paul's language is strong.

The Greek *aphormē* behind 'opportunity' means a starting-point for an attack, or even the resources needed for carrying out a military operation. In Romans 7:8,11 we read that sin takes 'opportunity' or 'occasion' through the commandment in order to generate spiritual death, the same word being used. Here Paul tells his Corinthian friends that he is giving them the means to attack those who remain hostile to him for no good reason. Even if the meek ultimately inherit the earth, in the interim they are not to stand by as the apostle becomes a target for character assassination.

Even if we do not know the names of Paul's opponents, we can sense something about their calibre — or lack of it. Although they made grandiose claims about themselves, all the time running the apostle down, they must have entertained a deep-seated uncertainty about spiritual issues for which they had little or no concern. They could not have been leaping for joy in the knowledge of the truth of God because they were power-seeking souls who had infiltrated the church. Unlike the apostle to the Gentiles, they were not 'obedient to the heavenly vision' (Acts 26:19), and this was because the Lord never summoned them to his service. Paul had no fears about opening his heart to the church, but theirs were carefully concealed.

Is the apostle employing irony, even sarcasm? One would think not. He spells out the realities of the situation, albeit with restraint. And in this lies an important principle. Although, as mentioned in the introduction to this commentary, not a few critics maintain that chapters 10-13 of what we know as 2 Corinthians were part of another letter written by Paul, this verse tells another story. Like Shakespeare's armourers on the night before Agincourt, the apostle gives 'dreadful note of preparation',[6] as yet remaining silent about the errors of those who would rid themselves of a turbulent apostle and reserving his assault for the last four chapters, where they will be mown down. For now it is enough to encourage comrades who refuse to be gulled by the hypocritical and hypercritical few.

By way of anticipation, far from being an 'add-on' to an original, truncated '2 Corinthians', chapters 10-13 are a fitting and needful climax to a letter that never loses sight of where it is going. The present verse points unerringly along that road.

5:13. For if we have lost our senses, it is for God; if we are sober-minded, it is for you.

This slightly difficult sentence gives dramatic effect to Paul's preceding remarks. Although the Greek *existēmi*, translated as **'lost our senses'**, can imply amazement, here it would mean being immoderate, travelling beyond the bounds of discretion. Instability might also be implied, as in Mark 3:21, which seems to give a parallel: 'He [Jesus] is out of his mind.'[7] Both in that passage and here in 5:13 the aorist is timeless, pointing back to occasions when allegedly the Lord (in Mark 3) or (in the present passage) Paul became permanently deranged. Reading between the lines, it might appear that the apostle is aware that some put it about that he is unbalanced. Although in later years the Roman governor Festus would make such an allegation,[8] here the accusers must have been nominal Christians, which makes the matter more grievous. But what is meant?

One possibility is that the verse is a refutation of the slur that Paul is unspiritual because he is never ecstatic in public. It is alleged that he is ice-cold and does not exude the warmth and enthusiasm that are so needful for a man of his station.[9] If so, the apostle indicates that there have been times when his spirit soared (as with the rapture to paradise, 12:4), but that he has been careful never to let it show. Unlike those who flaunt their capacities, his experiences are never divulged in order to prop up his authority.[10]

Be this as it may, Paul rebuts the accusation with what is probably a deft touch of irony, insisting that in his contacts with the Corinthians and others he remains **'sober-minded for'** them, whatever the agitations of the moment or, on the other hand, whatever the secrets locked in his soul. Because the church's interest is his paramount concern there has never been any display of undue emotion, mental aberration or empty boasting; nor will there be. The apostle, endeavouring to treat his hearers with the respect they deserve, is aware that exaggerated tendencies in the ministry are an insult.

There is another possible interpretation of Paul's admission that he has been known to take leave of his senses, which is that he concedes that his life's work has been an astonishment to many. 'The word of the cross is foolishness to those who are perishing' (1 Cor. 1:18), not to mention puffed-up Corinthian believers. Later in 2 Corinthians Paul will ask his readers to allow him to indulge in a little folly (11:1), the reluctant yet audacious mini-autobiography of 11:1 – 12:10 possibly giving some leverage to the charges implied by 5:13. In an absolute sense, of course, neither the messenger nor the message is disreputable, since the supposed instability lies in the eyes of hostile beholders. Accordingly, the apostle

may base his apologia on the viewpoint of those who
do not understand him, or who refuse to do so, as if
to say, 'If in some respects my message and my
lifestyle appear to you to be crazy, so be it. As you
see matters, only a fool would live as I do. But that
is your problem. My work is for God, and he knows
the truth even if you do not. The fact is that no man
can show that I am unbalanced. There may be
times, it is true, when I am at the end of my tether,
or may suspect that it is so (4:8), but I share this
only with the Lord. None other sees it.' This may be
the better interpretation of 5:13. In the celebrated
courtroom scene of Acts 26 it was Festus who lost
his equilibrium, not Paul. Let, then, the apostle's
critics think more carefully. The temperature is
being raised.

5:14-15. **For the love of Christ constrains us, we who have
judged this: that one died for all and that consequently all
died. And he died for all so that the living might never more
live to themselves — but rather for him who died and was
raised for them.**

In verse 14 Paul rises above the strife and controversy generated by some at Corinth. Of course he
does not lord it over the churches; of course he is not
out of his mind; of course he is not fleecing the
saints; and of course he does not purvey dubious
doctrine, misrepresenting Almighty God and thus
placing himself in peril.

Why, then, is he engaged in the ministry of the
gospel at, as others might see it, immense cost? Is it
because he endeavours to honour the one who called
him to the apostleship? No doubt, but this is not the
reason given here for a life of selfless commitment. Is
it because Paul hopes to improve his standing at the
last day? (cf. 5:10). Again, no doubt, but this is not

the stated incentive for his work. Yet again, it may be asked, 'Why?'

The answer is that the apostle is hemmed in by love: **'For the love of Christ constrains us'**, the Greek verb *synechō* behind 'constrains' meaning 'to restrain' or even 'to hold in custody'.[11] Paul is held in check by Christ's love so completely that there is no alternative for him: he *must* fulfil his ministry. Other issues — the pressures, the challenges, a hero's impatience for the day of battle, the care of the churches and holy indignation when truth is thrown to the ground — pale into near insignificance.

By 'the love of Christ' does Paul mean the love which he undoubtedly has for the Lord (technically described as 'subjective' love), or the love that Christ has for him ('objective' love)? Although some would disagree,[12] there can be little doubt that the latter is what he has in mind. A statement to the effect that Paul loves the Saviour so much that he can do no other than serve would be perceived as a sickly-sweet, holier-than-thou attitude. But if he admits that the love of Christ for him, a fallen sinner, is so deep, so vast and so intense that he has no choice and no desire to be other than he is, we understand immediately. And so did his friends — and enemies — down there in Corinth all those centuries ago. 'But God demonstrates his own love towards us, in that while we were still sinners, Christ died for us' (Rom. 5:8). Further, as Denney comments, 'Christ is not an instrument, but the agent, of the Father in all that He does.'[13] The love of Christ is the love of God. How may Paul not respond to the Almighty by giving his all?

There is more. The apostle has long since come to an understanding about Christ's love: **'... we who have judged this: that one died for all'**. Paul brings in a hint of autobiography, telling how at some time in the past — probably not long after the Damascus-

road theophany — he, Saul, the erstwhile fanatical
Pharisee from Tarsus, meditated carefully upon
Calvary, about which he must have had some factual
knowledge prior to his conversion. As a very recent
and concerned believer he reinterpreted the crucifixion of Jesus of Nazareth as a sacrifice for other men,
and did so to his total satisfaction; Scripture, the
Christians and his own recent experience testified to
the same truth. True, Saul had known that the cross
proved incontrovertibly that Jesus was accursed by
God (Deut. 21:23; cf. Gal. 3:13), but after he was
confronted by the risen and triumphant Messiah it
became his settled conviction that the Lord did not
perish as a heretic and blasphemer: 'One ['Christ',
the Messiah] died for [= on behalf of] all.' Indeed,
Saul became aware that had the Lord not suffered to
this end there would have been no full display of the
love of God, and there would have been no underlying rationale for a ministry to Jews and Gentiles. As
it was, 'Christ died for our sins, according to the
Scriptures' (1 Cor. 15:3).

Moreover, the apostle is conscious that this act of
self-sacrifice was not ineffective. He comments that
'and consequently [or, 'therefore']¹⁴ **all died'**. As
Hodge observes, 'It was because the apostle judged
that the death of Christ for his people not only placed
them under the strongest obligation to devote themselves to his service, but it secured this devotion.'¹⁵
Because Christ's death involved his judicial alienation from God in the interest of those for whom he
suffered, it follows that about A.D. 30 and at a place
called Calvary they suddenly became in principle
invulnerable to the penalties of God's broken law,
free from the dominion of sin and, in consequence,
the adoptive children of God. In other words, in the
infallible sequence of the plan of salvation they would
in the course of their lifetime be brought to God
(1 Peter 3:18), be united with the Lord in the likeness

of his death and become partakers of his resurrection glory (Rom. 6:5). It transpires that among the 'all' for whom Christ died and who died with him the apostle is included. This is why Paul is now a believer and also an emissary of the gospel.

Two questions arise.

1. Who are the 'all' to whom reference is made?

Does Paul mean all people, the totality of the human race, including, say, the persecuting pharaoh of the Exodus, Judas Iscariot and the ultimate Antichrist, the 'lawless one'? (see 2 Thess. 2:8). Or is he referring to a restricted constituency which, although presumably large, includes some but not others? This question will be addressed when we come to 5:19-21, but a provisional answer would be that the second view is correct because it fits both the context and Paul's other writings, and because the first approach is gratuitous, lacking hard evidence. Admittedly, 'all' often means every member of a particular block of humanity, but to predefine this block as the human race *in toto* is pure assumption.[16] To recapitulate, the apostle indicates that all for whom Christ died also died in that the cross was designed to have an absolutely certain effect upon them. Since this effect is nothing other than conversion, the only possible interpretation is that the 'all' of 5:14 are those who come to faith — that is, the elect. Christ 'loved the church and gave himself for it' (Eph. 5:25; cf. John 6:35-40). As Murray well says, there is an 'equation':[17] those who are raised to live with and for the Lord are all those for whom Christ suffered.

2. In what manner was our Lord's death intended to benefit men?

The answer has to be that he died in the place of others, as their substitute. The language employed in 5:14-15 is forensic, that of the courtroom, the sense being that when Jesus suffered he discharged the penalty owed to God by sinners. Even though very many of the latter were as yet unborn, they, along-side the saints who lived in pre-Christian times as well as during the lifetime of Jesus, were in principle relieved of all liability for their sins: they 'died' to (= were separated from) the just condemnation of God. Compare with Romans 5:12-21 and 1 Corinthians 15:21-22, which show that the union between Christ and his people means that the death and resurrection of the Lord precipitate the church's progress to glory. His death is our death, his life is our life and his exaltation is our exaltation.[18] Further, that the status of those guilty persons for whom Christ suffered moved from condemnation to justification *when* he died is indicated by the parallel between the two verbs: 'one died ... all died'.[19] In the words of Athanasius (A.D. 295–373), 'The death of all was fulfilled in the Lord's body.'[20]

That the little word **'for'** (Greek, *hyper*, followed by a genitive) in 5:14 does carry the idea of substitution is scarcely to be doubted.[21] Although there is another, more powerful way of expressing this concept, as when we read, '... just as the Son of Man did not come to be served, but to serve, and to give his life a ransom *for* [Greek, *anti*] many' (Matt. 20:28; cf. Mark 10:45), this does not mean that the somewhat less vivid construction employed here is inadequate. Indeed, in the Greek of the time *hyper* did carry the idea of substitution, as, for example, in the statement made by Josephus that Jonathan, one of the Maccabean brothers, was 'ready to die *for* them',[22] that is, in the place of his fellow-Jews. Further, the context, no less than the force of the preposition, must be allowed a verdict. As Plummer remarks, 'The ideas of representation and of substitution easily run into one another.' Moule notes that in most cases one who acts on behalf of another takes his place. Exactly so.[23] Had our Lord not intended to die as our representative he would not have allowed himself to be taken to Calvary.

A note is essential at this point. If the church died to, or lost, its legal guilt when Christ suffered, what, then, of the necessity for repentance and faith with a view to salvation? Does not the present exposition lead inexorably to the notion that the elect were justified before they come to faith, implying that they never need to believe because they are saved already? An immediate reply would be that even though the question may (perhaps) be proper, no full answer is called for just here. Although there is an appropriate response, no less definite than Paul's conviction that faith in Christ is a required obedience as a condition of salvation (see 10:5; Rom. 1:5; 15:18; 16:26; cf. 1 Peter 1:2,22), the task of this commentary is to expound the kernel of 5:13-14 and not to consider related issues, important though they are. Even so, I should add that I do not believe that what has sometimes been termed the doctrine of 'eternal justification' is to be found in the Bible. The elect sinner is deemed and declared righteous by God only *when*, by grace, he relies upon Christ for his salvation. But the fact that he does believe is a certain effect of our Lord's death, a truth which is inherent in these verses. Paul assumes that because the church died to sin when Christ died, each and every member of that church actually dies to the guilt and power of sin at some point in his or her lifetime.

Verse 14 flows naturally and necessarily into verse 15. A dead Saviour who remains dead would be an absurdity because he could not personally communicate the benefits of his death to the intended recipients. If he fails here, who else can succeed? No angel, let alone a human being, however saintly, would be adequate for such a task because no angel could qualify as the executor of the new covenant and the fount of the Holy Spirit. Mercifully, it was never within the plan of salvation that Christ should die, subsequently to be abandoned by God when it came to the vital matter of conveying redemption to other men. In revealing that Mary's son would save his people from their sins (Matt. 1:21), the angel meant exactly that. Even though the cross is central to the overall plan of salvation, it is not the whole plan. God the Father has, so the Bible teaches, sent his once-dead and now living Son to turn men from their wicked ways (Acts 3:26). Whereas dead men neither work nor receive pay for their labours, those for whom Christ gave his life become his remuneration *subsequent* to his death (Isa. 53:11). The stone which the builders rejected becomes the headstone of the whole building (Matt. 21:42), and this could not be said of someone permanently in his grave, forsaken by both men and God. In accordance with the eternal plan, our Lord 'was delivered up because of our offences, and was raised because of our justification' (Rom. 4:25). If Christ did not rise in order to benefit those for whom he died, why the resurrection?

Notice that Paul is as careful as he is insistent: **'so that the living might never more live to themselves but rather** [the powerful Greek *alla*: 'on the contrary'] **for him who died and was raised for them'**. The Lord both died for his people and rose on their behalf, which means that, even as he was their substitute upon the cross, so he represents them in heaven.[24] This was one reason for the resurrection, ascension and coronation.

Although the Holy Spirit is not mentioned in 5:15, his person and work are assumed. Paul builds on much that he has written, as, for example, his earlier statement that 'You are a letter of Christ ... engraved ... by the Spirit of the living God' (3:3); or his reference to 'the Lord, the Spirit' in 3:18. The apostle is fully aware that the ascended Christ, now seated at the throne of God, has been granted executive authority to assemble his body, the church — and all so that, as Paul writes, believers might live for the Saviour rather than for themselves.

This is powerful. Formerly the apostle was an unrepentant sinner, serving his selfish desires; the God of Israel had no real place in the affections of this arrogant Jew. Had he lived in Old Testament times he would have been no better, and sensitive saints in that era would have discerned that he was an Israelite in name only. Now, the Messiah has changed everything. Let the Corinthians not be unmindful of why the Lord has done this.

Application

Strange though it might seem, by itself and without interpretation the cross of Christ is a meaningless event. During the age when our Lord was upon earth thousands of men died in this way. What, then, is so special about Calvary? Standing by themselves, passion plays, symbolic crosses on ecclesiastical vestments and church buildings, or delicate golden crucifixes worn as necklaces, say nothing. As a man of his time Saul the Pharisee knew about Roman punishments and he must have been aware of what had happened to Jesus. Nevertheless, it was Calvary as an atoning sacrifice that changed his life, and in the providence of God he was enabled to interpret the cross retrospectively for the benefit of very many. Paul's assertion that 'we ... have judged' in 5:14 is vitally important. If we do not stand with the apostle in this, Christ's blood and tears will do us no good.

And, if we do follow his lead, we may discover that the only symbols of death and resurrection which we require are those ordained by our Lord himself: baptism and communion. Further, if we reflect with care upon what Christ has achieved for us, we shall find that we become driven men. Constrained by his love, we shall not want to flaunt ourselves.

How Paul considers Jesus, approaches the world and esteems the Christians (2 Corinthians 5:16-21)

The apostle is remarkably candid, telling the Corinthians that his attitude to the historic Jesus of Nazareth had been transformed, and in consequence his estimation of fellow-believers. He has come to appreciate that Jesus is the divine Messiah and that Christians constitute the renewed humanity which the Lord is creating. Building on this foundation, Paul outlines the kernel of the gospel message he presents to an unbelieving world and concentrates briefly, but in a spectacular fashion, upon what actually happened to Jesus at Calvary.

All this is a development of the apostle's response to Corinthian shallowness, which parades itself in at least two ways: first, a tendency to evaluate those within and without the churches in terms of worldly dignity, or the lack of it; second, giving heed to Jews who misinterpret Jesus to the detriment of authorized apostolic preaching. Because the church is virtually dismembering itself, Paul spells out the gospel alphabet to bring his readers to their senses.

5:16. So, from now on we know no man according to the flesh. And if we have recognized Christ according to the flesh, yet now no more do we do so.

Many at Corinth were unthinking. Because they failed to cultivate a close walk with the Lord they tended to assess fellow believers in terms of status and background, or the lack of them. This has come out powerfully in the first epistle: 'For you are still carnal. For where there are envy, strife and divisions among you, are you not carnal and behaving like men?' (1 Cor. 3:3). Some gloried 'in appearance and not in the heart' (5:12), and the apostle handles the problem by reflecting upon the sort of man that he used to be before he knew the Lord. Again, as in 5:14, a touch of autobiography creeps in.

The present verse is in effect an application of the previous one, which teaches that believers should serve the living Christ. Launching out, the apostle states that **'So, from now on we know no man according to the flesh.'** Putting himself forward as an example, Paul acknowledges that prior to his conversion he regarded others in the way that so many Corinthians have been doing subsequent to their baptism. This is a most severe criticism of the church: in spite of the fact that his readers are Christians, many estimate one another and ministers of the gospel, not excluding Paul, in a way reminiscent of the world. In a nutshell, they do not appear to be Spirit-filled believers. If they were, they would entertain new standards of judgement. Social caste, educational accomplishments, financial circumstances, or even proven usefulness as servants of the Lord, would be almost, if not totally, irrelevant. They would accord as much honour to the poor man as to the wealthy (cf. James 2:3). Unfortunately, there was preferential treatment of the most obnoxious kind in the church.

The following paragraphs give a sketch of the therapy administered by the apostle.

Prior to his conversion Paul obviously knew about Jesus of Nazareth, determining 'to do many things' against his name (Acts 26:9). The Greek, *ei kai*, behind **'and if'** in 5:16b concedes that he did at one time entertain a dismissive opinion of our Lord.[25] However, **'now'**, following his conversion, he has reinterpreted Calvary and appreciates that the cross was vicarious in both design and effect (5:14). He accepts the Lord for what he was and is.

This being so, Paul realizes that it is his calling to live for a man who, from the point of view of both Jew and Gentile, is at best a figure of fun and frequently an object of blasphemy. But the opinion of the world has not subdued him because Jesus was raised from the dead; men removed him from their scene, but God exalted him (5:15). No longer does Paul regard his Saviour as the man of sorrows, a fit target for ridicule. **'Yet now'** (Greek, *alla nun*) is strong: because there has been an irreversible reversal, so to speak, in the apostle's thinking, he expounds the Lord as **'Christ'**, the divine Messiah rather than simply as 'Jesus'.

An altered appreciation of the Saviour has led to a revised estimate of those who follow him. The Lord has chosen many who appear to be nonentities so that no man might boast in his presence (1 Cor. 1:27-28). In short, Paul has purposed to **'to know no man'** in a worldly manner, the way in which he contemplates Jesus determining how he casts his eyes upon the church. What the saints are in God's sight is all that matters, and the truth is that they are 'in Christ' (5:17). Their status cannot be higher, and the apostle strives to honour this perspective. In that 'no one' is followed by **'no longer'**, the two negatives imply a positive: Paul gazes at Christ *and* the Christians through the lens of the revealed gospel, and there are no exceptions. Will the Corinthians, please, imitate his example?

Furthermore, the English verb 'know' or 'recognize' occurs three times in the Greek text of the verse. The first instance translates a word, *oida*, which means 'to appreciate' or 'to acknowledge' (cf. 1 Thess. 5:12: 'Recognize those who labour among you'), and the remaining two represent another word, *ginōskō*, which here has much the same meaning. The verse cries for a genuine, beneath-the-surface understanding of matters as they really are.

It is not impossible that Paul is attacking those in the church who claim to be 'of Christ' (1 Cor. 1:12), who might have seen Jesus during his earthly ministry, and who possibly feel that they are superior to other believers.[26] That arrogant travellers from Jerusalem were circulating among the churches is shown by the statement in Acts 15:24 that 'Some who went out from us ... have troubled you,' and although these men were never endorsed by the pillars of the mother church, a few of them might have been stirring up trouble at Corinth.

Does Paul bring in 'according to the flesh' to describe how he used to think about Jesus, meaning that 'We thought superficially, in a fleshly way about Christ'? Or is he alluding to the outward appearance of Jesus, stating that 'We used to know Christ as he was in his flesh'? (cf. John 8:15: 'You judge according to the flesh').[27] If the latter, Paul might imply that at some stage he saw Jesus personally, perhaps in Jerusalem where, as a young and enthusiastic rabbi, the Pharisee had studied (Acts 22:3; 26:4). Although such a conjecture is not impossible, perhaps it is irrelevant. The apostle's point is that the truth that Jesus is the Messiah, a belief formerly anathema to him, is now the foundation of his life. In the second half of 5:16, then, 'according to the flesh' would balance with the first part of the verse, where Paul describes how he does not now estimate other believers.

5:17. Thus, if anyone is in Christ — a new creation! The old things have passed away and, look, new things have come into being.

Some versions read, 'If any man is in Christ, he is a new *creature.*' But instead of 'creature' it is better to read **'creation'** (Greek, *ktisis*). Paul, catching his breath in amazement, declares that, consequent upon Christ's death and resurrection, all who belong to him enjoy their happy state because they have undergone a radical re-creation (parallel this with our Lord's teaching concerning spiritual rebirth in John 3:3-7). When someone comes to the Lord he needs to realize that his new status is the sovereign handiwork of God and that his faith is not something he has manufactured by himself and for himself. This is why the believer looks at Jesus, the church and the world in a new way. In 4:6 the apostle likened a true conversion experience to the event of the first day of the creation week, when God summoned light into being, and the analogy resurfaces here (compare Gal. 6:15).[28]

The central idea is that the believer is a component of the new order to which redemption leads, 'new' in 'new creation' signifying fulfilment.[29] Although the church awaits the appearance of the Saviour, as indicated powerfully in the earlier part of chapter 5, a co-ordinate reality is that the age to come has already penetrated the present system and has done so in the persons of Christian people. We are, as it were, invaders in a doomed territory, simultaneously sounding the death-knell for the old and ringing in the new.

The apostle continues: **'The old things have passed away and, look, new things have come into being.'** His meaning is that for the Christian the present world remains visible but is in principle a thing of the past. 'Passed away' translates a Greek

verb, *parēlthen*, signifying the replacement of something that is exhausted and redundant by that which
retains its freshness and usefulness.[30] 'Old things' —
old preferences, old criteria, the old dispensation and
old ways of estimating others — have passed from
the scene, and 'new things' — new preferences, new
criteria, the new covenant and new ways of relating
to others — have come into being, never to fade
away.[31] How can this be? Because the believer is **'in
Christ'**.

This terse expression, often employed by Paul, is
too complex to permit a full exposition. Among other
truths, it tells of reconciliation, adoption, fellowship
with God, security and eternal hope.[32] If we are robed
by Christ and are seen by God 'in' him, we have all
things. To repeat, in context the spotlight falls on the
intrusion into the old by the new, 'the deposit' of the
Holy Spirit (1:22; 5:5) still being in the apostle's
mind. Standing in the dawn twilight we see ourselves
as the citizens of a not-so-far country whose hopes
cannot be long deferred.

Notice Paul's **'anyone'**: background and status are
irrelevant. Even though he does so in a loving fashion
and by a clear presentation of the truth, is the
apostle once again attacking those bent upon turning
the Corinthians back to a stale, racially orientated
Judaism? It could be.

His **'Look!'** is virtually a cry of jubilation. 'Behold,'
he writes, 'what is happening! When you gaze at your
fellow-Christians you glimpse the eternal glory shining from their faces. Everything is new' (cf. Isa.
43:19; Rev. 21:5). And this in spite of the fact that at
Corinth many of the saints lacked worldly status
(1 Cor. 1:26-28). How careful, then, should the anti-
Paul faction be if they propose again to aim their
javelins at the apostle and by implication at those
converted through his ministry!

A final point. The present verse (5:17) leads towards 5:19, which states that God 'was in Christ'. In the days of his flesh Jesus Christ was the God-man. (He still is.) This means that God was in Christ to ensure that we, in a somewhat different sense, should be 'in' Christ. In him God and man meet. There is mystery in this, but a mystery that points to one certain conclusion, which is that our Saviour is the indispensable focus of salvation. Again, the Judaizers need to beware.

5:18. And all things are from God, who reconciled us to himself through Christ and who gave to us the ministry of reconciliation...

From 5:11 onwards the apostle has written in the first person, both singular and plural, 'I' and 'we' (five times in 5:11; three times in 5:12; twice in 5:13; twice in 5:14 and three times in 5:16). All along the emphasis has been upon what Paul feels, what Paul does, what Paul hopes, how Paul does not vaunt himself, how Paul is motivated, how Paul has long since worked out his theology of the cross, and how Paul considers Christ, Christians and unbelievers.

There may be a danger of imbalance, and the apostle senses that a check is needed. He, the erstwhile persecutor but now a senior servant, though no higher than this, draws attention to someone infinitely more exalted than he. **'All things'** would refer to those for whom Christ died and rose (5:14-15), plus the world to come (5:17); it is all of God. Paul has his place, but he is subordinate. The Corinthians are not to suppose that he resembles the pseudo-apostles, arrogating to himself a prestige and authority to which he has no right. In the words of the hymn, 'To God be the glory, great things hath he done!' the emphasis being upon 'he'.

The key-words **'reconciled'** and **'reconciliation'** (Greek: verb, *katallassō*; noun, *katallagē*) appear for the first time in Paul's writings, and he is the only New Testament author to employ them. It is not impossible that the apostle's presentation stems from his experience of reconciliation when travelling to Damascus: then and there Saul knew that he had been forgiven. Of the ten occurrences of the word-family given to us, five are clustered in 5:18-20, suggesting that at this point there is an ultra-important concept. In fact, it is so important that a full consideration probably ought not to be restricted to the examination of a single group.[33] As Morris remarks, 'It is clear that the concept of reconciliation is sometimes present when the actual word does not occur, for example, when "making peace" is spoken of.'[34]

1. The meaning of reconciliation

Reconciliation is the restoration of a broken relationship by an initiative taken by one or both of two estranged parties. 1 Corinthians 7:11 teaches that a wife who has abandoned her husband is to come home and be reconciled to him. Who might be responsible for the breakdown is not the issue. (Did his bad behaviour drive her out, or was she wilful?) What is important is that she returns and thereby helps to heal the rift.

2. The broken relationship

The Bible teaches that man's numerous problems stem from his voluntary estrangement from God. This is why the book of Genesis, and particularly chapter 3 concerning the fall of Adam and Eve, is vital. Were there no sin there would be no death. When men break fellowship with the Lord they ruin themselves, and this is what happened in the Garden of Eden: alienation was the instant aftermath of Adam's sin. Many centuries later, the Lord put a question to wandering Israel: 'O my people, what have I done to you? And how have I wearied you? Testify against me' (Micah 6:3). The only possible answer was that God had done no wrong but that Israel had rebelled. This is how it always is: 'For all have sinned and fall short of the glory of God' (Rom. 3:23). In 5:18 the apostle builds upon this truth.

3. Who is responsible for seeking reconciliation?

Consider two persons, 'A' and 'B', who have an argument and who are no longer friends. Let's assume that one of the two, 'A' rather than 'B', is in the wrong, and that (contrary to what is sometimes said) it is not six of one and half a dozen of the other. Whose duty is it to get things moving in order to bring about a renewal of friendship? As the New Testament sees the matter, it is always the offender (in this case, 'A') who ought to seek reconciliation in order to mend his relationship with the offended party (in this case, 'B'). The latter has no prior obligation because the fault is not his. This is brought out in Matthew 5:23-24, where someone who has caused a rift takes steps to be reconciled to the person whom he has grieved. Within the context of 2 Corinthians 5:18 the onus is assumed to lie with offending sinners to placate God if they wish the relationship to be restored. And failure here must end in disaster because 'It is a fearful thing to fall into the hands of the living God' (Heb. 10:31).

This is why in 5:18 the emphasis falls upon believers being reconciled to God rather than God initiating reconciliation, even though the latter truth is the cornerstone of the peace process: it is the Lord who has provided an open door for the sinner. Bearing this in mind, Paul's words are consistent with the way the Bible looks at the matter: as professing believers we were the offenders, at one time self-alienated from the Lord. Now, by God's grace, we have been enabled to discover a way by which the angered and angry God can be placated. What is more, having taken advantage of it, we have experienced the benefits given by Christ.[35] Quite apart from a detailed interpretation of individual passages, it is clear that because God is hostile to evil it would be incorrect to say that we reconcile ourselves to the Almighty as if there were something about *him* with which we, children of dust, condescendingly need to come to terms.

But how does God arrive at a settlement with people like us? Is it that he takes into account practical repentance considered as a merit, or a profuse, well-meant apology, or a gift of some sort? The answer is strictly negative in each case. Paul takes us further.

4. Reconciliation as an effect

Notice that in 5:18 the apostle insists that, although we have found peace with God, this reconciliation has come about **'through Christ'**. That is, the reconciling act or offering, however it may be described, is not centred on anything that we may have brought forward. It resides in the person and activity of the Lord Jesus. Something that he did was so good that because of it God's righteous anger has been cancelled once and for all.

We have just been told what Jesus did so that sinners can be reconciled to God: he died (5:14-15). **'Reconciled'** is an aorist participle *(tou katallaxantos)* which does duty here as an adjective, implying an attribute of God and declaring what he provided at a particular time and place. Almost literally, 'All things are from the God-who-has-reconciled.' And the apostle will enlarge upon this in 5:19. Although sincere regret for being offensive plus commitment to Christ are essential for reconciliation, by themselves they are perfectly insufficient. An objective sacrifice of adequate worth given in the place of sinners ('on behalf of' or 'in the place of', 5:14) is needed to dissolve God's holy wrath. Christ provided this historically by offering himself. It follows that those who unite with the Lord Jesus by faith find by experience that God reconciles himself to them: at the same time that he does this, he lets them know.

5. The offender's unwillingness to seek reconciliation

Paul says more. The basis for reconciliation is Christ, and those who require this blessing are offending sinners rather than the offended God. But — and it is a considerable 'but' — the apostle implies that left to themselves sinful men would never aspire to reconciliation. 'There is no one who seeks after God' (Rom. 3:11). Rebels would never turn back to the Lord even though Christ may have died for them.

This is why 5:18 insists that God has 'reconciled us to himself through Christ'. It is true that in a relative sense when we believed we took the initiative in seeking reconciliation. Even so, how was it that we, uncharacteristically, chose to turn to the Saviour? The answer is that the Holy Spirit renewed us and made us want to be reconciled.

Although 5:18 does not mention the regenerating work of the Spirit of God, this glorious activity is assumed. Indeed, much of what we have read in 2 Corinthians is an exposition of the matter.[36] The God who was wrathful with us because of our faults loved us so much that he provided his Son as an offering for our sins *and* subsequently through Christ sent the Spirit to make us desire him.[37]

Perhaps Romans 5:9-11 ought to be read in parallel with these verses. There it is said that the objective reconciliation effected by the cross has obliterated God's holy anger (Rom. 5:9-10). But by itself the cross does not change hearts. It is through the living Christ, rather than a dead one, that we rejoice in God and that we have entered into the state of reconciliation (Rom. 5:11). This is Paul's immediate concern here in 2 Corinthians 5:18.

6. The ministry of reconciliation

The apostle continues: the God who brought about reconciliation has in his own interests given to **'us the ministry of reconciliation'**.[38] Previously in the epistle the work of the gospel is described as 'the ministry of the Spirit' (3:8) and 'the ministry of righteousness' (3:9). If we place these three expressions in line we see what look like three main points in an apostolic sermon: reconciliation presupposes justification and sanctification.

There is a slight difficulty with regard to the two occurrences of 'us' in 5:18. The first would appear to refer to all believers, in that all such are reconciled to God. Does this mean that the 'ministry of reconciliation' has been committed to all of 'us' (second occurrence)? Hodge thinks not because only ministers exercise a ministry, but Barrett observes shrewdly that 'The change from *us* Christians is abrupt and difficult.[39] It may be that Hodge has the stronger argument in that the apostle claims that God 'gave' the ministry to 'us', the past tense indicating a time when Paul and perhaps others received their vocation. If the first 'us' refers to the reconciled apostle and his colleagues all would run smoothly: Saul of

Tarsus has been transformed and now proclaims the
Jesus whom he persecuted. The immediate reference,
then, is probably not to all believers although all
believers are reconciled. In Barnett's words, 'Paul is
here saying, autobiographically, "God reconciled me
... gave to me the ministry of reconciliation,"' even
though the apostle may not point exclusively to
himself.[40]

There could be a sting in the verse's tail. Have the
false apostles been given a ministry? No. But Paul
has. Let the Corinthians be wary.

*5:19. ... that God was in Christ reconciling the world to
himself, not reckoning their transgressions to them and
having placed in us the word of reconciliation.*

Here and in 5:20 the apostle unfolds the message
that he proclaims to the world at large. Perhaps there
are few places in the New Testament where the heart
of the gospel is set out so plainly.

The opening, **'that God was in Christ reconciling
the world to himself ...'**, develops the preceding
verse.[41] The assertion concerning God and Christ is
capable of more than one interpretation:

1. It might mean that the man Jesus is God
incarnate. Christ is not only the agent of God
but is one with him: at that time 'God-in-Christ
was reconciling ...'

2. The sense could be that 'In Christ God was
reconciling the world to himself', 'in Christ'
showing *how* God was reconciling the world to
himself. God the Father and Christ are considered as distinct persons.[42]

3. Or, Paul may be saying that God was reconciling 'the world' in Christ, 'the world' standing for the elect people of God, both Jew and

Gentile, considered collectively as 'in Christ'.[43]
This perception is not far removed from the second suggestion.

None of these is grammatically impossible. If a
choice has to be made, one might opt for the second
because it continues the thought of 5:18, which tells
us that God reconciled us to himself 'through Christ'.
As for 'world', the Greek *kosmos* appears without the
definite article, 'the', which may suggest that it
reflects 'us' in verse 18 and 'all' in verse 14. If so, the
sense is that Christ came from God to install some
men from every age and race as the hub of his new
creation. The universalism of this statement consists
in the principle that the redeeming love of God ex-
tends worldwide, embracing both the Jew and the
Gentile, although not all Jews and Gentiles. Thus the
'world' is that new order yet to be manifested in its
completeness, the apostle interpreting salvation less
in terms of individuals reconciled to God and more as
the renewal of a system temporarily deranged by sin
(cf. Col. 1:20: 'and by him to reconcile all things to
himself'). As Kistemaker remarks, 'Paul's explanation
clarifies God's intention to achieve a reconciliation
that spans the entire world.'[44]

How God achieved this reconciliation is stated
clearly: '**... not reckoning their transgressions to
them**'. 'Not reckoning' is the obverse of what is said
in Romans 4:6-8, which expounds the imputation of
righteousness in terms of Psalm 32:1-2. This, in
turn, tells out the happiness of the man whose
transgression is forgiven and whose sin is covered.
The man whom God forgives is the man whom God
vindicates, non-imputation of sin being a sort of
prelude to the imputation of righteousness: the latter
does not come into being without the former. By
placing text against text it becomes evident that Paul
was a genius when handling Scripture. The apostle is

intensely biblical, writing with the awareness that the
ills of the world are due to Adam's fall and that the
reconstitution of the created order centres upon the
removal of sin and its effects. This, he indicates, is
what God does in Christ. Although the emphasis
rests upon the Father's initiative, there is no eclipse
of the action taken by the Son; it is assumed that he
was willing to suffer in the place of sinners, thereby
displaying the love of God towards the objects of his
righteous anger.[45]

As 5:19 comes to a conclusion the apostle picks
up and expands the last part of 5:18, stating that
God **'placed in us the word of reconciliation'**.[46]
'Word' (Greek, *logos*) implies a reasoned, logical
system designed to be set before thinking men. Paul
and his colleagues have (astonishingly) become the
fulcrum, the hinge-point, of the entire plan of salvation. The Greek *themenos* behind 'placed' points to
the call of the apostle to the ministry and is in the
middle voice, implying that in commissioning Paul
God acted in his own interests: love will identify and
secure both the means and the end.[47] Compare with
Romans 10:14-15, which shows that salvation is
through faith in the Christ *as heralded* by God's
messengers. Whereas without such men there would
be no hearing, no faith and no reconciliation, God
has deposited with his servant and his co-workers a
proclamation which, if understood and accepted for
what it is, introduces its hearers to the Lord.[48]

In 5:19 the apostle assumes, not for the first time,
the work of the Holy Spirit in bringing men to faith.
At Calvary Christ paid the price, and at conversion
God applies the benefits of the cross, our sins ceas-
ing to be reckoned to us. The objective act of self-
sacrifice leads via the medium of the preached word
to repentance and reconciliation.

5:20. On behalf of Christ, therefore, we are ambassadors as
if God is appealing through us: 'We beseech on behalf of
Christ, be reconciled to God.'

There is a very considerable problem with the second
part of this verse in the form offered by the English
versions. Take the New King James Version, for
example: 'We implore *you* on Christ's behalf, be
reconciled to God.'[49] Accordingly, in the name of the
Lord the apostle would appear to be summoning his
first readers, the Corinthians, to turn to Christ,
exhorting them in terms characteristic of a primary
evangelistic call to unbelievers. This is in spite of the
fact that, whatever their vagaries, they did believe.
Ponder the NKJV rendering alongside Paul's later
assurance that if the Corinthians examine themselves they will realize that they are 'in the faith'
(13:5; cf. 1:21-22; Heb. 6:9). Seen in this light, do we
detect at this point in the letter an aberration of the
apostolic mind and a monumental slip of the apostolic pen?

Apparently, some sort of reconciliation is needed.
Not surprisingly, over the years the difficulty has
been recognized, and there have been numerous
proposals. Here is one which is not uncommon, and
the Englishman John Gill, an eminent eighteenth-
century Calvinistic Baptist, will articulate it. He
writes that the apostle *was* addressing the Corinthians. In Gill's words, Paul exhorts the church to '...
let your wills bow, and be resigned to his [that is, to
Christ's], since he is the God of peace to you; and as
you are reconciled by Christ as a priest, be reconciled
to him as your King, and your God; to all his ordi-
nances and appointments; to all the orders and laws
of his house; conform in all things to his will and
pleasure, which we, as his ambassadors, in his name
and stead, have made known unto you. You ought to

be all obedience to him, and never dispute any thing he says or orders.'[50]

Let it be said that this view is reasonable *if* the apostle has the Corinthians in mind. And the distinctive employment of the second person plural 'you' in our English versions would seem to back this up, bearing in mind that everywhere else in this letter 'you' refers to the Christian readers. Can this be an exception?[51] On the other hand, the call to 'Be reconciled to God' is arguably inappropriate for those described in 1:1 as 'saints'. It is beyond doubt that at conversion the Corinthians were reconciled and that what was accomplished once and for all cannot have been undone in such a way that a fundamental restoration is now deemed necessary. To the Colossians Paul writes that 'You, who once were alienated and enemies in your mind by wicked works ... now he has reconciled in the body of his flesh through death' (Col. 1:21-22), and what was true for them was of universal application, Corinth not excluded. The difficulty with Gill's fairly conventional approach is the suppressed implication that Christians can be wholly alienated from their God. Further, the interpretation appears to anticipate the superficial cry not unknown in some more modern pulpits that if Christ is our Saviour he ought to become our Lord. But is this real? Can he be the one and not the other? In a sense, yes, because when Christians sin, as we all do, we fall out of fellowship with the Lord. Yet he does not cease to be our great advocate. Nor, when we lapse, do we cease to love him. We loathe the sin that drags us down. Even in our worst moments we do not forfeit our reconciliation. Although the Corinthians were not without their problems, to imply that they were alienated from the Lord as they had been before conversion is too strong.

Another route would be that exemplified by Kistemaker, who asks if Paul is 'addressing only the

members of the Corinthian church or does the
apostle have in mind all the people in the world?' He
concludes: 'The imperative "be reconciled" is directed
to both the Corinthians *and* the world' (emphasis
added).[52] This is difficult because the Corinthians
were already reconciled.

But perhaps there is another approach which, this
commentary would suggest, does excellent justice
both to the apostle's words and to acknowledged
Christian experience. As Bengel writes, 'Paul indicates not so much what he is doing [that is, pre-
senting overtures to the Corinthians], as what he is
doing in the discharge of all the duties of his office
[that is, as he preaches to unbelievers at large].'[53] Or,
as Lenski notes, 'Paul adds in brief how as ambassadors in Christ's stead his assistants and he speak
in Christ's name, or, which is the same thing, how
God speaks through them.'[54]

What these writers mean is that 5:20 develops
5:19, clarifying the basic gospel message which Paul
proclaims to unconverted men. This explains the
significance of 'therefore' as 5:20 opens up. Moreover,
in the Greek text of this verse the accusative 'you'
(humas) following 'beseech' is not introduced as a
distinct entity, the command to be reconciled being
strictly impersonal and undirected.

Here is the crux of the issue. The eloquent absence
of the distinct Greek pronoun 'you' implies very
strongly that the Corinthians are not the specific
targets for Paul's shaft. Because there is no grammatical necessity to bring in 'you' with reference to
the church, its arbitrary introduction in the English
versions can be considered as an over-dynamic
interpretation, diverting the reader from the point,[55]
which is that the apostle reports the kernel of his
preaching in the real world as he finds it. For a
fleeting moment the problems in the Corinthian
church are not on the agenda, Paul's immediate

tactic being to expound something of the charge given to Christ's ambassadors to go everywhere and preach the gospel. He declares that when he is out and about, in the market place or the synagogue or in court, or travelling en route to the next town, he directs unconverted men to 'be reconciled to God'. Because this imperative is cast as an impersonal second person plural, an application to the Corinthians would be awkward as well as out of context.

Here are verses 19 and 20 *en bloc*. Speech marks, which Paul's Greek did not possess, are added to help make the point:

> ... that God was in Christ reconciling the world to himself, not reckoning their transgressions to them and having placed in us the word of reconciliation. On behalf of Christ, therefore, we are ambassadors as if God is appealing through us: 'We beseech on behalf of Christ, be reconciled to God.'

Why this disclosure? The probable answer is that the apostle is widening his attack upon the hostile element in Corinth. He asserts the authority given to him by Christ, for whom he is an emissary and in whose name he begs men to turn to the Lord. His manner is astonishing in that an ambassador might be expected to stand upon his dignity, reflecting the greatness of the person whom he represents. As a rule, diplomats robed with authority do not plead, and Saul the Pharisee would never have done so.[56] But, as with his Master, authority, earnestness and humility are interwoven, and those who reject or distort the apostle's message grieve his divine and gentle Principal. Sadly, such is the state of affairs in the church to which he writes that it is necessary for Paul to make clear what he has to say to men in general. Do the false teachers match up to this? By

no means. Why not? Because they are not ambassadors appointed by God.

'On behalf of Christ' in the first half of 5:20 must
mean 'in the place of Christ'.[57] **'We are ambassadors'**
derives from a verb signifying action rather than a
passive retention of office. Compare with Ephesians
6:20: '… the gospel, for which I am an ambassador in
chains'.[58] Paul is on duty for the King of kings and
must herald accurately and faithfully what has been
committed to him. Nor is this an illustration: the
apostle really *is* an ambassador. He asserts that
when he preaches he is Christ's representative rather
than a subordinate agent. Therefore he is to be heard
as if he is the Lord.

That is not all. Because Christ is God, Paul is
Christ's mouthpiece 'as if God is appealing through
us'. 'As if' means 'seeing that', as in 2 Peter 1:3,
'Seeing that his divine power has granted to us
everything…'[59] 'Appealing' translates the Greek verb
parakalountos (hence the English 'Paraclete'): it is the
Almighty, no less, who exhorts the hearers as one
who is their helper and advocate. Notice that the
tenses are couched in the present tense ('we are
ambassadors'; God is 'appealing'; Paul does 'beseech')
to stress that urgent proclamation and encouragement are ongoing features of the apostle's ministry.

So what does God through Christ have to say
through this man? In brief, 'Be reconciled to God.'
The Greek verb *katallagēte*, in the phrase 'be reconciled', is both passive and a point imperative, implying the need for immediate, decisive acceptance of
that great thing which God will perform for men if
they turn to him: they are to take an initiative on the
understanding that resources are available for them.
Paul summons his fallen and intractable hearers to
hand themselves over to the offended but accessible
God so that he might operate in their lives, subsequently being at peace with them and they with him.

Moreover, this is a command rather than an option, a summons to be obeyed on the instant. Here is the will of God for all who find themselves exposed to the public 'ministry of reconciliation' (5:18). And because it is not a remote, impersonal will, Paul announces that 'We beseech on behalf of Christ'. 'Beseech' (from the Greek *deomai*) occurs in Romans 1:10, where the apostle tells how he *begs* the Lord to allow him to travel safely to Rome. Here, the ambassador of Christ not only issues an authoritative summons to his hearers, he urges them personally to obey, aware that God is pleading through him. Why should they die? The ambassador is concerned that the will of his Sovereign be obeyed, and this gives wings to his ministry.

Clearly, the present exposition raises not a few questions. For example, how can Christ desire and demand that all who hear the gospel repent when obviously some will not have been elected to salvation and therefore will never benefit from God's saving grace? How is it that the Most High can predestine some to glory, thereby leaving others as he finds them — in their sins — yet exhort all who hear the good news to come to Christ and find peace? That these are major issues is beyond dispute, but Scripture demands that we travel as far as it takes us, neither overstepping the mark nor falling short of it.

Perhaps there are three relevant points. First, systematic theology, an inductive discipline, ought to be the daughter of biblical exposition: working backwards, we hammer out our creed from what we perceive the Bible to say in a thousand places, of which this is one. Second, that we have in 5:20 an inexplicable antinomy, a seeming tension between two mutually friendly principles, is not to be denied. None the less, the Word of God lives with it and requires us to do so. Can we be unhappy?[60] Third, to quote Reymond, in Paul's day:

... there was only one lord of the world, the Roman Caesar. But according to the Christian gospel, he and all other kings now have a rival Lord who wears a crown that out-rivals all the lords of the earth, before whom every knee will bow and every tongue will confess his Lordship to the glory of God the Father. Therefore, 'to do the work of an evangelist' (2 Tim 4:5) is not simply to tell people 'how to be saved'; to 'evangelize' is to proclaim, to announce, from the housetops that Jesus Christ is Lord of lords. And to announce that Jesus Christ reigns as King and Lord of the universe is to announce to the Caesars of this world that they do not. To proclaim Christ's Lordship is *to confront* all the petty pretensions of the religious and secular pagan lords of this world with his true and sovereign Kingship which demands heart submission.[61]

Otherwise explained, evangelism should not, in the first place, concern itself with those for whom Christ did or did not die. Because Christ is Lord of all it is the responsibility of all who hear the good news to turn to him and thus be reconciled to God: faith leading to salvation is their duty. This is the heart of the message which Paul makes clear to the Corinthians.

5:21. He made him — who recognized no sin — sin on our behalf, so that we might become the righteousness of God in him.

1. Nevertheless, for whom did Christ die?

The apostle says in 5:19 that God reconciled men to himself through the death of Christ. In 5:20 he claims that he is a herald of the message of reconciliation, and in 5:21 he explains upon what basis sinners may experience peace with God: all who are urged to turn to the Saviour must be given good reason to suppose that their application will not be in vain.

In short, 5:21 is to be understood as an elaboration of the apostle's statement about the content of his gospel. But if this is the case, yet another question arises: may a preacher urge unregenerate and unrepentant sinners to turn to the Lord on the presumption that he suffered for them? Does he possess any scriptural warrant for saying this? If he has, must not such a warrant assume that Christ died for Adam and all his natural descendants? Following on from this, and in the light of the statement in 5:14 that 'If one died for all, therefore all died', must it not be accepted that corporate humanity has died both to guilt and (contrary to observation) to the power of sin? And, should this be so, does not Paul's doctrine of salvation begin to unravel?

It is at this point that balance — not compromise — has to be maintained. Scripture must be interpreted by Scripture. On the one hand, the New Testament is clear that God's good news for all people must explain Christ's death as the only basis for forgiveness. To put it in a back-to-front way, the fact that the Lord did die and was raised from the dead means that the cross has a very special significance. Peter told Cornelius and his household that 'Whoever believes in him [the crucified and risen Jesus] will receive remission of sins' (Acts 10:43). In the synagogue at Antioch in Pisidia Paul informed his hearers not only that our Lord was raised, but that

'Through this man is preached to you the forgiveness of sins' (Acts 13:37-38). To the Athenian idolaters the same apostle declared that everyone should repent because Jesus, whom God raised from the dead, will be the universal Judge (Acts 17:31). Before their conversion the Galatians learned about Jesus Christ 'crucified', with an emphasis upon why he died (Gal. 3:1).

Nevertheless, the New Testament gives us the clear impression that why our Lord died and for whom he died are distinct (not separate) issues. This is a point of the utmost importance. For example, we find that apostolic preaching never at any time exhorted unbelievers, both Jews and Gentiles, to turn to Christ on the prior assumption that he went to the cross for them personally.[62] Evidence for this supposition is lacking. Paul and others proclaimed the death, resurrection and return of the Lord to all and sundry, and explained the cross as a satisfaction to God for the sins of men, yet never assumed that their unconverted audiences were necessarily among those on whose behalf our Lord shed his blood. But — and here is another point of extreme importance — these ambassadors for Christ never failed to apply this principle retrospectively to those who were known to have turned to the Saviour. Paul can inform the Ephesians that 'Christ ... loved the church and gave himself for it' (Eph. 5:25) and acknowledges that the Lord 'loved me and gave himself for me' (Gal.2:20). In 2 Corinthians the apostle is adamant that the death of Christ makes the salvation of some certain rather than possible: 'If one died for all, then all died' (5:14). There are many other such statements.

These considerations infer a switch, a careful and subtle change of focus, between 5:19-20 and 5:21. In 5:19-20 Paul presents the message that he delivers to the world around him, and in 5:21 there is a pointer to distinctively Christian experience: our Lord was **'made ... sin so that we might become the righteousness of God in him'**. The expression 'so that' indicates certainty of purpose: the cross was designed as the instrument by which justification would become real.[63]

Why, then, the delicate shift in emphasis? The answer would be that we need to recall the traumas that were convulsing the church in Corinth. When he wrote this letter Paul rejoiced and wept, possibly simultaneously. In the light of what he was about to say in the next verse, 6:1, it was vital to assure the people that in his estimation they were the Lord's. The death of Christ was intended to change their lives, and it had not failed to do so. By God's grace they had heard Paul preach, understood what he had to say, turned to the Lord, and had consequently become 'the righteousness of God' in Christ. Paul abandons reticence and reserve, specifying those for whom our Lord laid down his life. He suffered for 'us', renewed believers.[64]

2. In what way, and why, was Christ 'made sin'?

The verse is staggering in its vivacity, and there are few, if any, passages in the New Testament which tell out as powerfully the basis upon which a sinner can be reconciled to God. Notwithstanding a switch in emphasis, as Paul contemplates the blessed situation of the believing Christian, 5:21 must not be read in stark isolation from 5:19-20. If men are to be summoned to reconciliation with God they need to know how this is possible. And if they are told that reconciliation is through Jesus Christ they need to be informed who he is, and what it is that he has done that will avail for them if they believe. And if (like the Corinthians) they have been reconciled they need to be reminded again and again of the foundation of their happy state.

First, Paul describes our Lord as a man who was unaware of any sin in his own life. An expansion might run as follows: **'He** [God] **made him** [Jesus Christ] — **who recognized no sin** [in himself] — **sin on our behalf.'** During the thirty or more years of our Lord's incarnate life he never at any time offended his heavenly Father, who always had reason to be well pleased with him.[65] Upon the cross he was heard to issue the rhetorical question: 'My God, my God, why have you forsaken me?' (Matt. 27:46; cf. Ps. 22:1), knowing full well that his sufferings were not due to any personal demerit.

The apostle continues: 'He [God] ... made [Christ] sin.' Paul's words are forceful to the point of violating the undiscerning mind. Notice, first, that the apostle does not claim that Christ was a sinner. He did not at some point become depraved, a slave to the sinful impulses inherent in other men. The period during which he knew no personal sin would have been his total lifespan, culminating in the hours spent upon the cross for the sake of others, hours in which he was conscious of his moral integrity. The meaning has to be that Jesus was, as it were, the individual personification and representative of the sinners for whom he perished. Paul has said as much in 5:14.[66] More importantly, if, as is likely, the apostle had Isaiah 52:13 – 53:12 in mind when he penned this statement, we are able to measure his meaning exactly.

It has sometimes been suggested that the 'sin' which Jesus was 'made' is the antitype to the Old Testament sin-offering.[67] That this was so is true, but it is not what is meant here. The interpretation is to be rejected for several reasons. First, in the Septuagint the Greek word for sin, *hamartia*, when used for 'sin-offering', is always in the genitive, 'for sin' or 'of sin'. This is not the case in 5:21. Second, the word 'sin' occurs twice in the verse, and consistency demands that it should have the same connotation in both instances. Since it means sin (not sin-offering) when Paul indicates that Jesus 'recognized no sin', the sense ought not to be changed in the second occurrence. Third, the apostle states that our Lord was made 'sin' so that sinners might be constituted the 'righteousness of God' in him. The only way in which they can become the 'righteousness of God' is that they are *regarded* as perfectly righteous even though, in themselves, they are not. It follows that our Lord was made sin in that he was regarded and treated as a sinner although he was not inherently sinful.

But why does Paul not describe Jesus as a 'sin-offering'? Perhaps the apostle wants to stress the solidarity of Jesus and all who belong to him. When the Father beheld our Lord at Calvary, although he did not loathe him he abandoned him to wrath, deeming the elect to be represented in his person. Similarly, when God sees him in glory he sees us (cf. Heb. 9:24: '... now to appear in the presence of God for us') — such is the intensity of the union between Saviour and saved. The introduction of the idea of the sin-offering would be inappropriate. As someone once wrote, this verse shows that Jesus endured 'what God does to sin, and makes visible what happens when man has God against him'.[68]

3. What is the meaning of 'that we might become the righteousness of God in him'?

In stating that God 'made' Jesus to be 'sin', 5:21 focuses upon the historic crucifixion. Equally, when we read that we **'become'** the righteousness of God 'in him', the meaning is that we have entered into a status which is irreversible.[69] Because of Jesus' death and his subsequent acceptance by God, as evidenced by his resurrection and ascension, our Lord's

righteousness will always be attributed to those who
are 'in him', that is, who are united to him by faith.
This imputation is of such a quality that believers are
said to be righteousness personified. The qualifier **'of
God'** may mean either that our righteousness is from
God, or that it is not dissimilar to that of God,[70] or
both. The statement is amazing.

Application

Brace yourself for a little slice (only a *little*) of church history! The
section which we have studied (5:16-21) relates to those to
whom the gospel ought to be preached, and the way in which it
should be preached. These are issues which have been known
to generate warm debate, particularly among Calvinists.

Since the time of John Calvin (1509–64) many have attempted to develop his theology. This is because 'Calvinism' did
not begin with the great French Reformer and because he was
not inspired. He loved the doctrines of grace but never gave
them their perfect expression, nor (no doubt) did he aspire to do
so. Hyper-Calvinism (or, high Calvinism), for instance, a school
of thought which manifested itself among English Baptists and
others in the late 1600s and since, has judged that the call to
trust in Christ is *not* to be addressed to the unbelieving world but
should be reserved for those who are perceived to be burdened
for their salvation. For example, in 1872 some 'Strict Baptists'
committed themselves to a rejection of 'the doctrine that man in a
state of nature should be exhorted to believe in or turn to God'.[71]
Two assumptions behind this radical statement are that the
unawakened sinner's alleged responsibility to obey the gospel
implies that he possesses an innate ability, or 'power', to do so,
and that a universal call to conversion denies the doctrine of
definite redemption, which properly teaches that Christ died to
save some men certainly rather than all men potentially. The
justly famed William Gadsby (1773–1844) had by this time
entered into print. According to him, 'To *preach* or *proclaim* God's
will is one thing, but to *offer* that which is the sole prerogative of

God to give and to make manifest, is quite another thing.'[72] In context, he is not slow to parody Arminian evangelistic appeals, and there is gold in much of what he says.

Nevertheless, in disagreement both with Gadsby's logic and the 1872 statement, one would respectfully suggest that 5:20 and its immediate context constitute a powerful tool to aid us in explaining what ought to be said to non-Christians who are oblivious to their need. This is not to say that there is no special word of comfort for those who do come under conviction of sin, a word which might be inappropriate for others. Nevertheless, does not hyper-Calvinism misinterpret the therapy partly because it fails to diagnose man's predicament with sufficient accuracy? Moral disinclination never cancels responsibility, and saving faith is presented by the New Testament as a required obedience (see Rom. 1:5). Paul entertained no reluctance whatever about confronting men with the demand that they turn to the Lord Jesus Christ in repentance. It was his life's work.

6. Paul's pastoral ministry

2 Corinthians 6:1 – 7:16

The day of salvation
(2 Corinthians 6:1-10)

It may be that these ten verses are the kernel of the whole letter. Through no fault of his own Paul has to some extent been alienated from a church that leans towards spurious apostles. He issues a challenge based upon the principle that the Corinthians have been privileged to see the turn of the ages, Moses' era having anticipated what Paul terms 'the day of salvation' (6:2, building upon Isa. 49:8). It follows that in distancing themselves from the apostle and his ministry, some Corinthians have walked away, not only from the Lord, but also from Moses and from the prophets who followed him and who awaited the Messiah. It is time for Paul's readers to repair their relationship, evaluate again Paul's gospel, and endeavour to lead fruitful Christian lives. It is neither too soon nor too late to turn from vanity.

It is not the case that the apostle has disgraced himself, giving the church some semblance of reason to look towards the Judaizers. Although beset by frailty and trouble, he has always honoured the

ministry of the new covenant. By implication, the
Corinthians are at fault in that some tend to boycott
him and all that he stands for.

*6:1. Working together, then, we exhort lest you receive the
grace of God in vain...*

It is possible that the apostle allies himself with a
fellow-worker or workers (**'we'**) to exhort the Corinthians not to **'receive the grace of God in vain'**. That
he does address the church is certain in view of the
occurrence of the separate personal pronoun, **'you'**,
reinforcing 'receive' and thereby contrasting with the
generalization, 'Be reconciled,' in 5:20, where the
pronoun is absent. But what is he saying? The superficial meaning might be that these 'saints' (1:1) are in
such a perilous position that, notwithstanding their
profession of faith, their salvation is at risk.

Such a meaning would tie up neatly with 5:20 if
we suppose that the latter verse is also addressed to
the church. On this understanding, 5:20 exhorts the
Corinthians to be reconciled to God, and 6:1 develops
the admonition by urging them not to receive the
grace of God 'in vain'. This expression is also found
in Galatians 2:2, Philippians 2:16 and 1 Thessalonians 3:5, in each instance the apostle stating that
he takes precautions so that his ministry might not
prove an empty thing. In 6:1 he is concerned not so
much for himself but for those to whom he is writing,
in that the outcome of their discipleship is hanging in
the balance.

The problem is that, as has been argued earlier,
5:20 is not directed to Christians but is a condensed
presentation of the gospel that Paul delivers to the
unbelieving world. It has been reasoned that because
the Corinthians are reconciled to God, 5:20 cannot
be meant for them. Their destiny is not in doubt, and
they await eagerly 'the revelation of our Lord Jesus

Christ' (1 Cor. 1:7). If this is so, 6:1 must have something else in mind.

Before suggesting a solution we ought to identify Paul's colleague or colleagues on behalf of whom he issues his plea. Most of the versions add 'with him' in italics, as if the apostle is speaking for God or Christ: 'Working together, then, *with him...*' This is legitimate, and we have only to compare with 1 Corinthians 3:9, where the apostle states that 'We are God's fellow workers', and with 5:20, where he says that he speaks for both God and Christ. This suggests that Paul's directive to the church is couched in the most solemn terms: because God in Christ, as well as the apostle, is working for the Corinthians, the latter are duty-bound to give earnest attention to this exhortation. If not, their reception of God's grace might turn out to be vacuous.

There is a puzzle in this. A Christian is someone who has come to know the love of God; mercy has been his experience. This being so, can omnipotent love be frustrated by human folly? The true answer, of course, is negative; in the final analysis the thing cannot be. He who began a good work will perfect it (Phil. 1:6), and Christ's sheep will never fall from his powerful hand (John 10:28). Because Jesus delights to fulfil his Father's will, he will not cast his people away (John 6:37-38). How can the 'everlasting life' granted freely to the believer (John 3:16) be everlasting if in some circumstances it can grind to a halt?

Yet if this is not the meaning, what does Paul imply? Is he referring to baptized unbelievers, to people who have no root, or who are choked by the thorns of worry, wealth and pleasure? (Luke 8:13-14). But the problem with such an interpretation is that there is not a breath of suspicion raised against the integrity of the Corinthians' faith. Childish they might be ('babes in Christ', 1 Cor. 3:1), but rank unbelievers they are not.

Perhaps the true meaning has its foundation in 5:10, where the apostle insists that 'We [that is, Christians] must all appear before the judgement seat of Christ.' He writes this because of the sad state of affairs in the church at Corinth, volatile people who allow themselves to be harassed by false apostles and their satellites (2:17; 11:13). Although the Corinthians are included in the book of life, it is doubtful that all will see their names inscribed on the honour-roll of heaven; some within the church are proven time-wasters and run the risk of being 'saved, yet so as through fire' (1 Cor. 3:15). If this is the crux of the matter, to 'receive the grace of God in vain' would mean that certain Corinthians failed to live intelligently for their Saviour (5:15) and that their version of Christianity was not serious. Without prejudicing his theology of grace, Paul counters an inconsistency which has raised its ugly head at Corinth. The apostle is realistic because he seeks to prepare the converts for glory.

If this approach is valid, Paul is telling the people that not only he, but also the Lord, who is deeply concerned, is aware of their slipshod discipleship. God in heaven and his servant on earth — fellow workers — are disconsolate, and summon the Corinthians to mend their ways. Do they want to shuffle towards Christ the King with heads bowed in shame?

6:2. (For he says, 'In a favourable time I listened to you and in a day of salvation I helped you.' Look, now the acceptable time; behold, now the day of salvation.)

And yet, is there salvation without sanctification? No. Where there is a healthy root there must be fruit, given time. But alongside blossom which yields nothing, a metaphor which did *not* necessarily apply at Corinth, some trees disappoint because their produce is surprisingly poor. This is Paul's burden. Remarkably, he takes his readers back to Isaiah 49:8 to remind them about where they are in the overall plan of redemption. He asks them why they aspire to set one foot only in the church of God, content to leave the other in the world.

Lesser men than the apostle would never have thought of citing this prophecy, and here we have a sure evidence, not only of Paul's broad understanding of the mystery of Christ, but of the fashion in which he brings doctrine to bear upon the lives of ordinary, humdrum Christians who find it difficult to be holy.

Isaiah 49:8 contains a word from God to his Servant, the Messiah who is to come. In the previous verses the Servant has revealed his disappointments and the fact that his God eventually justifies him. In consequence, not only will he restore the people of Israel, but he will be a 'light to the nations', bringing salvation to 'the ends of the earth' (Isa. 49:1-7). The present verse is brought in probably as an answer to the complaint of the Servant, who almost believed that his work was in vain (Isa. 49:4). In fact, this is not the case, because his God will help him in the 'day' of salvation, when Yahweh displays his favour both to him and to those whom he is to redeem. Without the assistance that God gives, the Servant must come to grief. But help cannot fail. The Septuagint, from which Paul cites, can be translated as follows:

At the right time I have given heed to you;
And in the day of salvation I have helped you.

As might be expected, this verse and the chapter in which it is found are frequently cited in the New Testament. One particular instance of this, the quotation of Isaiah 49:6 in Acts 13:47, is helpful because it sheds light upon 6:2. The apostle, preaching in the synagogue at Antioch in Pisidia, tells unbelieving Jews that the commission to the Messianic Servant to be a light to the nations and to bring salvation to far-away places applies to the missionaries also: 'For so the Lord has commanded us: "I have set you ['you', singular, referring to the coming Messiah] for a light of the nations, that you [again, singular] should be for salvation to the extremity of the earth."' Note the apostolic 'us'. The same thought comes through powerfully in 6:1-2. Paul believes that the original message to the Servant of Isaiah 49 embraces those who represent him. This is why he is able in 6:1 to commend himself to the Corinthians as a worker with Christ, 6:2 appearing as an important parenthesis. In a modern work it might show up as a footnote or be placed in brackets, dividing 6:1 and 6:3. Paul intends to show the Corinthians that they have been included in the scheme of redemption being accomplished by the Messiah, and that they are a local and partial fulfilment of the prediction of Isaiah 49. Can they not, then, recall the time when they first heard about the Lord Jesus and when they turned to him? If they do this, they must ask how they can be so lethargic, so biased against the apostle, and so prone to party divisions.

'He says' may point to Yahweh or to Scripture, the latter being the Word of God in that he continues to speak through the written Word. But the words, lacking as they do a specific subject, might be equivalent to our quotation marks, acting as a means of introducing a citation.[1] The apostle reinforces this with his own mini-commentary at the end of 6:2 in which he explains how Isaiah 49:8 has been fulfilled: **'Look, now** [between the time of writing and the second advent of Christ] **the acceptable time; behold, now the day of salvation.'** 'Acceptable' comes from a Greek compound word, *euprosdektos*, found also in Romans 15:16,31, developing the milder Greek term, *dektos*, for **'favourable'** in the first part of 6:2. This indicates the apostle's jubilation in that he, a former persecutor, has been enlisted to support the Messiah in his worldwide mission. He appreciates Isaiah's prediction that salvation will have its day, and is aware that the day has arrived. Twice he tells the church to behold in wonder: 'Can you not see the light blazing? Why do you live as if you belong to the world? Why do you not seize the golden moment?'

Because we live in the period between the first and the second advents of our Lord, this verse and its context apply to us also. The 'day of salvation' is still here.

6:3-4a. ... giving no one any cause for stumbling so that the ministry may not be blamed, but in everything commending ourselves as ministers of God ...

Paul continues from 6:1, the Old Testament citation and its commentary in 6:2 being, as we have noted, something of an insertion. The sequence goes like this:

> Working together, then, we exhort lest you receive the grace of God in vain,
> → verse 2
> → giving no one any cause for stumbling so that the ministry may not be blamed, but in everything commending ourselves as ministers of God...

Since there have been no grounds for impeachment, the apostle's moral authority enables him to admonish the church. Had he been a failure, the Corinthians would remain under no obligation to

listen to what he tells them. That this is not so is
owing, Paul assumes, to the grace of God and also to
his own watchfulness. He stresses the latter, implying that he has protected himself so that he might
care for others (cf. 1 Tim. 4:16). Paul, a driven man,
has thus far been enabled to commend himself to
every man's conscience in the sight of God (4:2).
Even if the gospel is a stumbling-block to the Jews
and folly for the Greeks (1 Cor. 1:23; Gal. 5:11), there
must be no personal misdemeanours.

This explains why Paul introduces the Greek
proskopē, behind **'cause for stumbling'**, a word
which is unique to the New Testament and which
means 'an occasion that would lead towards a false
step'.[2] **'The ministry'**, alias 'the ministry of the
spirit' (3:8), 'the ministry of righteousness' (3:9), 'this
ministry' (4:1) and 'the ministry of reconciliation'
(5:18), must be honoured. Compare with 8:20: '...
avoiding this: that someone may find fault with us in
this lavishness administered by us'. The Greek
mōmeomai behind 'find fault' also signifies ridicule in
that it is related to *Momus*, the name of the Greek
god of abuse. The world delights to learn that our
Lord's servants are disreputable.

From a negative Paul turns to a positive: **'... but in
everything commending ourselves as ministers of
God'**. In that 'no cause for stumbling' is balanced
nicely by 'in everything', the apostle asserts that all
things have been done well and that there are no
skeletons in his cupboard. Although he declines to
commend himself to others (3:1; 5:12), he is conscious that personal integrity speaks volumes (1:12;
4:2).

6:4b-5. ... in much patience, in troubles, in extremities, in
constraints, in beatings, in imprisonments, in disturbances, in
toils, in sleepless nights, in fastings ...

It is possible that the qualifier **'in much patience'**
should be attached to 6:4a: '... as ministers of God,
in much patience'. If so, the catalogue of difficulties
in 6:4b-5 splits up neatly into three sections, each
containing three elements. If not, we have a group of
ten burdens, ten possibly indicating fulness. Even so,
the first in the series would probably give colour to
the others in that it alone is distinguished by an
adjective, 'much'; in all his hardships the apostle has
exercised much endurance, thanks to which he
survives. He follows in the footsteps of our Lord, who
taught the necessity for this virtue.[3] More details
about Paul's trials and tribulations are given in
11:23-33 and in the Acts of the Apostles, although
the latter does not set out to give the whole story of
the apostle's life.

Going back to the first suggestion, if 'in much
patience' is associated with 6:4a, it might be, as
Bengel and others observe, that in 6:4b-5 the first
section (**'in troubles, in extremities, in constraints'**) remarks upon the rigour of Paul's sufferings in general terms, while the second section (**'in
beatings, in imprisonments, in disturbances'**)
refers to persecutions inflicted by his enemies, and
that the third focuses upon hardships which the
apostle has assumed voluntarily (**'in toils, in sleepless nights, in fastings'**).[4] Each adversity is mentioned in the plural (for example, Paul reveals that he
has been beaten on more than one occasion), and we
should note that when he wrote this letter the apostle
was at about the halfway stage in his life's work.
What would the future hold?

'Troubles' would refer to ongoing difficulties
generated by the clash between the gospel and an
ungodly world. The use of the word **'extremities'** (cf.
'in all our *affliction* and distress', 1 Thess. 3:7)
probably means that the solemn obligations thrust
upon Paul as an apostle are felt keenly; he has

subjected all to the task of proclaiming the gospel, and woe to him if he fails in this necessity! (1 Cor. 9:16). The reference to **'constraints'**, situations which have hemmed him in, suggests his being trapped by circumstances which he could not control. **'Beatings'** and **'imprisonments'** are self-explanatory, and will appear again in 11:23-25. **'Disturbances'** are mentioned because there was hardly a place to which the apostle travelled where his message did not precipitate some sort of public commotion.[5] He was reckoned to be trouble incarnate. By **'toils'** he means not only hard work, but also the fatigue induced by toil. In Luke 11:7 the unreliable householder feared exhaustion were he to react positively to an unwelcome request. **'Sleepless nights'** (perhaps more literally, 'sleeplessnesses') may mean nagging care and concern which denied slumber, the apostle having to spend more time on duty and less in rest. There must have been many such occasions. **'Fastings'** would refer to those times when Paul denied himself, or was denied, regular meals, because of the pressures of work and travel. Often lunch was late and sometimes it was not ready at all, which meant that he went without. On one occasion Peter was engaged in roof-top prayer while others were preparing his meal (Acts 10:10), but Paul did not always enjoy this boon. That he is not referring to ritual fasting is certain because he would never have mentioned it (cf. Matt. 6:16-18). There is also the consideration that the apostle might have gone without food because he could not afford it or because he refused to be a burden to others (1 Cor. 9:12-18).

6:6. ... in purity, in knowledge, in forbearance, in kindness, in the Holy Spirit, in love without hypocrisy...

The question arises as to how Paul has coped with such a range of hardships. He tells us: believers are enabled to overcome only when they develop their spirituality. In terms of Matthew 11:28-30, restfulness comes from the Lord.

'Purity' would be holiness of life and personal integrity rather than sexual chastity, although the latter must not be excluded.[6] **'Knowledge'** means the revelation of God in Christ granted to the apostle and which he disseminates (cf. 2:14; 4:6; 10:5; 11:6; see also Col. 2:2-3: 'Christ ... in whom are hidden all the treasures of wisdom and knowledge'). It is because Paul knows whom he has believed that he has been able to counter the rigours of ministry. The principle remains true for all servants of the Lord. **'Forbearance'**, or 'longsuffering', points to the manner in which Paul handles difficult Christians. According to the New Testament, the forbearance to be manifested by believers is worked out, or is required to be worked out, within the churches, indicating that it is never an easy matter for saints to stay and pray together. 'Love suffers long' (1 Cor. 13:4). We endure the world (6:4), but forbear with the servants of God, and there is a subtle but real distinction.

'Kindness' has a similar reference, that of a virtue to be manifested among the brethren. 'The fruit of the Spirit is ... forbearance, kindness' (Gal. 5:22). Paul implies that he is never rough-tongued when addressing Christians, knowing well that temper tantrums would destroy his ministry. But how can he not retaliate when abused within the churches? The secret is that because God is both longsuffering and gentle with his people[7] and because Paul is a man of prayer, his demeanour reflects the heart of the Lord. The Christian who controls himself can master the situations into which providence leads him.

Paul continues: **'We commend ourselves as ministers of God ... in the Holy Spirit'** [6:4,6]. If it

is asked why the Third Person of the Trinity is mentioned relatively late in the list — after all, the Spirit
is obviously the source of the 'fruit of the Spirit' (Gal.
5:22-23) — the answer would be that here is an
example of the apostle's literary ability. His elegance
of style comes to the fore in Greek but is not entirely
obscured by translation.[8] Yet if we feel obliged to seek
for systematization in what is almost a lyrical passage, 'in the Holy Spirit' might declare that the
apostle depends upon a God-given sanctity. The
primary grace bestowed by the Spirit is love, about
which Paul speaks.[9]

'In love without hypocrisy' signifies that in the
apostle's relationships there is no masked agenda.
He seeks the good of all, no man feeling compelled to
watch his back when Paul comes near. By implication, can this be said of the false teachers?

6:7a. ... in the word of truth, in the power of God ...

The apostle reminds the Corinthians that by God's
grace he is able to commend himself to other men.
'The word of truth' is probably equivalent to 'the
word of reconciliation' (5:19), and would be the
proclamation of the gospel as either the word which
is the truth, or the word which springs *from* the
truth, or — which may be better — the word which
tells out the truth, as in 4:2: 'the manifestation of the
truth'.[10] The point is that the man who preaches
faithfully recommends himself as well as his Lord to
the attention of others.

'In the power of God' refers to the work of the
Spirit by which those upon whom God sets his favour
are brought to faith when they hear the gospel[11] (cf.
1 Cor. 2:3-5). As Hughes well says, 'Power experienced becomes power communicated.'[12] When the
preacher senses that the Lord is with him in the
proclamation he may rest assured that the Spirit

operates among those who listen. As a secondary consequence he gains stature. In the light of what is to be said in 12:12 about the signs of an apostle, Paul confides that character is not less important than supernatural gifts.

Is he glancing yet again at his Corinthian opponents? Does he imply that they are less than truthful, that they remain ignorant of the power of God, and that, notwithstanding their bluster, they fail to commend themselves to their fellows? Probably, yes.

6:7b. ... by means of the weapons of righteousness, right-handed and left-handed ...

The apostle is engaged in a fight to the death, and although he has not travelled beyond the mid-point of his ministry he accepts that his work for the Master might cost him his life (as in the event it did). The Lord had informed Ananias about 'how many things he must suffer for my name's sake' (Acts 9:16). When the end draws near Paul writes that 'I have fought the good fight' (2 Tim. 4:7).

What, then, of his weapons? The extended metaphor of Ephesians 6:13-17 of the body armour and the sword of the Roman infantryman comes to mind. But the present verse is less elaborate, the apostle alluding tersely to miscellaneous weaponry which is righteous, by which he can attack (he does not overload the picture by being specific) and which may be deployed in every direction, to the right and to the left. The likely meaning is that Paul anticipates aggression from all quarters and that when it comes he retaliates vigorously.

Notice that 'in', which has occurred no less than nineteen times in the section 6:4-7a, is dropped in favour of **'by'**, meaning 'by means of' or 'through' (Greek, *dia* followed by a genitive). This relieves grammatical monotony and also makes a point: inward grace and strength manifest themselves *by* outward exertion.[13] The aggressive weapons deployed by Paul are summed up by a single word, **'righteousness'**, by which is indicated holiness of life in every situation, and possibly the justifying righteousness granted to the believer by God (= 'righteousness from God'). The expression may be variously interpreted owing to the flexibility of the possessive case which Paul brings in here ('...*of* righteousness'), but compare with Romans 6:13: 'Present ... your members ... instruments of righteousness to God.' Elsewhere Paul tells us that we ought to 'cast off the works of darkness, and put on the armour of light' (Rom. 13:12). A holy believer is an effective weapon in the hand of God: 'Blessed be Yahweh my rock, who trains my hands for war, and my fingers for battle' (Ps. 144:1).

6:8-10. ... through glory and dishonour, through ill report and good reputation, as deceivers yet true, as unknown yet being recognized, as dying, yet — look — we are alive, as being disciplined yet not being killed, as being grieved but ever rejoicing, as poor but enriching many, as having nothing yet possessing everything.

In 6:8a there is probably a subtle alteration in emphasis hanging on the nuance of the Greek *dia*, meaning 'through' or 'by means of'. As has already been noted, the preposition occurs in 6:7, in the phrase, 'by means of the weapons of righteousness', but at this point common sense would suggest that **'glory'** (not 'honour' as in NKJV') and **'dishonour'** are not instruments with which the apostle pursues his calling. The meaning, therefore, in this verse must be **'through'**: Paul passes through times when he is either praised or discredited by different persons. Seasons come and go.

'Glory' is the expression of favour, as in the statements, 'You receive glory from one another' (John

5:44) and, 'For they loved the glory of men rather than the glory of God' (John 12:43).[14] Paul knew what it is to be the centre of attention, as, for instance, among the Galatians who received him initially 'as an angel of God' (Gal. 4:14) but later changed their attitude to his message, and presumably to the apostle himself (Gal. 1:6; 3:1). Although brickbats were sometimes flung in his direction, no matter. He persevered. Notice that the apostle does not comment about the truth or otherwise of what is said. His head is not turned by congratulations, nor his heart soured by malice. John Calvin remarks that 'There is nothing harder for a man of character than to incur disgrace,' and that 'It is a sign of a mind well established in virtue, not to be diverted from its purpose, whatever disgrace it may incur. This is a rare excellence and yet a man cannot prove himself God's servant without it.'[15] Paul was such a man.

Then there were occasions when the apostle experienced what he terms **'ill report'**, although paradoxically basking from time to time in a **'good reputation'**. Both might be general assessments ('they say that …'), and it can be assumed that inaccurate whispers tended to be more frequent than loving comments. We may infer that when Paul was away from Corinth some individuals there criticized him destructively. The interesting thing is that the apostle usually seemed to be in receipt of intelligence about what was said, as witness 10:10: '"For his letters", they say, "are weighty and strong; the physical arrival, weak; and the word, contemptible."' His reaction, as 1 Corinthians 4:13 reveals, was to counter slander, and perhaps libel, by giving positive encouragement to others, including those who were treating him badly: 'Being defamed, we entreat.' It would be illuminating to know what Paul did say on such occasions. Equally, his partisans, plus those of discerning character who were more concerned for the ministry than for the minister, backed him up when he was travelling far from his home base. He was aware of this, too. Either way, the apostle journeyed **'through'** these situations avoiding both pride and depression. He was constant because he followed the Master and had a pure conscience.

According to 6:8b, matters were not always as they seemed, and in 6:8-10 we are given a series of seven antitheses, each beginning with **'as'** and concluding with **'yet'** or **'but'**, both terms asserting reality, that which is. The overriding idea is that the first impressions gained by those who gaped at the apostle were often deceptive. Therefore certain unthinking Corinthians needed to ponder.[16]

We remember that Paul has commended his colleagues and himself to the Corinthians 'as ministers of God' (6:4). He does so here. Although they are reckoned as **'deceivers'**, as **'unknown'**, as **'dying'**, virtually finished with regard to their ministry, as always **'being disciplined'** (by God), as **'being grieved'**, as materially **'poor'**, and as **'having nothing'**, he insists that they are to be heard. How does he counter these accusations? Whereas his adversaries strain to see one side of the matter only, again and again he adds, as in a litany, a blessed 'yet'.

So to the issue of deception. There were those, again unnamed, who regarded Paul as a false teacher, someone who deliberately misrepresented God, who sought to manipulate his adherents for selfish reasons and who claimed to be what he was not. The same epithet was hurled at our Lord posthumously: 'We remember, while he was still alive, how that deceiver said, "After three days I will rise"' (Matt. 27:63). Elsewhere, Paul and John allude to deceivers, human and demonic, at large in the churches.[17] Was Paul classed as such because he preached the resurrection? (See 1 Cor. 15:12: 'How

do some among you say that there is no resurrection
of the dead?') The possibility cannot be ruled out. It
is clear that the apostle remains sensitive to the
accusation of being dishonest.[18] Or, are his revised
plans about coming to Corinth (1:15 – 2:2) and a
supposed manipulation of finance (12:16) stimulants
for corrupt accusations? At any rate, Paul insists
that his conscience remains unsullied, as indicated
by 4:2 and 5:11. He will affirm in 13:8 that as a
dedicated servant of truth he is unable to do anything contrary to its interests.

'As unknown yet being recognized' is, like the
other antitheses in the sequence, in the present
tense:[19] this is how it has been for Paul at all times.
Pathos intensifies. Paradoxically, there is never a
moment when he is other than unknown and unap-
preciated, and there is never a moment when he fails
to gain the recognition due to him.

'Unknown' or, better, 'ignorant' (Greek, *agnoou-
menoi*), can be interpreted in either of two ways.
First, this might be an allusion to those critics who,
contrary to the evidence, deny that Paul is qualified
as an apostle. Consider again the implications bound
up in 3:1: 'Or do we need — as some do — commendatory letters to you or from you?' Alternatively, Paul
might be pointing to the time when he became both a
Christian and an apostle. Prior to the Damascus-
road theophany, Saul, 'a Hebrew of the Hebrews'
(Phil. 3:5), was a man of moment among his people,
but since then he has become 'the filth of the world,
the scum of all things' (1 Cor. 4:13). Had he remained the rabbi from Tarsus it is not certain that he
would have earned his bread by manual labour
(1 Cor. 4:12). On balance, it is better to accept the
second approach: his opponents *appreciate* what he
now is but refuse to acknowledge the transformation.
Paul surveys the wider field, not restricting himself to
tensions between the Corinthians and himself.

'**Recognized**' may point to the many Christians who accept him for what he is (cf. 1:14: 'You have recognized us in part,' where the same Greek verb, *epiginōskō*, is employed). Or, he may mean that if the world passes him by, the Chief Shepherd knows him.[20] Therefore Paul can handle the opposition. This interpretation is preferable.

The middle and end of 6:9 are probably a reminiscence of Psalm 118:17-18 (Ps. 117:17-18 in the Septuagint). Reflecting a Hebrew idiom for the sake of emphasis, the Greek can be translated with something like: 'I shall not die but live and declare the works of the Lord. The Lord in chastening has chastened me, but he has not given me over to death.' The psalmist reveals his assurance that he will live rather than perish, and that although (or possibly because) his God has chastised him, he survives. Paul identifies with the Israelite writer in that he also has approached death, yet he lives, although, with the emphasis of understatement, he declines to reproduce the psalmist's stress upon the intensity of the suffering.

And Paul does not romanticize. In Asia he had cause to despair, reckoning himself as good as dead (1:8). Nor was this an isolated incident, as 11:23 tells us: he was 'in deaths, often'. There was a reason for this: 'For we, the living, are constantly delivered to death because of Jesus so that the life of Jesus might be made apparent in our mortal flesh' (4:11).

'**Look — we are alive**' is exuberant, as if the apostle invites his readers to take a searching look at him. When all seems to be lost, lo and behold, Paul is back in action: once again he has been snatched from the jaws of death. It was so at Lystra on that first missionary journey when, stoned by the mob, he was thought to be dead. Dragged away, he found his feet and returned to the city (Acts 14:19-20).

Does the apostle have in mind the ultimate resurrection of the body? This cannot be ruled out. Time will be when the mortal shall be swallowed up by life (5:4). Present deliverances have prefigured the last and greatest miracle.

Remarkably, Paul confides that he has been the subject of divine correction.[21] Not even he was so holy that he did not need chastisement, and he mentions this explicitly in 12:7-9 with regard to the 'thorn for the flesh': it would be so easy for the apostle to exalt himself, but the Lord holds him back from the sin of pride. Here, Paul asks his readers to assess his sufferings as a heavenly tactic constraining him to trust and obey. Thus far he has not been handed over to death.

Paul continues. **'As being grieved'** does not mean that the apostle has a naturally miserable disposition.[22] Rather, sadness comes his way continuously and he never lacks for grief. Converts falter, churches entertain heresy, Israel remains in unbelief (Rom. 9:2), material needs are pressing, and friends can and do fail. The Corinthians have occasioned him much sorrow (2:1-4). **'But'** he is **'ever rejoicing'**, the Greek *aei* behind 'ever' implying a settled policy. To illustrate, the same turn of phrase is employed in Titus 1:12 when the apostle observes that 'Cretans are ever liars': when occasion suggests that the islanders might indulge in deceit, they do so without scruple. The sense here in 6:10 would be that when grief comes to Paul he rejoices because the compensations are by no means derisory. In the Philippian jail he praised the Lord even though he was beaten (Acts 16:23-25). He glories in tribulations, meaning that he rejoices because of them rather than that he celebrates despite his problems (Rom. 5:3). Let the Corinthians receive the testimony of such a person.

Materially, although the apostle remains **'poor'**, he is aware that he has been **'enriching many'**. The wealth which he imparts would be the treasure of the gospel (4:7), although some interpret this awkwardly as an allusion to the collection for Jerusalem. God has made known the 'exceeding riches of his grace in his kindness toward us in Christ Jesus' (Eph. 2:7; cf. Eph. 1:7; 3:8). And, notwithstanding the disappointments that flood in upon Paul, 'many' are being enriched by his ministry. He is not unlike the apostle Peter, who in a masterpiece of dry understatement, informed the beggar that although he lacked silver and gold, what he had he would give him (Acts 3:6). We know what happened.

The apostle's multiple references to himself attain their grand climax: **'as having nothing, and yet possessing everything'**. There is a difference between poverty and destitution. Although a poor man may have a home and be in employment even though his cash-flow is slender, to have nothing means just that: the individual has nothing he may call his own. Thus it was with our Lord: 'Foxes have holes and birds of the air have nests, but the Son of Man has nowhere to lay his head' (Luke 9:58); and so it is with Paul. Not a few of the Corinthians were poor (1 Cor. 1:26-28), but presumably they had houses in which to eat and drink (1 Cor. 11:22). The apostle admits that he possesses nothing. He is not his own master in that he is 'a servant [= slave] of Christ Jesus' (Rom. 1:1; cf. 1 Cor. 4:1), but even so the church ought to hear him. Or, because he is enslaved happily to Christ they must listen. Possibly the gifts which he has been known to accept from others plus his daily toil as a tent-maker stimulate ridicule.[23] He has come across as one who lacks credibility, yet credibility is his demand.

Admitted poverty is only one side of the picture: **'yet possessing everything'**. 'Possessing' means 'to hold down' or 'to retain' (Greek, *katechō*). To illustrate, in Philemon 13 the apostle tells his friend that

he has wished to hold on to the fugitive slave Onesi-
mus. In 6:10 he reveals that 'everything' — or perhaps 'all things' — is in his grasp,[24] meaning that he
is the master of circumstances rather than being
flotsam and jetsam carried along by forces which he
neither comprehends nor controls. There is a direct
parallel with 1 Corinthians 3:22: 'For all [things] are
yours.' Because he serves the Lord, and because the
Lord owns and governs everything, Paul is far from
being a pauper. The world falls before his feet. The
God who did not spare his Son will freely give his
people 'all things' (Rom. 8:32), and the apostle is
convinced that this includes him: marching to glory,
he is no longer held in bondage by the present age.
This being so, how foolish the Corinthians are if they
decline his ministry! Paul commends himself with
humility, with confidence in his apostolic mandate —
and with no affectation. Because his literary abilities
are those of a genius, there is nothing artificial in
what he writes. Rhetoric flows from within, as he
admits in the next verse: 'Our mouth has been
opened to you, Corinthians.'

Application

Sometimes we take Christianity for granted, as if the New
Testament has always found its home among the sons of men.
Not so. 'Blessed are the eyes which see the things you see; for I
tell you that many prophets and kings have desired to see what
you see, and did not see, and to hear what you hear, and did not
hear' (Luke 10:23-24).[25] Although the turn of the ages occurred
two millennia ago, we are blessed in that we live during the era of
the final revelation of God in Christ. This being so, our responsibilities are considerable. The Corinthians were in a similar
situation and needed to measure up to their privileges: darkness
was inappropriate for those who enjoyed the light of gospel day.

If Paul, a holy and humble servant of the Lord, whose ministry is presented by the New Testament as flawless, was allocated the discipline of chastisement throughout his apostolic career, what of ourselves? According to the New Testament:

1. Chastisement always presumes a *family relationship*. The Lord never chastises the world of unbelievers. Christ informed the Laodiceans that 'As many as I love, I rebuke and chasten' (Rev. 3:19). If you are being chastised it is because the Lord loves you.

2. It is always *with a view to our improvement*, designed to draw us nearer to the Lord 'that we may be partakers of his holiness' (Heb.12:10).

3. Chastisement is *unpleasant*. The Lord 'scourges every son whom he receives' (Heb.12:6), and whipping is, to say the least, not enjoyable.

4. It may take *a variety of forms*. The Word of God itself is a means of chastisement: 'All Scripture is ... profitable ... for correction [= chastisement] which is in righteousness' (2 Tim. 3:16). So is persecution, resistance to which is seen as bearing up under chastisement (Heb. 12:4-5). Paul's thorn in the flesh kept him humble (12:7). Apostolic excommunication, as in the case of Hymenaeus and Alexander (1 Tim.1:20), was intended to end their blasphemy, and some Corinthians were inflicted with sickness as a form of chastisement (1 Cor. 11:30,32). The revelation of the gospel is a chastisement for those who will hear (Titus 2:12), as is the minister who teaches patiently and earnestly (2 Tim. 2:25).

5. The chastisement process, 'of which all have become partakers' (Heb.12:8),[26] *remains with all Christians all the time*.

6. The experience *is effective*. 'Afterwards it [chastisement] yields the peaceful fruit of righteousness' (Heb.12:11).

Making space for Paul
(2 Corinthians 6:11-13)

It has been wisely remarked that the ministry of the gospel 'can never be a mere institution'.[27] Paul the man and Paul the apostle are one and the same, and in rejecting his message the Corinthians reject him. This hurts him and harms them. Conversely, if they are prepared to accept the apostle as a man of integrity — which they cannot deny he is — they will have to surrender to his teaching. It is for both that he pleads.

6:11. Our mouth has been opened to you, Corinthians; our heart has been enlarged.

Paul has stated his credentials in no uncertain terms. His ministry outreaches that of Moses and he has been given grace to bear up through years of affliction. For its part, the Corinthian church is the fruit of his ministry in that city, and he loves the people dearly, to the extent that his **'mouth'** remains **'opened'**, the open mouth being idiomatic for free speech.[28] The apostle feels free to raise any and every relevant issue with them.

Similarly, his **'heart'** remains **'enlarged'**, meaning that there is ample room in his mind and affections for the church,[29] and this in spite of an earlier visit which had proved uncommonly painful (2:1). How unlike the attitude of so many who are restricted or cramped in their care for Paul (6:12) and who think

little of his ministry! To demonstrate his concern for
the church the apostle addresses them directly:
'Corinthians' — a plainness which occurs only twice
elsewhere (Gal. 3:1; Phil. 4:15). At one time the Lord
had addressed Saul, the Pharisee, by name, and the
latter never forgot.[30] Paul, too, is capable of speaking
to the heart. If there has been a hiatus in the relationship between the church and himself, it is not
his fault, and he refuses to walk away.

6:12-13. You are not being restricted among us: you are
restricted in your affections. But in a similar exchange (I
speak to children), be enlarged — you also.

The apostle gives vent to profound emotion. It is not
the case that the Corinthians have been **'restricted
among us'**; that is, they are not being pushed out of
Paul's missionary and pastoral concerns. Rather, it is
they who are **'restricted in ... [their] ... affections'**.
The second occurrence of the verb 'restricted' (Greek,
stenochōreisthe) probably occurs in the middle voice,
meaning that there are those in the church who
deem it to be in their interests to exclude Paul.
'Affections', meaning literally the inward parts or
entrails but metaphorically the seat of a man's emotions, the inner self, occurs also in 7:15 with reference to Titus.[31]

The apostle calls upon their latent sense of justice:
'But in a similar exchange...' If he has room for
them, should they not also make space for him in
their affections? The word for 'exchange' (Greek,
antimisthia) appears in Romans 1:27 in the phrase,
'the due *penalty* of their error', and carries the sense
of something deserved or owing. The language is
emphatic: there ought to be a recompense, anything
other than at least a *quid pro quo* being unfair. Not
that this is solely a matter of simple justice. In that
Paul addresses his **'children'** in the faith, there

needs to be an in-house reciprocation. If the parent loves the children (cf. 1 Cor. 4:14: 'you ... my beloved children'), should not the latter respond in similar fashion? Less than this would be wrong. Let the church as a whole make room for the apostle. He needs to be loved, wants to be loved and ought to be loved (6:13). In Greek the verse concludes emphatically: **'Be enlarged — you also.'**

Application

One of the problems with Christians is that we are in the habit of frequently allowing our imperfections to show; we do not shelter ourselves as we ought. For his part, the apostle was remarkably skilful at preserving his integrity, achieving this by keeping near the Lord. The result was that his numerous critics did not have a leg to stand on. Paul knew that the only way to survive in the ministry is to cry to God for holiness.

What, then, of modern sick-hearts who ferret around for trouble? Let the apostle be our guide. At Corinth, Paul's therapy was love, and he flatly refused to shut tiresome souls away from his prayers and friendship. This was because he knew that one day they would inherit glory. It was not for nothing that he exercised 'much patience' (6:4).

Was 6:14 – 7:1 a part of the original '2 Corinthians'?

Over the years there has been considerable debate about the authenticity of these six verses and, as Barrett remarks, the passage is held by many to be 'an intrusion in the text of 2 Corinthians'.[32] There are four principal arguments in favour of the thesis. First, there seems to be no connection between 6:13 and 6:14, nor between 7:1 and 7:2. That is to say, the exhortation not to be mismatched with unbelievers, backed up as it is by a series of quotations from the Old Testament, is said not to fit the context. Guthrie notes that 'The change from vi. 13 to vi. 14 is unquestionably abrupt and different in tone from the preceding section.[33] Second, it is suggested that there are a number of words found nowhere else in those of Paul's letters which modern non-conservative scholarship accepts as apostolic, thus giving some weight to a theory of interpolation.[34] Third, were 6:14 – 7:1 to be removed there would appear to be a seamless fit between 6:13 and 7:2, which would then read: 'You also be enlarged... Have room for us.' Fourth, it is suggested that the section was written by Paul as part of another letter, possibly the so-called 'previous letter' mentioned in 1 Corinthians 5:9, or even that it has affinities with the Qumran literature.[35]

What is to be said? First, in the well-chosen words of Furnish, who holds that the passage was *not* original to Paul but was incorporated by him when

he wrote 2 Corinthians, there 'is distressingly little
hard evidence pertinent to the critical questions of
authenticity and integrity, and a great deal of the
scholarly discussion has been in effect a sharing of
opinions and a trading of conjectures'.[36] Martin
comments that 'There will never be a consensus on
the authenticity of this passage,' yet declines to
accept there is no *prima facie* evidence that the
passage could not have been written by the apostle.[37]

Such views are evasive because it cannot be
proved that 6:14 – 7:1 was imported by Paul or that
some early editing procedure introduced the section
from elsewhere, whether or not originally from the
apostle's pen. To entertain either hypothesis travels
beyond legitimate criticism. This consideration, plus
a conservative view of inspiration and inerrancy,
suggests that the age-old tradition that the canonical
2 Corinthians is a unit should be retained. The fact
that there are some words found in a passage which
do not occur elsewhere in the New Testament proves
nothing. As Plummer remarks, 'There are more than
three dozen of such words in each of the three
Epistles, Ephesians, Colossians, and Philippians,
and here these unusual words are needed by the
subject.'[38] Barnett observes that 2 Corinthians
contains fifty unique words, of which only six are
found in this passage.[39] Cannot the apostle, whose
scholarship is by common admission not inadequate,
be given leave to introduce new words as he sees fit?

Second, it must be asked *why* Paul wrote 6:14 –
7:1. Such a question, a necessity rather than an
option, is a task for legitimate criticism or — better —
for responsible exegesis. If we are prepared to view
the section within the overall context of 5:11 – 7:4 it
will be found that it makes excellent sense and, far
from being a square peg in a round hole, may be seen
as an essential link in Paul's train of thought.

Notice that from 5:11 onwards the apostle is concerned with reconciliation, and in 5:16-21 he defines the gospel which he delivers to the world at large. In 6:1-2 he directs his attention to the Corinthians because they need to avail themselves of the treasures of God's grace. This is followed up by a personal appeal. If the Corinthians turn back to the Lord and make the most of their Christian lives (their salvation is not in doubt, but their usefulness and ultimate reward are), they will accept Paul for what he is. All this must involve repentance because to return to God, to the gospel and to its accredited herald means abandoning the world. This is why the Corinthians are instructed not to be mismatched with unbelievers and are given a chain of promises as an incentive for holiness. In short, were 6:14 – 7:1 absent from the sequence there would be a vacuum. Far from being a literary cuckoo in the nest, the section takes its place with due decorum in a heart-felt address to the church.

Consider the problems addressed previously by 1 Corinthians: divisions within the church, a form of incest, drunkenness, litigation among believers, immorality, marriage to unbelievers, wrongful associations with idolaters, irregularities at the Lord's Table and a toleration of heresy concerning the resurrection.[40] All were the effects of stunted spiritual growth. Our canonical 2 Corinthians was written only a matter of months after 1 Corinthians, and it would be surprising if in that brief span the church had managed to right itself so as to attract the apostle's unreserved approval. On the contrary, because difficulties had been accumulating it is little wonder that 6:14 – 7:1 was brought in as a reminder that the congregation needed to reform.

Practical holiness
(2 Corinthians 6:14 – 7:1)

These six verses constitute the practical application of the lengthy excursus commencing at 2:14, in which Paul has expounded the superiority of the new covenant and the supersession of the old: because the Corinthians belong to the Messianic community they are duty-bound to separate themselves from sin. Reading between the lines, the apostle probably calls the people to reject links with local paganism and associated immorality, the imperative deriving from the fact that the Corinthians, collectively and individually, are nothing other than a temple for the Holy Spirit.[41] Although their status as saints is irreversible, if they do not apply what is soon to be read to them they will aggravate tension between themselves and God.

6:14a. Do not be unevenly yoked with unbelievers...

The verse turns on Paul's prohibition, 'Do not be unevenly yoked with unbelievers' — almost certainly a recall of the Septuagint text of Leviticus 19:19. An English translation of the Hebrew text of this verse might be, 'Do not breed together two kinds of your cattle,' but the Greek version teaches that two different species of draft animals must not be bound together by a double yoke suitable for the one but not for the other.[42] Such an arrangement would break down and therefore be dishonouring to the Lord.

Deuteronomy 22:10 repeats the principle: 'You shall not plough with an ox and a donkey together.' Paul asserts that if a believer yokes himself inextricably to an unbeliever there must be damage. Note that the prohibition implies the converse: if circumstances arise believers may properly be tied to fellow Christians. For example, in Philippians 4:3 the apostle addresses someone as a 'true yokefellow'. Clearly, in 2 Corinthians Paul does not advocate isolation from society (cf. 1 Cor. 5:10: '... since then you would need to go out of the world'). We breathe its air, eat its food and associate with its people. None the less, because labour for the Lord is our prime concern, care must be given to relationships which may affect our usefulness. If we bear Christ's yoke (Matt. 11:29), how can we be attached to those who do not serve him? When Paul stresses that he would be 'all things to all men' (1 Cor. 9:22), he does not imply any sacrifice of principle.

'Do not be' could mean 'do not continue to be'. Either the Corinthians are being told to break off unequal relationships, should they exist, or, as some commentators think, the apostle warns his readers against future illicit alliances: unless precautions are taken, tomorrow's temptations might be overpowering.[43] The first approach is better because Paul does not look for trouble, there being little doubt that he takes into account snares present at the time of writing. Concerning the nature of these dubious relationships, the apostle is vague, although, as we have seen, 1 Corinthians gives some pointers. Marriage must be in his mind, and we have here a subtle hint that matrimony ought to be an instrument of service: man and wife are to be one in the Lord's work. Is Paul also warning the Corinthians away from his false rivals (11:13), whose satellites some are becoming? It is not impossible.

6:14b-16a. ... for what partnership is there for righteousness
and lawlessness, or what fellowship is there for light with
darkness? And what is Christ's agreement with Belial, or
what portion for a believer with an unbeliever? And what
concord for God's shrine with idols?

Now follows a five-link chain of rhetorical questions,
to which the obviously negative answers are to be
supplied by the reader. The dramatic contrasts
selected by Paul serve to point out the gulf between
the Christian and the unbeliever. **'For'**, which introduces 6:14b, shows the absoluteness of the opposites. Taken in isolation, each relationship constitutes an unequal yoke, and in the aggregate they
must lead to a breakdown of Christian discipleship.

First, what **'partnership'** can there be for **'righteousness and lawlessness'**? (6:14b). None. By 'righteousness' the apostle personifies believers, those who
have become 'the righteousness of God' through faith
in Christ (see 5:21 for an explanation). 'Lawlessness'
represents unbelievers who are 'not subject to the
law of God, nor can be' (Rom. 8:7). The polarization is
hostile and does not admit any common ground.
Compare with Hebrews 1:9 (and also Ps. 45:7), which
says of Christ that 'You have loved righteousness and
hated lawlessness.' Our Lord rejected the unequal
yoke, and his final word to spurious Christians will
be: 'Depart from me, you who practise lawlessness!'
(Matt. 7:23).

Second, **'What fellowship is there for light with
darkness?'** (6:14). Again, none. By 'light' is meant
the Christian who has seen the truth, and by 'darkness' the person who prefers to live in spiritual
oblivion. Because he refuses to face up to reality and
loves darkness rather than light,[44] true fellowship
with him is as impossible as it is undesirable. That
the Corinthians, notwithstanding all their entangle-
ments, enjoy 'the light of the knowledge of the glory

of God' (4:6) is certain. Therefore they have to protect themselves.

Third, **'And what is Christ's agreement with Belial?'** (6:15a). There is none. 'Belial' is a Hebrew term, here transliterated by Paul into Greek and preserved as such in the English versions, meaning something like 'beastliness' or 'worthlessness', and almost certainly standing for Satan, the adversary of Christ (cf. Heb. 2:14).[45] Occurring nowhere else in the New Testament, the epithet may have been introduced here to imply that Satan is the lord of the stained unbeliever even though the latter is unaware of it. How, then, can such a person agree with a Christian about any matter of spiritual importance?

Fourth, **'What portion** [= possession] **for a believer with an unbeliever'** within the kingdom of God (or, for that matter, anywhere else), whether present or future? (6:15b). None. 'Blessed are the meek, for they shall inherit the earth' (Matt. 5:5), the 'meek' being those of humble mind and repentant heart. Others will be excluded. Only the saints have an inheritance in light (Col. 1:12).

Fifth, **'And what concord for God's shrine with idols?'** (6:16a). 'Concord' (Greek, *sygkatathesis*) suggests an agreed decision, and a shrine is the central sanctuary within a temple complex, the dwelling-place of deity (whether imagined, as in heathen temples, or symbolic, as in the Jerusalem temple). In 1 Corinthians the apostle likens both the church and the individual believer to a shrine because the Lord makes his residence within them (1 Cor. 3:16; 6:19), and this is a doctrine common to the rest of the New Testament. Believers are 'living stones' being built up into a 'spiritual house' (1 Peter 2:5), and both Stephen and Paul announce that the Almighty does not dwell in any human construction, whether or not it has been authorized by God (Acts 7:48; 17:24). The apostle inveighs against contact with effigies (1 Cor. 10:7,21), stating dogmatically that no idolater can have a part in the kingdom of God (1 Cor. 6:9), the reason being that the worship of a created thing blurs the separation between the Almighty and what he has made. Basically, since men are sufficiently aware of the personality of the transcendent Creator (Rom. 1:18-25), the confusion is a deliberate sin. That the early Christians understood that they should have nothing to do with handmade images is shown by the decree of the Council of Jerusalem prohibiting the consumption of food knowingly offered to them (Acts 15:20). If idolatry was banned within the temple at Jerusalem — which was still standing when 2 Corinthians was written — how much more should the true shrine, Christ's body, the church, be free from contamination?[46] This is the issue.

The cumulative effect of these contrasts is staggering. The Christian is righteousness, light and a partner with Christ. He does believe and is a shrine for God. The non-Christian is in a state of rebellion, is spiritually blind, is dominated by the Evil One, neither credits the good news — should he hear it — nor trusts in Christ. Given a Corinthian-type situation, he is probably a functioning idolater. It follows that saint and sinner can have no bonded relationship, no vital common interest, no agreement about things that matter, no mutual foundation for life in this world, and no share together in the eschatological state.

6:16b-18. For we are the shrine of the living God, even as God said:

'I will dwell with them and will walk with them,
    and will be their God
    — and they will be my people.'
'Wherefore, come out from their midst

and be separated,' says the Lord.
'Also, do not touch what is unclean
— and I will admit you
and be a Father to you
— and you will be sons and daughters to me,'
says the Lord Almighty.

In 6:16b the apostle travels swiftly from general principles to recalls of Scripture. Because the church constitutes **'the shrine of the living God'**, its members cannot in any circumstances enjoy a fruitful association with idols. Paul drives the lesson of 6:16b home with force, knowing that idolatry remains a snare for the Corinthians.[47] On the one hand, they have to spare no effort to keep the shrine free from contamination; on the other, they may expect that if it is clean the Lord will maintain his residence with them. After all, a shrine *is* meant to be the home of God. The Old Testament's history of the kings of Israel and Judah is replete with examples of temple desecration, and we know what followed.

This is why Paul introduces a series of Old Testament texts to expound the promise that if the conditions are met, the Lord will be pleased to dwell with his people. Before we examine these quotations, notice the high view that the apostle takes of the Hebrew Scriptures. He writes, **'As God said ...'** (6:16c). This is the only place in the New Testament where this emphatic formula occurs. Paul clearly intends his readers to be impressed, pricking up their ears because an important statement is about to issue from the divine throne. In more detail, within this statement and its continuation the apostle takes for granted what we know as the doctrine of inspiration. He cites from Leviticus, Ezekiel, Isaiah, 2 Samuel and, again, Isaiah and 2 Samuel, these books being taken as words which God spoke and which remain on record.

Next, as we shall see, the quotations are updated and made to point away from the Israel of the Old Testament to contemporary Messianic churches populated with believing Jews and Gentiles. Neither is the relevance of the Old Testament for Christians ignored, nor does Paul forget that he is a minister of the new covenant.

Third, the apostle applies the doctrine which could be termed 'providential preservation'. The copies of the Hebrew Scriptures available to him and to his readers are, he implies, sufficiently accurate transcripts of the original autographs. What, for example, God said through Moses in Leviticus has been preserved over the centuries (in Paul's case, about 1500 years) for later generations. What the Lord placed on record is kept on record.

Finally, Paul does not hesitate to take into account the Greek Septuagint, perhaps the earliest translation of our 'Old Testament' (originating in Alexandria, Egypt, from about 250 B.C. onwards), acting on the assumption that the words of God, originally breathed out (2 Tim. 3:16) in classical Hebrew or, in some cases, in Aramaic (mainly Daniel and Ezra), were metamorphosed into another language in later years by non-inspired scholars, and that in translation they retain their validity. To discuss this last point in detail would be to stray from our subject, but it is not hard to realize the relevance of Paul's use of an Old Testament *version* for an approach to the question of the authority of Bible translations.

The opening citation is a combination of Leviticus 26:12, where God says, 'I will also walk among you and be your God, and you shall be my people', and Ezekiel 37:27, where the Septuagint version reads: 'And I will be God to them, and they shall be my people.'[48] The dual quotation is apposite in that although Leviticus 26 promises blessing to Israel when the law is obeyed (Lev. 26:1-13) and issues

warnings in the anticipated event of disobedience
(Lev. 26:14-39), there follows the reminder that the
Lord will never forget his original commitment to
Abraham and his family (Lev. 26:40-45). Ezekiel
37:27 predicts the regeneration of Israel, God's
people being led by David the Shepherd King, that is,
Christ (Ezek. 37:24). In short, it appears that Paul
cites both from Moses and a prophet of the exile to
show that the Corinthians belong to the true Israel
which delights in holiness. Therefore, let them be in
practice what they are in principle; obedience must
lead to blessing.

Further, if the Corinthians have become the bene-
ficiaries of the promise of Leviticus 26:12, what of the
Judaizers lurking in the wings of the church? The
apostle implies that their Jewishness is of no avail.
'But he is a Jew who is one inwardly' (Rom. 2:29).
Paul attacks.

The next citation is from Isaiah 52:11: 'Depart!
depart! Go out from there, touch no unclean thing;
go out from the midst of her, be clean' (6:17a). Paul
retains neither the order of the Hebrew text nor that
of the Greek version, not indulging in wooden literal-
ness but opting for flexibility in order to bring out the
relevance. Moreover, he prefaces the citation with
'wherefore' (Greek, *dio*) because he intends to convert Isaiah 52:11 into an application of Leviticus
26:12. To enjoy the presence of the Lord, the people
of God must leave the citadel of sin to its fate and
return to the land of promise. For Isaiah this meant a
prospective departure from Babylon, then the centre
of world heathendom; for the Corinthians, giving up
the idolatries of the society in which they lived. What
is unclean is left to conscience.

In 6:17b Paul returns to Ezekiel, citing part of
Ezekiel 20:34: 'And I will bring you out from the
peoples and receive you out of the countries where
you are scattered, with a mighty hand, with an

outstretched arm, and with fury poured out' (Septuagint). Ezekiel recalls Leviticus 26, assuming that the
day is coming when a regenerate and obedient Israel
stands before the Lord. Notice the astute manner in
which these carefully selected Old Testament texts
are handled: Isaiah informs God's people what they
ought to do, and Ezekiel tells of the blessings they
will receive in the event of obedience. Paul aims both
shafts at the Corinthians.

In 6:18 the final Old Testament recall takes the
form of a couplet of allusions, to 2 Samuel 7:14 (cf.
1 Chr. 28:6) and Isaiah 43:6. The first reference falls
within God's promise to David concerning the duration of his kingdom: 'I will be his [that is, David's
son's] Father, and he shall be my son.' In Scripture
as a whole there are three applications of this promise: first, to David's immediate son, Solomon; second,
to Christ (see Heb. 1:5); third (as here in 6:18) to all
who are united to Christ by faith. In Isaiah 43:6 the
Lord addresses the north and the south — the extremities of the earth — calling upon them to surrender 'my sons' and 'my daughters' in a second exodus.
Formerly separated from the Lord, the escapees will
be in relationship with him. In context, the verse is
Messianic, the Corinthians being reminded that they
live beneath the panoply of the Christ. As well as
being the shrine of God (6:16), they are members of
his family. God is Father **'to'** them, and they are
children **'to'** him.[49]

The God who placed himself on record within the
Old Testament (6:16) is presented as the **'Lord Almighty'** who **'says…'** 'Almighty' is a direct recall of
2 Samuel 7:8 (Septuagint) — 'This is what the Lord,
the Almighty, says' —[50] uttered when God directed
Nathan to address David concerning the monarch's
family. Paul is impressing upon the minds of the
Corinthians the principle that the Old Testament is
part of God's word to them and is still speaking. Even

so, we ask if the Gentile element in the church would have had easy access to Old Testament scrolls in order to interpret this mini-cluster of allusions and references. Possibly so, probably not; we cannot tell. The point to bear in mind is that *we* have such access and are challenged to delve deeply. As a wise master builder (1 Cor. 3:10), the apostle is laying foundations for serious discipleship.

In sum, if the Corinthians realize the chasm which exists between the Christian and the unbeliever they will take pains to decline the unequal yoke. If they do they will discover that these wonderful Messianic promises must be fulfilled in their situation. God will be their Father and make his abode with them (John 14:20,23). He who is 'Almighty', who rules over all, has said so. There can be no room for doubt.

7:1. Therefore, having these promises, beloved, let us cleanse ourselves from every defilement of flesh and spirit, perfecting holiness in the fear of God.

Long-standing principles have been followed by incentives, 6:14-16b leading to 6:16c-18. In turn, these promises are applied. Although the apostle experiences what it is to be disparaged by some Corinthians, he addresses them as **'beloved'**, a relatively rare term which he employs only seven times when writing to churches.[51] Verbal economy highlights his love and commitment even if the church has tended to mask any maturity it might possess. **'Let us'** is a friendly exhortation, again bringing to the fore Paul's identification with his readers.

'These promises' to which the apostle alludes concern the present rather than the future, and, having been formulated in terms of meticulously selected Old Testament texts, are specific. These things being so (**'therefore'**), the readers are to

undertake two actions, one negative and basic, and
the other positive and complementary.

First, *Christians must cleanse themselves from
known sin.* **'Let us cleanse'**[52] signifies action to be
undertaken here and now, with no second thoughts
later on: every form of **'defilement'**, **'of flesh and
spirit'**, public and private, in thought and deed,
must be excised. 'Flesh' occurs here in a non-
technical sense and means the bodily frame. Compare with 'Our flesh had no rest' (7:5), and 'holy both
in body and spirit' in 1 Corinthians 7:34.

Second, *we are to be pure.* Paul's words are well
crafted: **'perfecting holiness in the fear of God'**.[53]
The desired action is cast in the present tense, developing what has just been written. Having renounced
defilement, the believer's ongoing task is to ensure
that his life remains spotless, the stated motivation
being 'the fear of God'. Since his redemption is sure
and because he must give account to Christ, the
Judge of all saints (5:10), the Christian is to prepare
himself by pleasing his Lord in this world (5:9). God
will not be mocked, and sin in the life of the believer
will reap its own sad harvest both now and afterwards, when he may suffer loss (1 Cor. 3:15). At this
juncture the apostle is probably not pointing to the
need for spiritual development, although this is
important (cf. 3:18), but is concerned with disen-
gagement from the temple-cults at Corinth.

Application

William Edwin Sangster, a celebrated twentieth-century Method-
ist preacher, tells the following story against himself. As a junior
officer in the British army he found himself placed in charge of a
small building which his men had turned into a gambling den.
When this was brought to his notice he consulted his regimental
sergeant major about what to do. 'Don't take any notice,' the

RSM cautioned. 'It is wise not to see some things.' Sangster let matters rest, although the men knew that he knew.

One day a soldier came to him in distress. He wanted to borrow a considerable sum of money because he had lost heavily at gambling and the debt was to be repaid immediately. When told that he had only himself to blame, the soldier retorted, 'Well! You knew that it was going on — and you didn't object!' He had interpreted his officer's silence as consent. Sangster confesses that he had been *too* smart in following policy rather than principle. In trying to avoid being decisive and keep the peace he helped neither himself nor anybody else.[54]

Paul teaches that if a relationship is wrong we must walk away from it, whatever the consequences. If we do what is right we shall be honoured.

An appeal and an expression of confidence (2 Corinthians 7:2-4)

These brief verses are strategic. Summing up 2:14 – 7:1 and the exposition of the new covenant, they extend Paul's earlier appeal to the church to make room for him in its affections (6:11-13). Expressions of confidence are prominent, and these lead directly into 7:5-16, verses which in turn resume the thread of 1:15 – 2:13 where the apostle refers to the alteration in his travel plans, raises the vexed matter of the anonymous offender and explains why he wrote the previous letter, the one we know as 1 Corinthians. And this resumption constitutes the platform for all that is to be written concerning the collection (chs. 8-9) and the false apostles (chs. 10-13), issues that must be settled prior to a return to Corinth.

In short, 7:2-4 is probably the hinge upon which the complete letter turns.[55]

7:2. Make room for us: we have wronged no one; we have corrupted no one; we have disadvantaged no one.

Either 6:14 – 7:1 is an interruption in the flow of thought linking 6:11-13 and 7:2, or Paul — not illogically (he never loses his way) — puts his finger on a besetting sin of many Corinthians: reversion to the grossness of the indigenous culture. This commentary has argued for the latter approach. In 7:2 the apostle reconnects with 6:11-12, which declares that there is abundant space in his heart for them

and that they are to be found there. The burden of
6:13 is repeated in 7:2 in order to tie ends together:
ought not the church to make room for him? He
instructs the people to do so.

There are three reasons why the Corinthians
should respond to the apostle's plea. First, **'no one'**
in the church has been unfairly treated (had Paul
been criticized because of what some might have
considered an unjust treatment of the formerly
incestuous church member? — see 1 Cor. 5:13).
Second, **'no one'** has been corrupted, either by bad
doctrine or misbehaviour, or by both (contrast the
Judaizers, 11:3). Third, Paul has taken financial
advantage of **'no one'** — perhaps, it might have been
alleged, in the matter of the collection for Jerusalem
(cf. 12:16-18). In the Greek text the three occurrences of 'no one' come first for emphasis. Moreover,
the three verbs, 'to wrong', 'to corrupt' and 'to disadvantage' are each set in a simple past tense, possibly
alluding to a previous visit to the church.[56] If so, Paul
defends himself against an undercurrent of disap-
proval. Perhaps Titus reported this to him when he
met the apostle in Macedonia (7:5-7).

Paul is conscious that he has not offended (cf.
1:12; 1 Cor. 4:4) and is no less aware that personal
holiness remains the indispensable prerequisite for
meeting error head-on. Not only is the apostle sure
that the Corinthians are unable to contradict him,
but he comes across as a discerning pastor who
declines to name and shame. There is pathos in his
plea.

7:3. I do not mention this for condemnation, for I have said
previously that you are in our hearts to die together and live
together.

Paul could indulge in recrimination, but to what
effect? Relationships, strained by unspirituality and

bad manners on the part of the Corinthians, might snap. Anyway, the issues to be addressed are far too serious for self-justification. Therefore he indicates that he refuses to indulge in **'condemnation'**. This powerful word implies deftly that, yes, his readers are in the wrong and that the apostle has always been in the right.

Gentleness abounds because Paul loves these people and will not abase them; he leaves it to their consciences to fulfil that melancholy office. As for the apostle, he repeats what he has **'said previously'** — perhaps in 6:11-13 and prior to the sharp near-digression of 6:14 – 7:1 — that, come life or death, the people remain in his heart. In fact, both sides are living and dying **'together'**, possibly meaning that they have all died to sin and are now alive with Christ. If so, note Paul's confidence in the Corinthians. They are not unreconciled, contrary to some interpretations of 5:20. Or the apostle may be hinting that more suffering is in prospect, in which event the Lord will rescue him (cf. 1:9-10; 4:11,14) so that the Corinthians will see him again.

None of this is spurious sentimentality but a needful expression of concern, bearing in mind what comes later in the epistle. Note that in 7:3,4 Paul abandons his diplomatic first person plural ('we' / 'us'), and picks up the first person singular: **'I have said previously'**; **'for *me*, much boldness ... *for me*, much boasting ... I have been filled with comfort; *I* superabound with joy ...'** He wants the church to understand that this is how it is.

7:4. For me, much boldness with you; for me, much boasting concerning you. I have been filled with comfort; I super-abound with joy in all our trouble.

When a man is sure of what he believes he will have little difficulty in expressing himself. Paul is in this

happy situation with regard to the Corinthians. They
are locked in his affections, and he is confident that,
notwithstanding the present tension in their relationship, all will be well. In fact, Titus has given him good
news (7:7). Even before the two men foregathered in
Macedonia the apostle never quite lost the assurance
that the Lord would uphold his people in Corinth.
The flickering flame was never extinguished, even to
the extent that Paul has shared his hopes for the
church with others. Not only has he great **'boldness'**
— either freedom of speech or confidence in them —
when writing this letter,[57] he indulges in **'boasting'**,
no doubt informing brethren elsewhere, probably in
Macedonia and Asia, that the Lord had been blessing
the work in Achaia. The apostle is replete with **'comfort'** and overflows **'with joy'**. The Greek *hyperperis-
seuomai* behind **'superabound'** occurs also in Romans 5:20: 'But where sin increased, grace
abounded much more.' In 7:4 the idea is that of
immense over-compensation, all Paul's troubles
being far outweighed by the joy given to him by the
church.

The extended exposition of the new covenant and
of the integrity of its apostolic messenger which
began at 2:14 now comes to its end. It is remarkable
that although Paul can remind the church that they
squeeze him out of their affections (6:12; 7:2), he
affirms at this point that he is more than comfortable
with the Corinthians. How can this be? The answer is
given in the following verses: notwithstanding pressing needs, the church has responded positively to the
previous letter. Even if the superstructure requires
considerable attention, the foundations are not
unstable. Paul is able to be objective, distinguishing
between fundamental and peripheral issues, a capacity which has enabled him to thread his way
through a labyrinth of difficulties which would have
caused lesser men to give up in disgust. As it is, even

though they have a long way to go, the Corinthians manifest growth in grace. The apostle is refreshed, the pains of ministry have been justified — and there is time for an all-too-brief rest along the way before disclosing the content of his meeting with Titus, addressing the question of the collection and then, in the letter's climax, turning to the false apostles.

Application

Has someone ever approached you, saying, 'I want to speak to you in Christian love,' or, 'I would like a heart-to-heart talk'? If so, your antennae twitched and you sensed that you were about to learn some unpleasant home truths, possibly rammed home in a less than kindly spirit. Paul had much to say to the Corinthians but he prefaced all by declaring his profound appreciation for the church. And he was guileless because sweet talk was unthinkable. For him, what was really important was that these volatile folk belonged to the Lord, were treading the upward path and were not completely insensitive to his ministry, even though they appeared from time to time to exclude him from their affections.

Most things in life are relative, and credibility, a two-way process, is no exception. If we can show our appreciation of others we will be more likely to win their trust. In his day the apostle was a master of the art of friendship.

Paul has occasion to rejoice
(2 Corinthians 7:5-16)

Paul takes up the vexatious issue, put to one side at 2:13, of his transfer to Europe from Asia and his meeting with Titus somewhere in Macedonia. Titus, we recall, had been to Corinth to deliver the epistle we know as 1 Corinthians, sent in lieu of a promised but rescheduled visit, and the writing of which was exceedingly painful for the apostle. The younger man has travelled north to report the effect of the letter, bringing excellent news, although it is recognized by Paul and by Titus himself that stormy winds still blow. At this point in 2 Corinthians the apostle expresses his joy that the church have evidently searched their hearts, that an anonymous offender has at last been given due care and attention, and that Titus was encouraged by his visit. The path is opening up for Paul's suspended third journey to Corinth.

7:5. For when we came to Macedonia our flesh had no rest, but we were troubled in everything: on the outside, conflicts; within, fears.

The apostle resumes the thread from 2:13: 'I did not have rest in my spirit in that I did not find Titus my brother; but having taken my leave of them [the church at Troas, in Asia], I went away to Macedonia.' This being so, we are obliged to consider the lengthy section 2:14 – 7:4 — a massive eighty-three verses, no less — as a planned digression, inserted as a plea for a renewed appreciation of the glory of the new covenant and of the authoritative status of the apostle, and, as a concomitant to these, for separation from sin.

A point needs to be made. Because this parenthesis, accepted by even the most radical critics as an original part of the canonical 2 Corinthians,[58] is so long it follows that any attempt to slice up the remainder of the letter must remain suspect. Of all the various parts of the epistle, 2:14 – 7:4 is thought to have almost impeccable credentials. If, then, the section is allowed to remain in place, why not afford the same respect to the final four chapters?

It is also the case that 2:14 – 7:4 fits well into the overall pattern of the epistle. There is no discernible isolation. May this not also be the case with 10:1 – 13:14? The spontaneity of a man who perceives that the whole of his mission is in jeopardy does not give rise to an editorial pot-pourri of heart-cries to a church rending itself asunder. Arguably, the letter is seamless, a unitary production by someone who understands well how to weave strands of love, indignation, doctrine, pastoral concern and apostolic authority together in an entirely subtle fashion. Some may, it is true, gain the impression that a later redactor has left his fingerprints across the work, but to the careful student who maintains the twin doctrines of inspiration and inerrancy the thirteen chapters come across as one letter.

Arriving in Macedonia, and possibly basing himself at Philippi, Paul had no rest for his **'flesh'**. Although separated by many verses, 'spirit' and 'flesh' are co-ordinated as descriptive of the apostle's mind-set in that he was absorbed totally by the ups and downs of God's people. Compare with 7:1, where 'flesh' and 'spirit' appear in conjunction as representing the whole man. But why 'spirit' in 2:13 and 'flesh' in far-

away 7:5? Possibly because they signal the beginning
and end of the long digression. Whereas Troas had
been an open door through which Paul found a
measure of tranquillity (2:12), in the north of Greece
matters were different. **'On the outside'**, surrounding him as he went about his business, there remained **'conflicts'**. Antagonism was his daily burden. **'Within'**, in mind and heart, **'fears'** bubbled up
continuously. The man was evidently in pain when
(to paraphrase) he writes that **'Our flesh** [= weak,
tired body] **had no rest, but** [the strong Greek *alla*]
we were troubled in everything.' The perfect tense
inherent in 'had' (Greek, *eschēken*) implies that
stress had not vanished. Even so, Paul had the self-
control which enabled him to focus upon the state of
affairs further south.

*7:6. But God — he who comforts the lowly — comforted us
by the arrival of Titus...*

The apostle found himself at his wits' end in Macedonia. Nevertheless, God stepped in to help. First,
the Father is described as **'he who comforts the
lowly'**, a statement formulated to imply that it is God
alone who offers comfort of this quality, and that
apart from him there is no true source of strength. A
somewhat similar affirmation has been given in
1:3-4.

Further, it is presumed that God's comfort is
always given to *all* the lowly, a generalization incapable of exception anywhere or at any time. By
'lowly' the apostle would almost certainly mean those
who are of a humble, God-fearing disposition. Compare with Matthew 11:29: 'I am meek and lowly in
heart.' But, with others, Hughes suggests that 'lowly'
carries a psychological connotation, 'dejected' or
'depressed' (see Luke 1:52; James 1:9), rather than
pointing solely to ethical and spiritual qualities.[59] If

so, might not Paul entertain a double meaning, alluding to the lowly in heart when they are feeling low?

'But [yet again, the Greek *alla*] **... God'** is a typical apostolic formula implying sovereign initiative.[60] The Almighty, not allowing any of his believing people to be carried off permanently to a dungeon of despair, meets them before disaster supervenes. Paul is no exception in that the Lord has intervened to retrieve the apostle from intolerable stress. Divine comfort is much more than unmediated sympathy, the help granted to Paul having come **'by'**, or 'in', the timely arrival of Titus from Corinth.[61] The latter's appearance in Macedonia was a heaven-sent tonic for uplifting a worried saint.

It is likely that when he wrote 7:6 Paul had Isaiah 49:13 in mind, which says, 'For Yahweh has comforted his people and will have mercy on his afflicted.' The apostle has quoted from Isaiah 49:8 in 6:2, and the context no doubt still hovers in his mind as he recalls Isaiah's promise that in the era of salvation the God of Israel will aid his lowly people.[62] He realizes that the prediction had been fulfilled in his own experience during a period of acute distress.

7:7. ... and not only by his arrival, but also in the comfort with which he was comforted when with you, reporting to us your desire, your lamentation, your zeal for me — so that I rejoiced even more.

Paul needed good friends as well as trustworthy colleagues, and Titus qualified on both counts. Crossing over to Macedonia from Asia, the apostle waited for his associate to arrive from the south. The latter's eventual appearance gave his mentor considerable joy, and the two men had opportunity to walk and talk together. **'But'** — and Paul draws attention to this with the Greek *alla* — their shared pleasure

was not so much in their fellowship as in the fact
that Titus brought good news. His abiding concern,
as that of the apostle, was for the welfare of the
Corinthian church. Without such assurance, gloom
and even despair might have prevailed.

As it was, Titus' ministry among the Corinthians
had been blessed by God, and the people responded
warmly to him in his capacity as Paul's delegate.
During his stay he received much comfort, the glow
of which he relayed to the apostle: **'God ... comforted us by the arrival of Titus, and not only by
his arrival, but also in the comfort with which he
was comforted when with you, reporting to us
your desire, *your* lamentation, *your* zeal for me —
so that I rejoiced even more.'**

For the sake of emphasis the pronoun 'your' is
repeated by Paul three times, and in the Greek text is
placed in front of each associated noun, as in English, but — and this is the point — this would not
necessarily be the case in the original. This suggests
that the apostle was convinced by Titus that the
Corinthians were at last showing a positive reaction.[63] They longed to see Paul again because they
understood that, through no fault of his own, he had
felt it necessary to reschedule a promised visit (1:16;
2:1). The way for him to return to them is wide open
in that most have come to regret their follies and the
grief they caused him.

Their desire, lamentation and zeal probably signify
that they want to put the recent past behind them, or
even to face up to those who persist in disparaging
Paul. The Galatian Christians showed a not dissimilar support for the apostle (Gal. 4:18), zeal for the
messenger being a reflection of an underlying concern for the truth. In Paul's situation the two went
together because he would never flaunt himself. He
has yearned, lamented and been zealous for the
Corinthians; they have now repaid him in kind, and

the apostle is overjoyed. And this in spite of the fact that some still exclude him from their affections (6:12; 7:2). Titus has not only been comforted, he has been 'refreshed' and given cause to rejoice (7:13). In short, the Lord has honoured his servants' concerns and Paul is sure that the steps he took to remedy the difficulties were from God. Not that problems are at an end; far from it. But the apostle acknowledges that progress has been made. He rejoices 'even more', meaning that spasms of grief have dissipated, giving way to relative euphoria: always joyful, now he is more so.

7:8-9. Because if I grieved you by the letter, I am not regretful. If I was regretful (for I see that that letter perhaps grieved you for an hour), now I rejoice, not because you were grieved, but that you were grieved towards repentance. For you were grieved according to God — so that in nothing did you suffer loss from us.

Titus had been comforted and he has comforted the apostle. It was because Paul had sent an earlier letter that the church paused to think seriously about where it was going, and it is to this previous correspondence that reference is now made.

This commentary has argued that the letter in question was the canonical 1 Corinthians, and proceeds here upon that assumption. The apostle learned from Titus that his written rebukes distressed the church, but he has no regrets. Although the letter was not intended to cause heartache but rather to demonstrate Paul's concern (2:4), given the admonitions which make up so much of 1 Corinthians, it is no wonder that a document which moved Paul to tears caused many Corinthians to weep also.

'Regret' (Greek, *metamelomai*) can mean to change one's mind, as with the sorrowful Judas Iscariot who returned the thirty pieces of silver (Matt.

27:3). Not unsurprisingly, it often implies remorse. In the Old Testament it is said that God himself does not regret the appointment of his Son as King-Priest: 'Yahweh has sworn and will not relent, "You are a priest for ever according to the order of Melchizedek" ' (Ps. 110:4).

In 7:8-9 the apostle indicates that he does not regret having written 1 Corinthians; it was right to send it even **'if'** he knew that the letter would cause distress (an awareness that made him wince at the time), even **'if'** after issuing it he doubted the advisability of his action, and even if upon its receipt the people were **'perhaps'** grieved.[64] Having dispatched the epistle, but before he received encouraging news from Titus, Paul's heart was heavy about what he had done, even though he must have been conscious that his word was given to him by the Lord and that the letter *in toto* was the Lord's commandment (cf. 1 Cor. 2:13; 14:37).

It is fascinating to observe that the consciousness of inspiration never cancelled out or overrode anxiety and pastoral distress. In the event, when Titus met up with the apostle in Macedonia the latter's fears took to their heels because it was clear that the Lord had seen fit to use him to bring the church to godly repentance. This is why Paul indicates that **'that letter'**, a document written in anguish of heart, caused the Corinthians grief **'for an hour'**, that is, for a very brief time.[65] The degree of hurt and its duration were minimal and no harm was done. Literary surgery wounded in order that it might heal, and when pen was put to parchment Paul knew that acute pain would be generated. Even so, he found then, and finds now, no personal satisfaction in the awareness that consciences have been pricked. On the contrary, he is vexed because he vexed them. The arrow finds its mark and the deer limps into the covert to lick its wounds. The kindly archer refuses to congratulate himself because of his excellent marksmanship.

'**Now**', since Titus has shared his news about the Corinthians' response, the apostle rejoices because he can '**see**' that they '**were grieved towards repentance**'. By this he means that the people acknowledged that there were issues calling for rectification: they needed to turn from sin and, prompted by the apostle, they have resolved to do so.[66] Thus, their hurt and grief have been '**according to God**'[67] so that in the final analysis they will '**in nothing suffer ... loss from us**'.

The implication is that had the Corinthians maintained their numerous follies they would have been deprived of God's blessing both now and perhaps even in the world to come ('saved, yet so as through fire', 1 Cor. 3:15). Paul, aware of the possibility, has battled to help the church by writing 1 Corinthians. Had he failed, the church would have lurched on, deprived of so much that the Lord would otherwise have given it, the principle being that sin cannot be retained with impunity. The apostle had a tearful duty to perform, and he has not been unfaithful. The easy way out would have been irresponsible, the Corinthians being abandoned to muddle through for themselves. Bereft of guidance, they must have suffered loss 'from us' by a silence tantamount to negligence, Paul contributing to their decline. In the event, if the church does happen to lose out, it will not be his fault.

7:10. For grief according to God works repentance — not to be regretted — leading to salvation, but the world's grief works death.

The apostle has indicated that he rejoices, not because the Corinthians were grieved by what he wrote, but because they sorrowed '**according to God**', perceiving their miserable conduct from the divine (and apostolic) viewpoint. The introductory **'for'** shows that Paul is explaining what godly sorrow is and in what respect it differs from the species of grief characteristically displayed by the world.

The distress experienced upon the receipt of 1 Corinthians effected **'repentance ... leading to salvation'**, a repentance which is said '**not to be regretted'**. There is a play here on 'regret', taking us back to 7:8. Paul's point is that he had briefly re-gretted sending the epistle, but had then changed his mind, particularly when he received cheering news from Titus. Then he realized that the letter had stimulated genuine remorse which, for their part, the Corinthians would never regret. On this view the descriptive 'not to be regretted' should be attached to **'repentance'**, although an attachment to **'salvation'** is not impossible. Against the latter, when we are in the glory we shall have no regrets, and so why state the obvious? Paul is really saying that repentance leading to salvation is a benediction that no one ever regrets if he has attained it. Sorrow of the calibre experienced at Corinth always induces repentance, and repentance always leads to salvation. Paul particularizes because this is the position to which, by God's grace and through the influence of 1 Corinthians, the church as a whole (though with some possible exceptions) has arrived.

Having said this, there might be another way of looking at 7:10. The statement would be a truism if applied solely to the Corinthians. Of course, they will never regret sorrow which led to repentance, which in turn led to salvation. Notwithstanding their faults, they are converted Christians. Why, then, Paul's remark? What he might be saying is that *he* does not regret having fulfilled his painful duty, 'not to be regretted' exhibiting his personal relief. Sorry no longer, the apostle has experienced the joy of the skilled pastor and is unashamed about having had to endure, and even to inflict, pain.[68]

There is, Paul indicates, another species of sorrow, that of the world, which **'works death'**, 'death' being alienation from God, the lot of those who do not repent. To understand the apostle's meaning we can draw a parallel with Romans 7:13, where Paul states that 'Sin ... was producing ... death.' The same Greek verb, *katergazomai*, occurs in both verses, and the principle giving rise to the apostle's words here in 7:10 is that because worldly sorrow is inherently superficial it cannot lead to reconciliation with a holy God and thereby to salvation. The world grieves for the effects of sin, but not for sin itself, and lacks shame for having offended God. At one point Job was tempted to ask if sin is sinful: 'Have I sinned? What have I done to you, O watcher of men?' (Job 7:20), his problem at that moment being that if God is so great, of what significance are the offences perpetrated by men in their minuteness? Does 'sin' matter? At heart Job knew better, and so did Paul and the Corinthians. It is because God created Adam and his posterity in his image and likeness (Gen. 1:26) that it matters when we offend him. Sadly, whereas Christians accept this as a principle, others do not. Even though Esau wept because of the consequences of his folly, he was never penitent (Gen. 27:38; Heb. 12:17).

Perhaps the apostle passes these remarks for two reasons. First, he wants to encourage the Corinthians by reminding them that, notwithstanding their problems, they remain the children of God and have brought forward satisfying evidence to show themselves as such. They have not been abandoned. Although their sorrow has encouraged Paul — an encouragement which he needed — the important thing is that it has brought them nearer to the Lord. This is what counts and this is what has happened.

Second, their humility, which has led to a positive response to 1 Corinthians, will bring about their **'salvation'**. This statement needs to be considered. Paul is not claiming that salvation is based upon repentance and subsequent good works. Rather, it stems from the initiative of grace (1:2) and is based upon the work of Christ (5:21). Nor does the apostle make out that the Corinthians' numerous sins tore them away from the Lord but that now, thanks to their sorrow and penitence, they have retrieved themselves. His subtle implication is that because their initial response to the gospel was God-given, in spite of setbacks they remain on the highway to heaven. In Calvinistic terms, the Corinthians have shown that, persevering in their faith, they will continue to rejoice in the prospect of salvation.

7:11. Look, this thing itself — to have been grieved according to God! How much eagerness it produced in you! What defence! What indignation! What fear! What desire! What zeal! What vindication! At every point you commended yourselves as pure in the matter.

'Look' develops the previous verse, the apostle leaping for joy, so to speak, and desiring his readers to share his exultation. Thanks to the report conveyed to him by Titus he sees in his mind's eye the Corinthians ready to welcome him with open hearts and faces. Paul is concerned not with aspiration but with reality, and bids the people contemplate themselves: **'Look, this thing itself — to have been grieved according to God! How much eagerness it produced in you! What defence! What indignation! What fear! What desire! What zeal! What vindication! At every point you commended yourselves as pure in the matter.'**

The sixfold **'what'** translates the strong Greek *alla*, 'but': '... what apology (etc.)'. The multiple employment of the word in this way is dramatic and can be compared with 1 Corinthians 6:11: '... *but* you were washed, *but* you were sanctified, *but* you were justified'. The overall idea is that the apostle had almost hoped against hope for a change of heart in Corinth, *but* it happened. Having had a tendency to limit the Lord, Paul has been wondrously surprised. **'This thing itself'** is none other than godly sorrow on the part of the Corinthians, mentioned also in verses 9 and 10. Paul is thrilled. Grief of this calibre generated so much 'eagerness', and this has manifested itself in a number of ways. **'How much'**, inserted to qualify 'eagerness', may be assumed before each of the other six nouns. For example, there has been so much 'defence' and so much 'indignation'.

First, there has been **'defence'** (Greek, *apologia*), meaning not so much an apology for being offensive as giving an account of where the church now stands in relation to Paul's admonitions.[69] At an earlier time it did not matter to the Corinthians what he thought about them; now they are eager to share with him and restore their reputation even if this means showing regret for the way in which they have let the apostle and themselves down.

Second, their zeal has manifested itself in so much **'indignation'**. This means almost certainly that the dismay felt by the Corinthians has been turned upon themselves rather than upon any individual miscreants in the church: they are shocked by their ill-behaviour — a revulsion, nevertheless, which ensures that troublemakers do not escape rebuke.

Third, there is **'fear'**. The church accepts that Paul is an apostle of Jesus Christ and has been granted spiritual authority over them. What, then, if he should come to exercise the rod rather than arrive in a spirit of gentleness? (1 Cor. 4:21). Although Paul would never be unpleasant, he is prepared, if necessary, to insist upon severe discipline in order to purify the church from within, and it is about this that the Corinthians are in trepidation. When Titus arrived at Corinth they knew that he represented Paul. They remain apprehensive (7:15).

There has been so much **'desire'**, repeating from 7:7. Paul has deferred his visit to the church until the time is right, and now the Corinthians long to see him to ensure that the original happy relationship between the shepherd and the sheep is back in place.

They have shown **'zeal'** (again, repeating from 7:7), which means two things: first, the Corinthians are eager to give Paul the respect due to his office; and, second, they are keen to prove to him that they refuse to be led away by the pseudo-apostles. They sense that they are basically sound in the faith.

Sixth, their godly sorrow has generated **'vindication'**, by which must be meant the exercise of church discipline.[70] The offender mentioned in 7:12 has been dealt with by the people in the manner required by Paul: neither was the guilty individual allowed to remain in the church, nor was the offended person (presumably his father — see 1 Cor. 5:1) permitted to wallow in grief because of the church's evil toleration of the former's misdeeds. Although there is more work to be done, in principle the congregation has vindicated itself by expelling the wrongdoer pending repentance, which, according to 2:7-8, he has since shown.

The apostle concludes by observing that at every point, or in every way, the people have shown themselves to be pure in this matter. This could mean that, as Paul sees it, the church had never soiled itself by identifying with the incestuous son's evil behaviour, or — much better — that although formerly negligent, they have taken action, albeit at a late stage, against the individual, thus cancelling

guilt by association. Now they are without fault.[71] The
nature of the offence is not stated because the Corinthians were aware of the apostle's meaning, and
tact was in everybody's interest. The **'matter'** is
closed; it is yesterday's history, not today's agenda.

7:12. So, even if I wrote to you, it was not on account of him
who did wrong, nor on account of him who was wronged, but
in order that your eagerness for us might be made apparent
to you before God.

At this point the commentary departs from the
NKJV's reading for 7:12b, '... that *our* care for *you* in
the sight of God might appear to you', and accepts
the United Bible Societies' Greek text, yielding, '**...
that *your* eagerness for *us* might be made apparent to you before God**'. But the alternatives come
down to the same meaning: Paul writes to cement the
bond between the Corinthians and himself.

To repeat, it is assumed here that the earlier letter
to which the apostle refers was the one we know as
1 Corinthians, that the offending individual was the
incestuous son and that the offended person was his
outraged father, both of whom are mentioned in
1 Corinthians 5:1.[72] If this is so, the issue of discipline in this sordid affair is nothing less than 'the
matter' referred to in the previous verse, as also in
2:5-9.

Paul has disclosed that he sent 1 Corinthians to
his 'beloved children' (1 Cor. 4:14) in order to evaluate their obedience to his instructions (2:9). Now, as
we read between the lines, it becomes clear that the
rupture between a spiritual father and his children is
being employed in the interests of a much more
fundamental matter, that of retrieving a healthy
relationship between the Lord and the church. The
apostle was able and willing to seize any opportunity,
however unpleasant or even bizarre, to further the

interests of the gospel, which explains the burden of the present verse. Paul wrote to the Corinthians to urge the removal of the leaven of sin from among them (1 Cor. 5:7), and at the first level of discussion he was concerned for the welfare of the sinning son and the sinned-against father, issuing directives for both their sakes. Nor does he deny this.[73] What he reveals now is that local interests are subservient to the greater end: 'but in order that your eagerness for us might be made apparent to you before God'.

When a man spends time in prayer before the throne of grace he can hardly be dishonest; the thing is virtually impossible. Elsewhere and with other people he may delude himself and act the hypocrite, but not when he is in the presence of Majesty. This is what Paul means when he brings in the qualifier **'before God'**. His concern is for the spiritual growth of the Corinthians, and growth is dependent upon their acknowledgement of what he terms 'our gospel' (4:3) and also of his integrity. After all, the apostle has never preached untruth and has never let his hearers down by ill-conduct; his conscience is clear.[74] No ordinary minister has the authority to define the good news, and no church should expect its pastor to do so. But Paul was extraordinary. He spearheaded the mission to the Gentiles, had established the church at Corinth (among not a few others), and was self-consciously an inspired author of Holy Writ (1 Cor. 2:12-13). He discovered that evil men had penetrated the Corinthian community (11:4, 12-13) and was convinced that the church was in acute peril. This is why he issued 1 Corinthians. Let the people now read his words and let them bow in prayer. Let them ask themselves if, after all the trouble that has been stirred up, Paul is not Christ's servant, and let them ask this when they pray. Others who have been busily tearing him down were never sent from God.

Thanks be, Titus came north to Macedonia and has informed the apostle that the letter did its work, that the church was now examining itself and that it had banished its suspicions concerning Paul. Although reverberations from the trouble-makers may linger, turbulent times are past and the Corinthians realize where their priorities lie. The apostle wrote to them so that their diligence on his behalf might be apparent to them. And he has not been unsuccessful. Their inflated self-esteem has almost gone.[75]

One further point. 1 Corinthians is a massive letter with much practical and doctrinal content. If 7:12 refers to that epistle, it should not be forgotten that both in 2:4 and here Paul implies that it was sent with particular reference to immorality tolerated by a majority in the church. Here is the touchstone: if the Corinthians can tackle *this* issue, surely everything else will fall into place. It is precisely because they have resolved the problem for the benefit of the individuals concerned and for themselves that 2 Corinthians does not raise other matters discussed in the previous letter. Questions about marriage, about the Lord's Table, about the resurrection and about the status of women in the church appear to have been settled. Paul requests his secretary to put down his writing instrument for a moment, and rejoices.

7:13. Because of this we have been comforted. And in our comfort we rejoiced so much more at Titus' joy, because his spirit has been refreshed because of you all.

The apostle picks up the thread from 7:6, where he states that the Lord encouraged him through Titus' news when the two men met up in the north of Greece. The intervening verses (7:7-12) are a mini-digression expanding the background to Paul's grief and subsequent joy. In 7:13a, finishing off from 7:12, he sums up his remarks about himself: **'Because of**

this we have been comforted,' 'this' being the good news conveyed to him by his colleague. 'Comforted' appears in the passive voice and perfect tense (Greek, *parakeklēmetha*), meaning, first, that God encouraged Paul at that time, and, second, implying that the sense of reassurance remains; a burden of anxiety has been removed. Now the apostle enlarges upon Titus' experience when in Corinth and upon his relationship with his friend.

Importantly, Paul reveals that he is no island and that his has been no ordinary comfort. Here we have an expression of more than personal relief: the apostle was elated because of Titus' news and also because the latter had been overjoyed and refreshed by the Corinthians. He, no less than Paul, was grieved by the state of affairs in the church and must have visited Corinth with deep apprehension. What would he find? What would happen to him? He knew that the issue was nothing less than the survival of the work of the gospel in that part of the world, and that if Paul's labours there were to come to nothing the ripple effect it would set off must be dire. This was particularly the case because the apostle and his colleagues were committed to organizing a collection for the churches in Judea (8:6; 1 Cor. 16:1). If, for whatever reason, the Corinthians withdrew from the scheme the damage to Paul's credibility would be massive. Of course Titus trembled as he approached Corinth.

Happily, 1 Corinthians was effective. It appears that the church accorded Titus a welcome in the knowledge that he was Paul's representative. Hence the qualifier, **'refreshed because of you all'**. Anxiety was relieved, which is why the apostle employs the verb 'refreshed' in the perfect tense (Greek, *anapepautai*): not only was he himself at peace since receiving Titus' news, but the latter's ease had not evaporated. In confessing that his co-worker's relief was for him a source of special joy (**'we rejoiced so much more'**), Paul shows that he had been, and still was, concerned more for the workman than for the work, which explains why he never lacked friends and helpers. Nor does he show jealousy over the fact that Titus seems to have been granted a warmer reception than that afforded to Paul himself on a previous occasion, to judge by the criticism quoted in 10:10 that 'His physical arrival is weak', which implies contrasts. He hints that when Titus returns to the church to arrange for the collection (8:16) *they* need not be fearful.

7:14. For if I have boasted to him in any way about you, I have not been made ashamed; but even as we spoke everything to you in truth, just so our boasting about you to Titus has come true.

Paul warms to his theme. Why was he so relieved when Titus met him? The answer would be that he was vindicated in the eyes of his co-worker and that a potential source of division between the two men was laid to rest. This is important, and we need to look at the dialogue between Paul and Titus before and after the latter was in Achaia.

The apostle has informed his readers that he glories in them (1:14; 7:4), and now he reveals that when his relationship with the Corinthians was deteriorating to the point of rupture (through no fault of his own), he shared his joy in the church with Titus. Superficially, this had been a bold — some might have said foolhardy — step, but the apostle took it because he was convinced that because the Lord had begun a work of grace in Corinth he would see it through to the end. Notwithstanding the set-backs, the church will do more than survive: it will reassert its ties with Paul. In other words, the apostle informed his colleague that because all must be well

Titus had no need to fear anything from the Corinthians, and that armed with this assurance he ought to be on his way. Nevertheless, the apostle might have been a touch hesitant, which would explain **'if I have boasted to him in any way about you'**, 'if' bringing out his slight trepidation when encouraging his associate.[76]

What did Titus think about all this as he found himself en route to Achaia? In effect, Paul's reputation was at stake because had his predictions failed there might have been a crisis of confidence. Titus would have felt that the work of mission was collapsing thanks to Paul's indiscretion and false analysis of the situation. His frustration would not have been kept to himself, and he and others might have melted away.

But it did not happen, which is why Paul writes that just as he had always spoken the truth to the church, not excluding the matter of travel arrangements, so his report about that church **'to Titus'** (Greek, *epi Titou*) was given in good conscience; there was no attempt to apply whitewash. In the event, Paul's expressions of pride have been justified, as he knew would be the case; he had not been embarrassed by the younger man when a relieved Titus returned from Corinth. Not only was the link between the apostle and the church restored, but that between Paul and his adjutant became firmer than ever.

The apostle makes this disclosure because he wishes to administer a gentle rebuke, his expression of confidence in the Corinthians being intended to shame them for having doubted his integrity. There was never an occasion when Paul did not have room in his heart for them, and there has never been good cause for them to squeeze him out of their affections.

7:15. And his affection for you is so much greater, remembering the obedience of you all when you received him with fear and trembling.

Opening with **'and'** as a development of the previous verse, Paul reveals what Titus said to him about the church's reaction to his arrival. They made an open show of genuine **'obedience'**, among other matters in the vexed matter of disciplining the incestuous brother, and accepted Paul's colleague with **'fear and trembling'**, knowing that their responsibility was great.[77] They held Titus to be what he was, an emissary of the apostle to the Gentiles and therefore a man invested with authority. Conversely, had Titus failed, the campaign would probably have been lost and Paul might have become permanently *persona non grata.*

Aware that the false apostles were blackening him, he drives a wedge between the church and them. Had the Corinthians not accorded Titus respect, Paul would have planned to visit at a later date to deal with them severely. This the people did not want, which explains why they welcomed the younger man. Later, when he departed from Corinth to meet Paul in the north, Titus continued to remember how they had taken him to their hearts. His affection for the church has deepened to the extent that it remains **'so much greater'**, as emphatic as possible.[78] The apostle perceives that only good can flow from a relationship of this calibre.

7:16. I rejoice because I am confident in you in everything.

Paul has been given proof by Titus of what he knew all along to be the case: that as a whole the church would maintain its loyalty to apostolic doctrine and to those who proclaim it, a commitment which has now been demonstrated by obedience to his written instructions. The apostle concludes the present section with an assertion:[79] he rejoices because **'in everything'**, in all that bears upon the life of the church and their relationship with Paul, they show maturity. Because he has rejoiced at Titus' good news (7:7), at the church's repentance following their receipt of 1 Corinthians (7:9) and at Titus' joy (7:13), Paul is **'confident'**, the Greek verb being *tharrō*, as in 5:6: 'We are always courageous.' The apostle is boldly optimistic because he has come to see that these are people upon whom, at long last, he can depend.

And he needs this persuasion: Paul justly praises his readers for what they have done in order to stimulate them to further achievements. The next two chapters, 8-9, will focus upon the crucial matter of sending money to Judea, and the final four chapters, 10-13, upon the false apostles. A mishandling of each issue would be more than enough to undo the good work undertaken by Paul and Titus, but the apostle can continue the letter because he has brought into the open the mutual sense of regard between the church and himself. The air is now clear.[80] If we understand this we shall comprehend why there is no need to dabble in theories of editorial redaction beyond any possibility of demonstration.

Application

Although there are occasions when Christians give cause for disappointment, a minister should always exercise confidence on their behalf. If they are regenerate, grace still reigns and will continue to do so. Better days and better ways must come, even though immediate action might be necessary. The apostle was faced with some appalling problems at Corinth, yet, as 7:5-16 shows, he never gave up on the church. In the last analysis, the children of God are not to be condemned as failures. Perhaps it works the other way, too: churches should bear with and care for their ministers if occasionally they appear to be less immaculate than the archangel Gabriel.

In this letter Paul displays his ability to distinguish between godly sorrow and worldly grief, and his summing up of the Corinthians' response to his earlier letter is exactly right (7:10-11). For us, how difficult it can be to tell the difference between the man who is ready to make a superficial profession of faith and someone who is genuinely grieved because he has offended God! Those who hold office need to pray for discernment — and remain on the alert.

Notes

Introductory matters

1. From Richard S. Lewis, *Space Exploration: A Comprehensive History of Space Discovery* (London: Salamander Books, 1983), p.246.
2. With acknowledgements to Trotter's metaphor in his introduction to the Penguin Classics *Great Expectations* (London: 1996), p.vii, where he points out that Dickens' great novel reacts to the stress of Victorian social issues.
3. If this scheme is deemed to be arbitrary, it does not stand alone. Barnett, in his *The Second Epistle to the Corinthians*, subdivides his translation and commentary into sections which parallel very closely those of the UBS Greek Testament.
4. Guthrie provides an excellent refutation of the arguments against the unity and integrity of 2 Corinthians (Donald Guthrie, *New Testament Introduction,* London: IVP, 1974, pp.421-49). Philip Edgcumbe Hughes, *Paul's Second Epistle to the Corinthians* (NICNT Series, Grand Rapids: Eerdmans, 1988), pp.xxi-xxxv should also be read. The present work cannot, and does not need to, match the detail given in these volumes. They say just about everything that needs to be said on the subject. Concerning the date of 2 Corinthians, it is also suggested that the Corinthian letters were written during the years A.D. 55-56 (e.g. F. F. Bruce, *Paul: Apostle of the Heart Set Free,* Grand Rapids: Eerdmans, 1998 [first published 1977], p.475; Merrill C. Tenney, *New Testament Survey,* London: IVP, 1961, p.296; Paul Barnett, *The Second Epistle to the Corinthians,* NICNT Series, Grand Rapids & Cambridge: Eerdmans, 1997, p.14f.).
5. A. Plummer, *A Critical and Exegetical Commentary on the Second Epistle of St Paul to the Corinthians* (ICC series, Edinburgh: T. & T. Clark, 1915), p.xx.
6. This issue will be considered when we arrive at 6:14.

7. R. V. G. Tasker, *The Second Epistle of Paul to the Corinthians: An Introduction and Commentary,* Tyndale New Testament Commentaries, (Leicester: IVP, 1983 [first published 1963]), p.24.

8. Hughes, *Paul's Second Epistle to the Corinthians,* pp.54-8, provides essential reading, as also Guthrie, *New Testament Introduction,* pp.425-38.

9. From the Englishman William of Occam (*c.*1280-1349).

10. R. V. Jones, *Most Secret War* (London: BCA, 1978), p.371.

11. Betz, commenting on the view of Johann Salomo Semler (1776) that 2 Corinthians as we know it is a composite production, admits that chapters 8 and 9 cannot be shown to have been inserted by a later editor: 'It has never been successfully proved or disproved' (Hans Dieter Betz, *2 Corinthians 8 and 9: A Commentary on Two Administrative Letters of the Apostle Paul,* ed. George W. Macrae: Philadelphia: Fortress Press, 1985, p.xi). That is, the numerous theories of editorial redaction are uniformly precarious.

12. *The London Baptist Confession of Faith of 1689* (Choteau, Montana: Gospel Mission, n.d.), p.9; *The Westminster Confession of Faith* (Free Presbyterian Church of Scotland, 1958), ii. 8.

13. Kruse, writing in 1987, accepts that Paul wrote no less than five letters to the Corinthians, that what we know as 2 Corinthians 1-9 is the fourth in the series, and that chapters 10-13 are the major part of the fifth letter (Colin G. Kruse, *The Second Epistle of Paul to the Corinthians: An Introduction and Commentary,* Tyndale New Testament Commentaries, Leicester: IVP, 1997 [first published 1987], pp.26,33,34). But Barnett noted as recently as 1997 that 'In our view 2 Corinthians is not a pastiche of letters of independent origin. Rather, the letter was always a unity, written in the cultural mode of an apologetic letter' (*The Second Epistle to the Corinthians,* p.24). His arguments are well developed and should not be ignored.

14. C. K. Barrett, *A Commentary on the Second Epistle to the Corinthians* (London: A & C. Black, 1973), p.5.

15. *Ibid.,* p.18.

16. *Ibid.,* p.21.

17. *Ibid.,* p.17.

18. *Ibid.,* pp.3-11.

19. Although this is never actually said, Bruce also accepts that Paul wrote five letters to the Corinthians, the last coming to light as our 2 Corinthians 10-13 (*Paul: Apostle of the Heart Set Free,* p.276). But Bruce never discusses inspiration and inerrancy.

20. Simon J. Kistemaker, *New Testament Commentary: Exposition of the Second Epistle to the Corinthians* (Grand Rapids: Baker Books, 1997), pp.5-6.

21. *Ibid.*, p.75.

22. *Ibid.*, p.7.

23. For example, Héring writes that 'When the curtain arises in 10, we are immediately aware of a complete change of scene. Titus and the Macedonians have disappeared, along with the collection-plates. The Apostle, himself alone before the Church, is playing a very different rôle' (Jean Héring, *The Second Epistle of Saint Paul to the Corinthians*, trans. A. W. Heathcote & P. J. Alcock, London: Epworth Press, 1967, p.69). Yet a shift in mood and emphasis, which may be acknowledged, is not necessarily the same as a change of scene.

24. So Tenney: 'There is no satisfactory external evidence for partitioning II Corinthians. Every manuscript of the Pauline epistles contains it as it is, so that its integrity cannot be challenged on grounds of manuscript variation' (*New Testament Survey*, p.299).

25. Plummer, *The Second Epistle of St Paul to the Corinthians*, p.xxxvi.

26. W. Robertson Nicoll, *2 Corinthians* (The Expositor's Greek Testament, vol. 3, 1903), pp.24-5.

A century ago, Denney observed sensibly that the theory which posits that the 'sorrowful letter' is other than our 1 Corinthians 'appears with an infinite variety of detail', and 'that the grounds on which it rests are subjective; it is a question on which men will differ to the end of time' (James Denney, *The Second Epistle to the Corinthians*, London: Hodder & Stoughton, 1894, p.4).

27. Margaret E. Thrall, *The Second Epistle to the Corinthians* (ICC Series, Edinburgh: T. & T. Clark, 1994), vol. ii, p.10.

28. Victor Paul Furnish, *II Corinthians* (Anchor Bible, vol. 32A, New York: Doubleday & Co.), p.36.

29. Ralph P. Martin, *2 Corinthians* (Word Biblical Commentary, vol. 40, Waco, Texas: Word Books, 1986), p.xlvif.

30. The fundamental problem about sectioning various books of the Bible is that no primitive strand material has ever been discovered. Where is 'Q', an alleged early document behind the Synoptics? Where are 'proto-' and 'deutero-Isaiah'? What of 'J', 'E', 'D' and 'P' — materials which, it has been said, were woven together to produce the Pentateuch? Rather like neo-Darwinism, the strand theory of composition awaits the appearance of a

'missing link'. Realistically, the literary vacuum must be allowed to speak for itself.

31. Guthrie, *New Testament Introduction*, p.429.

32. Cf. 1 Cor. 4:14-21; Gal. 5:11-12; 6:11-18; Phil. 3:1-7; 2 Thess. 3:12-15; 2 Tim. 4:14-18, where the apostle vindicates himself against opposition within the churches.

33. Robertson Nicoll, *2 Corinthians*, p.13.

34. 8:10 ('a year ago') and 9:2 ('last year'), both translating ἀπὸ πέρυσι, need not mean a twelve-month period. Because both the Macedonian and the Jewish civil New Year commenced in September, Passover in A.D. 57 would have been in the previous year if Paul wrote 2 Corinthians in the autumn. Having woken up on New Year's Day, 1 January 2000, we might well have alluded to the day before, 31 December 1999, as 'last year' (or even in terms of the 'last millennium').

An outline of 2 Corinthians

1. E.g. 1:15-17; 2:17; 3:1; 5:12.

Chapter 1 — The introduction to the letter

1. See Rom. 1:1-7; 1 Cor. 1:1-3; Gal. 1:1-5; Eph. 1:1-2; Phil. 1:1-2; Col. 1:1-2; 1 Thess. 1:1; 2 Thess. 1:1-2; 1 Tim. 1:1-2; 2 Tim. 1:1-2; Titus 1:1-4; Philem. 1-3.

2. χαίρειν, 'to rejoice', is an imperatival and elliptical infinitive, that is to say, a command which lacks words needed to fill out the sense. Cf. Rom. 12:15: '[to] rejoice with those who rejoice ...' This will be referred to again in volume 2 in the note on 13:11.

3. Acts 19:21; Rom. 15:26; 1 Thess. 1:8.

4. Note the remark of the writer of the Muratorian Fragment (c. A.D. 170, lines 23-6) to the effect that although Paul wrote a second letter to the Corinthians, 'yet one church is recognized as being spread over the entire world'.

5. 'From' ← ἀπό. Cf. James 1:17.

6. Greek, κύριος, from יְהוָה.

Hughes suggests that the application of the word κύριος to Jesus may derive from Hellenistic religion as well as the Septuagint (*Paul's Second Epistle to the Corinthians*, p.8). Although this is possible, it cannot be proved. For the New Testament, Jesus of Nazareth is the God of Israel manifest in the flesh. The idea of a Hellenistic connection is a throwback to early twentieth-century liberal theories concerning the origin of Paul's religion.

7. Rom. 1:8-12; 1 Cor. 1:4-9; Phil. 1:3-11; Col. 1:3-8; 1 Thess. 1:2-10; 2 Thess. 1:3-4; 2 Tim. 1:3-7; Philem. 4-7.

8. Cf. Gen. 14:20; 2 Chr. 2:12; Ps. 28:6; 66:20; 124:6; Luke 1:68. There are many other similar references.

9. 1:15-16; 1 Cor. 16:5-6.

10. 11:7-8; 1 Cor. 9:12,18.

11. E.g. Phoebe, Rom. 16:2; Aquila and Priscilla, Rom. 16:4; Stephanas, 1 Cor. 16:15; Tychicus, Eph. 6:21; Timothy, Phil. 2:19-22; Epaphroditus, Phil. 2:25-30.

12. From παρακαλῶ. Note the late Latin confortare, 'to strengthen'.

13. The Greek πᾶς can mean 'all', the totality of a set, or 'each', each item within a set. Hence, God is the source of all comfort, however it may occur, or he is the source of each and every experience of comfort enjoyed by his people.

14. Matt. 10:38; 16:24; Luke 9:23; 14:27; cf. Acts 14:22; Rom. 8:17-18; 2 Tim. 2:12.

15. The second occurrence of 'salvation' is not included in some important manuscripts. Its omission would make sense in that Paul can hardly be suffering in the interests of the Corinthians who are saved. This commentary departs from the NKJV, Textus Receptus and Codex Vaticanus, which duplicate 'comfort and salvation'.

16. The Greek adjectival participle ἐνεργουμένης is probably active ('comfort which is energetic') rather than passive ('comfort being energized'). When comfort comes, it works.

17. There is a double use of the Greek ὑπέρ, 'beyond', 'above', 'over': καθ᾽ ὑπερβολὴν ... ὑπὲρ δύναμιν, stressing that pressures have been intolerable.

18. Josephus, Antiquities, 14. 210.

19. ἀλλά, indicating a contrast to what precedes.

20. The perfect participle πεποιθότες, 'remain persuaded', has the force of an adjective: 'that we might not remain persuaded in ourselves ... but in God'. Remarkably, Paul's attitude had to mature.

21. τηλικοῦτος, 'so great', 'so large', 'so mighty' (e.g. 'so great a salvation', Heb. 2:3).

22. Moule notes that the verse apparently travels beyond the confines of strict grammar (C. F. D. Moule, An Idiom-Book of New Testament Greek, Cambridge: Cambridge University Press, 1960 [first published 1953], p.108). But this does not mean that Paul is ungrammatical. He does no more than write to the Corinthians in a way that they would have understood.

Chapter 2 — Misunderstood flexibility

1. Although the UBS Greek text gives 'in simplicity' (accepted by Charles Hodge, *A Commentary on 1 & 2 Corinthians*, Edinburgh: Banner of Truth Trust, 1974 [first published 1857/1859], p.389), the manuscript evidence seems to support 'in holiness' (see R. C. H. Lenski, *The Interpretation of I & II Corinthians*, Minneapolis: Augsburg Publishing House, 1963 [first published 1937], p.837; and Hughes, *Paul's Second Epistle to the Corinthians*, p.25, n.2). But 'simplicity' seems to fit the context better than 'holiness'.

2. Boasting in the Lord: cf. 10:17; Jer. 9:24; 1 Cor. 1:31;
    an unclouded ministry: cf. Rom. 1:9; 12:3; 15:15; 1 Cor. 15:10; Eph. 3:2.

3. ἐβουλόμην → 'I intended'.

4. δἰ ὑμῶν.

5. προπεμφθῆναι, used here, means to accompany or escort a traveller, or to help someone on his journey by contributing food or money etc.; cf. Acts 15:3; 17:14-15; 20:4,38; 21:5; Rom. 15:24; 1 Cor. 16:6,11.

6. ἐλαφρία → 'lightness', almost 'frivolity'.

7. Cf. with ascriptions of divine faithfulness: 1 Cor. 1:9; 10:13; 2 Thess. 3:3. Kistemaker considers that Paul writes an oath formula, calling God as his witness to his truthfulness (*II Corinthians*, p.60). This approach is not impossible.

8. μήτι ἄρα, 'so did [I]?', implying a negative answer.

9. οὐκ ἐγένετο → 'did not become'.

10. γέγονεν → 'became and remained "yes".'

11. διά governed by the genitive.

12. Luke 1:46-55,67-79; 2:25-35,38; 24:25-27,44-45.

13. Assuming the 'South Galatian' theory, according to which the churches of Galatia were those of Antioch, Pisidia, Iconium, Derbe and Lystra, established during Paul's first missionary journey, and that the letter to these churches (the one we know as Galatians) was probably written prior to the Council of Jerusalem (Acts 15).

14. εἰς Χριστὸν, indicating motion into. There is a dynamism in the Christian life.

15. Kings: 1 Sam. 16:13 (taking David as an example).
    Priests: Exod. 29:7.
    Prophets: 1 Kings 19:15-16. But is Elisha a fair example? E. J. Young remarks that 'There is no recorded instance in the OT of the anointing of a prophet. The only exception seems to be I Kings 19:16. In this passage Elijah was commanded to anoint Elisha, but he seems never to have

done so' (*The Prophecy of Daniel: A Commentary*, Grand Rapids: Eerdmans, 1957 [first published 1949], p.203, n.8).

Christ: Ps. 45:7; Isa. 61:1; Luke 4:18; Acts 4:27; 10:38; Heb. 1:9.

16. 1 Kings 21:8; Esth. 3:12; Jer. 32:10-14.

17. σφραγισάμενος is an aorist middle-voice participle, showing that God has sealed us in his own interests. Barnett observes helpfully that Paul never connects baptism with the sealing of the Spirit, and that it was not until the time of Irenaeus and Tertullian, in the early second century, that 'seal' became a term for baptism (*The Second Epistle to the Corinthians*, p.112, n.50).

18. Greek: ἀρραβών; Hebrew: עֵרָבוֹן.

19. So, Gen. 38:17,18,20; cf. Jer. 30:21; Neh. 5:3.

20. For the overlap between 'in' and 'into', see Moule, *An Idiom-Book*, p.77.

21. Lenski maintains that our anointing occurs when we are baptized in the same way that Jesus was anointed at his baptism. He maintains, too, that it is 'most difficult' to place our anointing elsewhere than in baptism (*I & II Corinthians*, p.854). It may be asked, 'Why?'

22. So, Barnett, *The Second Epistle to the Corinthians*, p.115.

23. 'Against': ἐπί + the accusative.

Lenski argues against this, claiming that Paul simply calls upon God to stand with him, even as, in 1:19, Timothy and Silvanus stood by him when proclaiming the gospel to the Corinthians (*I & II Corinthians*, p.860). But, it may be answered, what if Paul was lying?

24. Cf. Ruth 1:17; 1 Sam. 14:44; 25:22; 2 Sam. 3:35; 1 Kings 2:23; 19:2.

25. 5:10; Rom. 14:4,9-10; 1 Cor. 3:12-16; cf. 1 Peter 5:1,3.

26. Christian joy: Rom. 15:13; Phil. 4:4; 1 Peter 1:8. It is probable that Paul's co-evangelists were Silas and Timothy (1:19).

27. ἐξ ἐμοῦ rather than ὑπ᾽ ἐμοῦ; contrast Gal. 1:11: 'the gospel which was preached by me [ὑπ᾽ ἐμοῦ]'.

28. Thus Bengel, among others.

29. Although most modern commentators would not agree.

30. 'I wrote' is a true aorist (ἔγραψα), not an 'epistolary aorist'.

31. ἐκ, 'away from [much trouble ...]'; διά, 'through' / 'by means of [many tears]'.

32. περισσοτέρως appears in: 1:12; 7:13,15; 11:23; 12:15; Gal. 1:14; Phil. 1:14; 1 Thess. 2:17; Heb. 2:1; 13:19. Contrast with others is absent. To back up the point, Paul places ἀγάπη at the

beginning of the clause: '... but τὴν ἀγάπην ['love'] — that you might know I have περισσοτέρως ['more especially'] for you'.

33. Cf. Acts 20:19,31; Phil. 3:18; 2 Tim. 1:4.

34. The Greek εἰ μή, 'but', 'except', would probably have been used had Paul been referring to his own hurt feelings: 'He did not grieve me, *except* in part.' The use of the adversative ἀλλά, 'but', shifts the emphasis from Paul to the grieving church: 'He did not grieve me, *but* (that I might not press the matter), you all in part.'

35. Kistemaker remarks that 'The incident is well known to the recipients of this letter, so Paul has no need to be specific' (*II Corinthians*, p.76). True, but this does not justify Kistemaker's virtual denial that the apostle is alluding to the incestuous brother of 1 Corinthians 5. Barnett claims that 'There is no compelling reason' for such an identification (*The Second Epistle to the Corinthians*, p.124). Perhaps not, but, as we have seen elsewhere, ambiguity on this point clouds the interpretation of the letter.

36. This is the only occurrence of the noun ἐπιτιμία, 'censure', 'rebuke', in the New Testament. The related verb, ἐπιτιμάω, is not uncommon. For example, Jesus spoke severely to the disciples, and Peter proceeded to speak severely to Jesus (Matt. 16:20,22). Timothy was required to 'rebuke' as part of his pastoral function. As in the Septuagint (e.g. Gen. 37:10; Ruth 2:16; Zech. 3:2), the idea is that of censure.

37. The verb καταποθέω, 'swallow', 'engulf' (e.g. 1 Cor. 15:54; Rev. 12:16) is intensive: the man was in danger of being gulped down by extreme sorrow.

38. κυρόω occurs in Gal. 3:15, 'a man's covenant ... when it has been *ratified*'. The essential meaning is 'to decide in favour of', and possibly to do so publicly.

39. E.g., 1 Cor. 4:1; 5:13; 6:18; 11:34; 14:13; 16:2.

40. 'Also' (Greek, καὶ) in 2:9 has sometimes been taken to mean that at one stage Paul actually spoke to the Corinthians to test their obedience, and that 1 Corinthians develops the examination. A better interpretation would be that 1 Corinthians was written to answer questions and to instruct the church, a related reason ('also') being to bring their obedience to light.

41. Cf. Rom. 15:15; 1 Cor. 5:11; 9:15; Philem. 19,21; 1 Peter 5:12; 1 John 2:13,21,26; 5:13.

42. Concerning 2:9, Plumptre writes that 'It scarcely seems like St Paul to make the punishment a trial of obedience' (*Ellicott Bible Commentary*, *1 Corinthians*, p.368). If 'discipline' is substituted for 'punishment', why not?

43. 'Face' (πρόσωπον) carries a variety of related meanings in addition to (of course) 'face': 'person' or 'appearance', or even 'presence'. In 2:10 there may be a Hebrew turn of phrase, לִפְנֵי, 'in the presence of', behind Paul's Greek. This would fit the context.

In 2 Corinthians, where the word is employed frequently, 'face' may carry the following meanings: 'persons' (1:11); 'presence' (2:10; 8:24); 'face' or 'countenance' (3:7,13,18; 4:6 [probably]; 11:20); 'appearance' (5:12); '(personal) presence / appearance' (10:1); '(outward) appearance' (10:7).

44. Had Paul been acting officially, he might have written, 'in the name of Christ' (cf. 1 Cor. 5:4).

45. 2:11; 11:14; 12:7; 1 Cor. 5:5; 7:5.

Chapter 3 — The ministry of the new covenant

1. Troas was not the Troy of Homer's *Iliad*, but was situated some fifteen kilometres away from that site.

2. 'Did not have' is perfect but probably takes an aorist sense, meaning that at that time the apostle was restless, but later found consolation. For the 'spirit' of a man, see Rom. 8:16; 1 Cor. 2:11.

3. Thus the perfect passive participle, ἀνεωγμένης, 'opened'.

4. The verb θριαμβεύειν does not mean primarily 'to cause to triumph', but 'to lead in triumph'. See William F. Arndt & Wilbur F. Gingrich, *A Greek-English Lexicon of the New Testament and other Christian Literature* (Chicago: University of Chicago Press, 1979 [first published 1957]), p.363. Even so, 'to cause to triumph' is not to be ruled out entirely.

5. In A.D. 51 the British leader Caratacus was brought to Rome in chains. Led in procession before Claudius, he was set free, together with his wife and brothers. His cry before Caesar was: 'Spare me, and I shall be an everlasting token of your mercy!' (Tacitus, *The Annals of Imperial Rome,* trans. M. Grant, London: Penguin Books, 1989 [first published 1956], 12.33-37). Paul, who may have known about this triumph, had been released to the praise of God's grace (Rom. 9:23). So have we.

6. 2:14,16; cf. John 12:3; Eph. 5:2; Phil. 4:18.

7. Cf. Rom. 12:1; 15:16; of Jesus, considered as a fragrance in the sight of God, see Eph. 5:2.

8. Hughes suggests that this interpretation is unlikely because it involves too much explanation (*Paul's Second Epistle to the Corinthians,* p.80, n.18). Perhaps so.

9. καπηλεύω; Josephus, *Against Apion,* 1.61.

10. Again, the Greek word is εἰλικρίνεια, 'judged in sunlight' (cf. 1:12; 1 Cor. 5:8).

11. Throughout the commentary the epithet 'Judaizer' is employed with regard to those within the churches who sought to make proselytes to Judaism. But the verb 'to judaize' means to live like a Jew, which is another matter (cf. Gal. 2:14).

12. Cf. 1 Cor. 4:18; 15:12; Gal. 1:7.

13. The reading 'our' is much better attested than 'your', even though some commentators consider that 'your' makes more sense in context. But the apostle is at pains to show that his own confidence, no less than that of others, needed bolstering.

14. A perfect participle, from ἐγγράφω, to record.

15. Cf. 7:3; Jer. 31:33; Rom. 2:15; 10:8; Heb. 8:10.

16. 'Being recognized [γινωσκομένη]' and 'being read [ἀναγινωσκομένη]'; cf. 1:13.

17. See the notes for 2:6.

18. Cf. Mary I, Queen of England, who was said to have the name of Calais, lost to France in 1558, written on her heart. The town was, it seems, infinitely precious to her.

19. As here, many commentators interpret the participle φανερούμενοι as 'you show' rather than as 'it is evident' or 'you are being made apparent [by God]'.

20. The underlying Greek is not the easiest, but the meaning would probably be as suggested.

21. See also Exod. 31:18; 34:1; Deut. 9:10-11.

22. Cf. Prov. 3:3; 7:3; Ezek. 11:19; 36:26.

23. This is not to deny that throughout the Sinai dispensation the saints honoured Moses' law as the necessary expression of their love for the God of Israel. This was because they lived in the era of promise (see, among a host of examples, Luke 1:5-6). But Paul writes as a servant of the Messiah to God's people who have witnessed the inauguration of the era of fulfilment. Because the focus has changed once and for all, Moses' legislation is suddenly and comprehensively redundant.

24. The prepositions need to be noted: ἀπό, 'sufficient *from* [= 'away from'] ourselves'; ἐκ, '*from* [= 'from within'] ourselves ... *from* [= 'from within'] God'.

25. 'But': ἀλλά.

Hughes observes that *El Shaddai*, as an Old Testament name for God, is occasionally translated in the Septuagint by ἱκανός, 'the Sufficient One' (Ruth 1:20-21; Job 21:15; 31:2; 40:2 [39:32 in *LXX*]; Ezek. 1:24). He suggests that Paul *might* have had this in mind in 3:4-5 (*Paul's Second Epistle to the Corinthians*, p.92, n.16). This is not impossible because the apostle could, and did, think both in Hebrew and Greek, and (conventionally) wrote in Greek. But would such a play on words have been meaningful to the Corinthians?

26. Leon Morris, *The Apostolic Preaching of the Cross* (London: Tyndale Press, 3rd ed., 1972), p.87, deserves to be read.

27. Andrews offers a helpful exposition of this point (Edgar Andrews, *Free in Christ: The Message of Galatians,* Darlington: Evangelical Press, 1996, p.165).

28. This assertion may be slightly inaccurate. Uniquely, σύνθηκη, translating בְּרִית, appears in 2 Kings 17:15 in the *Codex Alexandrinus*: 'And they rejected his [God's] statutes and his covenant.' But this meagre evidence does not overthrow the principle. In any case, other manuscripts do not have this term.

29. Cf. Luke 22:20; Heb. 8:8; 9:15.

30. Hodge queries this: 'It is not always easy to determine whether the words "new covenant" refer to the gospel dispensation introduced by Christ, or to the covenant of grace inaugurated in the first promise made to our fallen parents' (*1 & 2 Corinthians,* pp.430-31). With respect, one would disagree. New Testament references to the 'old covenant' show that it was a needful interlude, to be superseded by something which, unlike Moses' ministry, would always remain relevant and new. This is consistent with Jer. 31:31-33.

31. Hughes suggests that 'spirit' points to the inner spirit of the believer (cf. 3:3) rather than to the Holy Spirit (*Paul's Second Epistle to the Corinthians,* p.101). But John 6:63 and Rom. 8:11 might suggest otherwise.

32. Does the qualifier, 'but of the Spirit', refer to Paul as a minister, or to the 'new covenant', or to both? Possibly to both, insofar as the apostle and others proclaimed the new covenant.

33. γράμμα → 'letter' (but not an 'epistle').

34. This is not to deny that Moses looked to the long-term future, when a repentant Israel will presumably turn back to the Lord and when God will remember the original covenant with the patriarchs (e.g. Lev. 26:40-45; Deut. 30:2-10).

35. The tension between letter and Spirit does not deny in any way the usefulness of, or the necessity for, Holy Scripture. Schröter, noting that for Paul the Spirit is manifested in the regeneration of the heart rather than by written demand, writes that 'Eine kleine Ironie besteht darin, dass er dies selbst in einem mit Tinte auf Papier geschriebenen Brief darlegt' ('It is somewhat ironic that he himself sets out this in a letter written with ink on

paper' — 'Jens Schröter, Schriftauslegung und Hermeneuitik in 2 Korinther 3', *Novum Testamentum*, 40 [1998], p.275).

36. The verb: διακονέω, 'to minister'; nouns: διάκονος, 'servant', and διακονία, 'ministry'.

37. The careful reader will become aware at this point that this commentary does not identify with the typical Puritan view that believers 'are never *sine lege* [without law], nor are they *sub lege* [under law] in respect of justification, but they are nevertheless *in lege*, that is, within the compass of the Law for instruction, for subjection, and in so far as it is written within their hearts' (citing from Ernest F. Kevan, *The Grace of Law: A Study in Puritan Theology*, London: The Carey Kingsgate Press, 1964, p.185). That is, the Puritans held that regenerate Christians are under the rule and direction of the moral law of Moses for Christ's sake. In response, it can be argued that Paul does not anticipate the notion that Moses' Torah is made up of separable elements, one of which being a perpetuating moral component, and that herein lies the nub of the issue. Unless the thrust of their presentations of Christian ethics remains elusive, it seems that the failure of both the *Westminster Confession* and the 1689 Particular Baptist Affirmation to refer to 1 Corinthians 9:21 may hint at some embarrassment.

38. The verb ἐντυπόω occurs only here in the New Testament, and just once in the Septuagint version of Exod. 39:30 [36:39 in *LXX*], with reference to inscribing 'Holy to the Lord' on the golden plate attached to the high priest's turban. To illustrate, the Essenes apparently educated other men's children by mentally *impressing* upon them their own principles (Josephus, *Wars*, 2.120). The meaning is the same.

39. See also 1 Cor. 1:28; 6:13; 13:8,10,11; 15:24,26; Gal. 3:17; 5:4,11; Eph. 2:15; 2 Thess. 2:8; 2 Tim. 1:10.

40. This is a fair assumption. Van Unnik observes that 'No help can be derived from later Jewish traditions; they hardly mention the story and if they do so, they simply state that Moses made a veil without explaining his motives. If they speak about the "glory" of Moses' face they stress its permanent character. Therefore the only possibility for a correct exegesis lies in the text itself' (W. C. Van Unnik, '"With unveiled face", An Exegesis of 2 Corinthians iii 12-18', *Novum Testamentum*, 6 [1963], p.157).

41. Hodge, *1 & 2 Corinthians*, p.436.

42. The negative πῶς οὐχὶ presupposes an affirmative response.

43. Although Kistemaker takes this as a further rhetorical question (*II Corinthians*, p.113).

44. This is a tentative statement. Love certainly exists within the Godhead (e.g. John 17:24), and this love must by definition be righteous.

45. Acts 7:38,53; Gal. 3:19; Heb. 2:2.

46. In 9:3 the same expression, ἐν τῷ μέρει τούτῳ, 'in this respect', is used. A comparison may serve to fix the meaning in 3:10. The degradation of the glorious by something more glorious is an oxymoron, a 'sharp foolishness'.

47. The Greek adjective is ὑπερβαλλούσης, meaning extraordinary or outstanding. Cf. 9:14; Eph. 1:19; 2:7; 3:19 — all referring to the extraordinary work of grace revealed in Christ.

48. Greek, διά + genitive; cf. 6:8: 'through [= accompanied by] glory and dishonour'. Moule suggests that διὰ δόξης is adjectival, meaning 'glorious' (An Idiom-Book, p.58).

49. This is not contradicted by the occurrence of the same phrase, 'in glory' (ἐν δόξῃ) in 3:7. There, the phrase expounds the circumstances of the revelation rather than its abiding essence. Hodge would query the distinction suggested here (1 & 2 Corinthians, p.439).

50. Cf. John 7:4, where acting 'in secret' is opposed to being known publicly. 'Publicly' translates the Greek ἐν παρρησίᾳ, the word taken up in 3:12 as 'boldness'.

51. Barnett fails to ask how Paul knew why Moses veiled his face (The Second Epistle to the Corinthians, p.189). So too does Kistemaker (II Corinthians, p.118). Nevertheless, is not the question important?

52. ἐτίθει, an iterative imperfect: 'he [Moses] used to place'.

53. '... that the sons of Israel should not look at' implies initial design and not merely the end result. Moses did not want Israel to see what was happening beneath the veil, πρός meaning intention. To repeat, the Greek behind 'end' is τό τέλος, probably signifying the termination of 'the thing being brought to nothing' (cf. Rom. 10:4). But both 'end' and 'purpose' could be implied. (See T. E. Provence, 'Who is sufficient for these things?', An exegesis of 2 Corinthians ii 15 – 3:18', Novum Testamentum, 24 [1982], p.61).

54. At this point the comments of Hughes need to be taken into account. Sensibly, he observes that during all the years in the wilderness Moses must have appeared among the Israelites with an unveiled face. Further, Hughes asks if Moses could have perpetrated the untruth that what was fading was not fading. His conclusion is that Moses had no desire to cover up the fading nature of the covenant. Accordingly, the prophet's design was to

allow the people to behold the glory of the administration, but not without interruption or concealment, that which is hidden and spasmodic being, by definition, imperfect (*Paul's Second Epistle to the Corinthians,* pp.109ff.). There is truth in this because there were interludes in the process of revelation through Moses: he ascended and descended. Even so, the suspicion abides that this interpretation is too complicated. Admittedly, Moses did not veil his face at all times during the forty-year journey because there was no need to do so. He must have donned the veil only when he had spoken *ex officio* as the mediator, the reason being (surely?) to conceal the fading away of the glory.

55. As Tasker expresses it so well (*2 Corinthians,* p.64).

56. Hanson argues that Moses put the veil over his face to prevent the Israelites from seeing the reflected glory of the pre-existent Christ (A. T. Hanson, *Jesus Christ in the Old Testament,* London: 1965, pp.28ff.). The present commentary would not disagree.

57. Deut. 18:15-19; cf. John 1:21; 5:46; 6:14; 7:40; Acts 3:22-23.

58. This is not the place to discuss the mechanisms undergirding the hardening process, although Paul indicates that God is the agent (Rom. 9:13-18). The aorist $\dot{\epsilon}\pi\omega\rho\dot{\omega}\theta\eta$ is probably ingressive: 'became hardened'.

59. Exod. 16:2; 17:2; 32:1; Num. 12:1; 14:2; 16:3; 20:2-5.

60. Although it is implied by Matt. 9:16-17; Mark 2:21-22; Luke 5:36-39.

61. According to rabbinic tradition, Moses' face shone until his death, and then afterwards in his tomb, signifying that the Torah was supremely glorious. Paul refutes this principle (see Hughes, *Paul's Second Epistle to the Corinthians,* p.110, n.7).

62. Pearle and Brookes state, 'However evil be the sin of a man, Judaism holds out the glorious promise of atonement. To atone for one's sins is the purpose of one of the great festivals in our religious calendar. Atonement must be preceded by a sincere repentance on the part of the sinner who not only regrets his past sins but resolutely determines not to sin again. In the case of a sin against one's fellow man, we are taught that God does not forgive until restitution is made. In Judaism there is no intermediary between God and man and every man approaches God directly through prayer' (Chaim Pearle and Reuben S. Brookes, *A Guide to Jewish Knowledge,* London: Jewish Chronicle Publications, 4th ed. [revised], 1965, p.112). In the light of 1 Tim. 2:5, which states, 'For there is one God and one mediator

between God and men, the man Christ Jesus', this comment on the alleged sufficiency of repentance without an objective sacrifice acceptable to God speaks for itself.

63. Paul employs ἐπί + the dative, meaning that the veil lies inertly upon the public reading of the law. The hearers do not comprehend.

64. The apostle seems to say that it is the old covenant rather than the veil that is being cancelled. On the other hand, the second part of 3:14 *might* be translated thus: '... the same veil remains upon the reading of the old covenant, not being uncovered — because in Christ it is being brought to nothing.' This has the merit of associating 'veil' and the verb 'uncover', as by implication in 3:18, but gives some confusion because of the change of subject from 'veil' to 'covenant'.

65. That Paul is not discussing a future widespread conversion of ethnic Israel is indicated by his discussion of what occurs 'whenever' (Greek, ἡνίκα δὲ ἐὰν) someone turns to the Lord'. The historic event, whenever it is to be, is not on the agenda.

66. In the New Testament the verb occurs in 3:16; Acts 27:10,40; 28:13; Heb. 10:11.

67. סור, hiphil.

68. A mild proviso is necessary. In Exod. 34:34 the Septuagint gives περιερεῖτο, middle voice: Moses took off the veil. Here, in 3:16, we have περιαιρεῖται, probably in the passive voice: the veil is taken away (by the Spirit).

It might be noted, too, that the Septuagint of Exod. 34:34 employs ἡνίκα, '*whenever* Moses entered the presence of the Lord'. This virtually confirms the existence of an allusion in 3:16, which employs the same word.

69. The verb occurs coincidentally in the Septuagint of Exod. 34:31: 'Aaron and all the rulers ... *returned* to him [Moses].' Paul is almost certainly not alluding to this.

70. Thus the expanded form of the Nicene Creed at the Council of Constantinople (A.D. 380): 'We believe ... in the Holy Spirit, the Lord and the Life-giver, that proceedeth from the Father' (Bettenson, *Documents*, p.37). This seems to be a clear allusion to 3:17.

71. Paul's teaching elsewhere is that Christians are not 'under law', which means that we have nothing to do with Moses' legislation considered as a unitary code, nor the latter with us (e.g. Rom. 6:15; 7:4,6; Gal. 3:25; 4:21). Nor does the New Testament allow us to pick and choose between an artificially separable 'moral' law and a confessedly redundant 'ceremonial' law. This does not mean that the new dispensation is (to pick up the

jargon) 'antinomian' (= 'against law'). All depends on an identification of the Christian's rule of conduct (note 37 above discusses
this).

72. This is the usual meaning of κατοπτρίζομαι, found here.
Most commentators cite Philo, *Allegorical Interpretation*, 3.101,
where the Alexandrian expands Moses' prayer to God in Exod.
33:13: '... nor would I find the reflection [κατοπτρισαίμην] of Thy
being in aught else than in Thee Who art God, for the reflections
in created things are dissolved, but those in the Uncreated will
continue abiding and sure and eternal.'

73. ἀνακεκαλυμμένῳ, perfect passive participle from ἀνακαλύπτῶ:
what has been removed will not be set in place again.

74. Cf. 1 Cor. 15:48-49; 1 John 3:2.

75. Basically, however, the Greek κατοπτριζόμενοι means to
look at something in a mirror (as implied by 1 Clement 36), or,
secondarily, to reflect (See Arndt & Gingrich, *A Greek-English
Lexicon*, p.424; Barnett, *The Second Epistle to the Corinthians*,
p.205, n.38).

76. Lenski argues that we reflect the reflection of God (*I & II
Corinthians*, p.948). So, too, Dupont (R. J. P. Dupont, 'Le chré-
tien, miroir de la gloire divine d'après II Cor. III,18,' *Revue
Biblique*, 56 [1949], p.397), and Plummer (*The Second Epistle of
St Paul to the Corinthians*, p.105). Van Unnik is insistent ('With
Unveiled Face,' p.167).

77. For a similar grammatical construction, cf. Gal. 1:3: 'God
[who is] our Father'. But see Barnett, *The Second Epistle to the
Corinthians*, p.209, n.54, in favour of the interpretation that
'Spirit' means the Holy Spirit.

78. For Paul's conversion and call: Acts 9:15-16; 22:15-16;
26:16; 1 Tim. 1:12-17.

79. καθῶς might mean 'as', 'to the degree that'. Or it could even
have a causal sense: '*Since* we have received mercy, we are not
discouraged.'

80. These are some of the nuances of ἐγκακῶ ('I am weak'). It has
been suggested that the orthography should be ἐκκακῶ, which
suggests falling away to evil. The former is usually preferred.

81. In 4:3, the opening εἰ δὲ καὶ means 'even if, as I allow '. Cf.
4:16; 5:16; 7:8;12:11.

82. The perfect participle, κεκαλυμμένον, 'has been covered up',
is probably adjectival, with little reference to the time when the
covering up was put into effect.

83. Hughes, *Paul's Second Epistle to the Corinthians*, p.125.

84. αἰών → 'age'. Cf. Matt. 28:20; 1 Cor. 2:6.

85. νόημα → 'mind'; 'thought'; 'mind-set'.

86. The suggested 'upon them' demands that the verb αὐγάζειν be transitive. Barnett takes this view, and provides a useful discussion (*The Second Epistle to the Corinthians*, p.218, n.41). Lenski disagrees (*I & II Corinthians*, p.963).

87. Cf. Rom. 2:16; 2 Thess. 2:14; 2 Tim. 2:8.

88. Matt. 4:9; Luke 4:7.

89. 1 Cor. 10:20; Gal. 4:8; Rev. 14:9,11; 20:4.

90. Cf. Mark 3:22 and parallels; John 12:31; 14:30; 16:11; Eph. 2:2; 1 John 5:19.

91. Cf. Gen. 1:26 (Septuagint) and 1 Cor. 11:7. Because he derives from God and retains his image, man enjoys personality.

92. Cf. Col. 1:15; 2:9; Heb. 10:1.

93. United Bible Societies' Greek text: 'Jesus Christ [the] Lord'; NKJV: 'Christ Jesus the Lord'.

94. Cf. Acts 2:36; 10:36; 1 Cor. 12:3.

95. Lenski takes 'our hearts' (plural) to refer to all who believe, and not just to Paul in particular. He may be right, although this would not reduce the implied allusion to the Damascus-road theophany (*I & II Corinthians*, p.972).

96. Acts 9:3,8; 22:6,11; 26:13.

97. But see Moule, who suggests that 'in' might overlap to 'to' — i.e., 'revealed *to* me' (*An Idiom-Book*, p.76).

98. It is possible that the apostle is alluding to Isaiah 9:2: 'The people who walk in darkness will see a great light.' Did Isaiah have the Genesis record in mind also?

99. 'Shine' and 'shone' are almost certainly intransitive, verbs lacking objects. So, 'He shone ... with a view to [πρός] illumination.'

100. Cf. John 1:14; Col. 1:12; Heb. 1:3; 1 John 1:5.

101. Richard Dawkins, in his highly readable defence of Darwinism, frowns on theologians who accept evolution. Allegedly, they 'smuggle God in by the back door' (*The Blind Watchmaker*, London: Penguin Books, 1991 [first published 1986], p.316). Moreover, 'Divine creation, whether instantaneous or in the form of guided evolution [and certain other theories] ... give some superficial appearance of being alternatives to Darwinism, whose merits might be tested by an appeal to evidence. All turn out, on closer inspection, not to be rivals of Darwinism at all' (*ibid.*, pp.316-17). In making such a grandiose claim, this exponent of non-random survival as the explanation for life is surely right. Paul, I think, would have agreed. But Paul would have accepted the historicity of Genesis, as does this commentary.

Chapter 4 — Earthly and heavenly homes

1. Hughes suggests that Paul may have in mind here the custom by which precious metals were deposited in earthenware containers to be carried in triumphal processions — cf. 2:14; 1 Cor. 4:9; Col. 2:15 (*Paul's Second Epistle to the Corinthians*, p.136). Herodotus, 3.96, records that Persian kings poured molten gold and silver into earthenware jars to cool, chipping off the shell when the metal solidified. But the connections are surely speculative.

2. Greek: ὑπερβολή, ὑπερβάλλοντος, ὑπερβαλλόντως: 1:8; 3:10; 4:17; 9:14; 11:23; 12:7; Rom. 7:13; Gal. 1:13; Eph. 1:19; 2:7; 3:19.

3. 'In everything' ← ἐν παντί.

4. Is Paul alluding to a public gladiatorial combat? Perhaps.

5. Cf. Rom. 4:19: 'the deadness [νέκρωσις] of Sarah's womb'.

6. Cf. 11:23; Rom. 8:36; 1 Cor. 4:9; 15:31.

7. Hodge, *1 & 2 Corinthians*, p.469.

8. 2:14; 3:3; 4:10,11; 5:10,11; 7:12; 11:6.

9. ἀεί → 'always', 'constantly'.

10. Cf. Acts 7:51; Heb. 3:10.

11. Lenski tends to the view that Paul, like the other apostles, was being delivered to death *by* the world because of his evangelistic success (*I & II Corinthians*, p.980). The sentiment is true, but might it not depreciate the principle of divine sovereignty?

12. Alford, *2 Corinthians*, p.621.

13. See Warfield, *The Inspiration and Authority of the Bible*, p.318.

14. The NASB could be right when it gives the rendering: 'I believed when [Hebrew: כִּי] I said, "I am greatly afflicted."' That is, when he cried out in anguish the psalmist nevertheless retained his trust in the Lord. It all depends on the semantics of כִּי, usually translated 'because' or 'for'. But 'when' is by no means uncommon (See Francis Brown, S. R. Driver & Charles A. Briggs, *A Hebrew & English Lexicon of the Old Testament*, Oxford: Clarendon Press, 1959 [first published 1907], p.473).

15. Cf. 1 Cor. 4:21; Gal. 6:1.

Barnett considers that the reference to the Holy Spirit is 'probable' on the ground that Paul acknowledges the work of the Spirit in the life of the psalmist (*The Second Epistle to the Corinthians*, p.240, n.7). It may be so.

16. In his letters Paul refers to three species of resurrection: initial, spiritual resurrection (e.g. Eph. 2:6), providential 'resurrections' and the final resurrection.

17. 'Knowing that' sometimes leads into a statement that is known already by the readers (e.g. 1:7; 5:6; 1 Cor. 15:58; Gal. 2:16; James 3:1; 1 Peter 1:18).

18. 1 Cor. 15:20; cf. Col. 1:18; Rev. 1:5.

19. δὶ ὑμᾶς, not ὑπὲρ ὑμῶν.

20. 'Increasing numbers' instead of 'many' is suggested by Moule (*An Idiom-Book*, p.108).

21. 'Yet' (or 'if'): εἰ; 'rather' (or 'on the other hand'): ἀλλά.

22. Cf. Eph. 3:16.

23. Cf. Eph. 4:23.

24. With acknowledgements to Barnett, *The Second Epistle to the Corinthians*, p.250.

25. Cf. 5:5; 7:10,11; 9:11; 12:12. In the New Testament κατεργάζομαι occurs twenty-three times, and, with two exceptions, in Paul's letters. Of the twenty-one, six are in 2 Corinthians.

26. ὑπερβολὴν, meaning excess: 1:8; 3:10; 4:7,17; 9:14; 11:23; 12:7; Rom. 7:13; 1 Cor. 12:31; Gal. 1:13; Eph. 1:19; 2:7; 3:19. Paul's καθ᾽ ὑπερβολὴν εἰς ὑπερβολήν, 'in excess leading to excess', is taken here neither as solely adverbial, qualifying κατεργάζεται, 'makes effective', nor solely adjectival, qualifying 'an eternal weight of glory'. Process and destination are alike beyond comprehension. Cf. Gen. 7:19; 17:2.

27. With acknowledgements to Robert J. Sheehan, *The Word of Truth* (Darlington: Evangelical Press, 1998), p.31.

28. βάρος and δόξα, usually translating כָּבוֹד.

29. The first person plural in 4:13-14 undoubtedly refers to Paul and his colleagues, but it would be hard to prove that 'we' has this narrow connotation. Does not 4:18, not to mention 5:1-10, apply to all who are in Christ?

30. This is a genitive absolute which could be translated loosely as, 'We are not gazers at seen things.'

31. With acknowledgements to Barnett, *The Second Epistle to the Corinthians*, p.254.

32. πρόσκαιρα → 'for a time / season' rather than 'temporary'.

33. Marcus Aurelius, *Meditations*, 3.16; 7.68.

34. Hodge, *1 & 2 Corinthians*, pp.485ff., as also Tasker, *The Second Epistle of Paul to the Corinthians*, p.78.

Others have proposed other interpretations: that the house / building is (1) the body of Christ, the church; (2) the new Jerusalem; (3) the heavenly temple of the Lord's presence.

35. John 14:2; Heb. 11:10,14; 13:14; Rev. 21:10.

36. Cf. Matt. 24:36; 1 Cor. 15:51; 1 Thess. 4:13-14; 2 Thess. 2:1.

37. John: λύω; Mark: καταλύω.

38. Cf. Col. 2:11; Rom. 2:28-29; Heb. 9:11,24.

39. Hodge does not allude to Rom. 8:23 in his claim that 'the house from heaven' is heaven itself, the abode of believers when they die (*1 & 2 Corinthians*, p.490). Hughes properly chides him on this score (*Paul's Second Epistle to the Corinthians*, p.167, n.28).

40. ἐπιποθέω: 9:14; Rom. 1:11; Phil. 1:8; 2:26; 1 Thess. 3:6; 2 Tim. 1:4.

41. Greek, ἐπενδύω: Lev. 8:7; 1 Sam. 18:4; 2 Sam. 13:18. Cf. Josephus, *Antiquities*, 5.37, 'putting [ἐπενδύντες] sackcloth upon their apparel' (with reference to Israel after the defeat at Ai, Josh. 7:2-6).

42. Barrett writes that 'The metaphor is hopelessly mixed' (*The Second Epistle to the Corinthians*, p.152). Mixed, perhaps, but not 'hopelessly'. Subtlety and elegance combine.

43. ἐνδύω and ἐπενδύω → 'put on' and 'put on over the top'.

44. εἴ γε καὶ → if indeed'; or, εἴπερ → 'if after all', in some important manuscripts.

45. 'Having put on' ← ἐνδυσάμενοι; 'having put it off' ← ἐκδυσάμενοι (a few manuscripts).

46. Cf. Heb.12:23.

47. Philo, who was roughly contemporary with Paul, commented thus on Moses' desire for death and removal to a better world: 'The body, the shell-like growth which encased him, was being stripped away and the soul laid bare and yearning for its natural removal hence' (*On the Virtues*, 76). The apostle did not think like this.

48. For ἐφ ᾧ, behind 'because', cf. Rom. 5:12; Phil. 3:12; 4:10.

49. As Vos neatly expresses it (*The Pauline Eschatology*, p.207, n.1).

50. Cf. 4:17 etc.

51. Barnett, *The Second Epistle to the Corinthians*, p.265.

52. 'Guarantee', as in the NKJV, is not a good word because it suggests recompense or a free repair in the event of breakdown. But does a Rolls Royce ever come with a guarantee? One suspects not.

53. Cf. Eph. 1:14.

54. Barnett suggests that at this point Paul may have been correcting an 'overrealized eschatology', whereby some triumphalist Corinthians believed that they were already 'with the Lord' (*The Second Epistle to the Corinthians*, p.269). But even if

the congregation overflowed with spiritual gifts, they were still consciously awaiting the final revelation of Christ (1 Cor. 1:7).

55. There is mystery here. Our Lord ascended to heaven in bodily fashion (Luke 24:51; Acts 1:9), and now accepts the worship of spirit-beings (Heb. 12:23).

56. Here and in 7:16; 10:1,2. Elsewhere only in Heb. 13:6.

57. Cf. Luke 3:22; 9:29; John 5:37; 1 Thess. 5:22.

58. Note the present tense, $\epsilon\dot{\upsilon}\delta o\kappa o\hat{\upsilon}\mu\epsilon\nu$, 'we are pleased'. Cf. Matt. 3:17: '... in whom I am well pleased'. Coupled with $\mu\acute{a}\lambda\lambda o\nu$, as in 5:8, the verb means 'to wish rather', 'to prefer'.

59. So, Barnett, *The Second Epistle to the Corinthians*, p.273; Hodge, *1 & 2 Corinthians*, p.500, citing Rom. 14:8 as a back-up.

60. Cf. Rom. 15:20; 1 Thess. 4:11.

61. See also Matt. 25:31-46; John 5:22; 2 Tim. 4:1. This interpretation is more narrow than that, say of Hodge (*1 & 2 Corinthians*, p.501), or of Hughes (*Paul's Second Epistle to the Corinthians*, p.180) who both apply this judgement to all men, as does Calvin (*2 Corinthians*, p.71). That Christ will judge all men is clear (Acts 10:42; 17:31), but 5:10 is surely not concerned with this. And the immediate context, as well as the parallels offered by 1 Cor. 3:13; 4:5, is compelling. Alford is careful: 'I may observe that no more definite inference must be drawn from this verse as to the place which the saints of God shall hold in the general judgement, than it warrants; viz. that they as well as others shall be manifested and judged by Him (Matt. xxv.14)' (*The Greek Testament*, vol. ii, p.629). It may be asked why he assumes that the trial of the saints is to be incorporated within the sphere of the universal judgement. Admittedly, there is mystery here, but not ambiguity. Kistemaker comes closer: 'But here the Greek construction shows that he [Paul] addresses the Corinthian Christians and presumably his opponents in that church' (*II Corinthians*, p.180). Barnett does not raise the issue (*The Second Epistle to the Corinthians*, p.276).

62. Verb: $\phi a\nu\epsilon\rho\omega\theta\hat{\eta}\nu a\iota$; adjective: $\phi a\nu\epsilon\rho\acute{o}\nu$.

63. According to some manuscripts, Rom. 14:10 reads, 'the judgement seat of God'.

64. Matt. 27:19; John 19:13; Acts 12:21; 18:12,16,17; 25:6,10,17.

65. Cf. Matt. 13:12; 25:29; Mark 4:25; Luke 8:18; 19:26, 1 Cor. 3:10-15; 4:5.

66. This is the force of $\pi\rho\grave{o}\varsigma$ $\mathring{a}$ $\mathring{\epsilon}\pi\rho a\xi\epsilon\nu$: we face both the Lord and our deeds.

67. κομίσεται → 'shall receive'. So, Eph. 6:8; Col. 3:25; 2 Peter 2:13.

A variant reading, translated into English, gives 'that each might receive his own things of the body' (τὰ ἴδια τοῦ σώματος instead of τὰ διὰ τοῦ σώματος, inserting an iota before διά). If this is the original wording the idea of personal retribution is intensified.

68. ἀγαθόν → fit, capable, useful; φαῦλον → base, evil, worthless.

69. Grudem, *Systematic Theology*, p.1144, deserves to be read.

Chapter 5 — The ministry of reconciliation

1. Cf. 7:1; Acts 9:31; Eph. 5:21.

2. Hodge observes that persuasion can mean to seek to please or win over, and cites Matt. 28:14, Acts 12:20 and 1 John 3:19 (*1 & 2 Corinthians*, p.505).

3. As argued by Barnett (*The Second Epistle to the Corinthians*, p.280, n.8).

4. Cf. 1:12,14; 4:2; 6:3; 7:2.

5. 'Giving [διδόντες] you', Paul employing a participle instead of the finite verb, may be an example of the Jewish mind at work, the use of the participle being common in Biblical Hebrew. The apostle could be showing his background.

6. Shakespeare, *Henry V*, Act III, Scene 6. The battle of Agincourt was fought out between the French and the English in 1415.

7. Cf. John 8:48, where the Jews assert that the Lord is demon-possessed.

8. Acts 26:24-25, although noun and verb are both different: μανία and μαίνεσθαι.

9. Thus Kruse, *The Second Epistle of Paul to the Corinthians*, p.121.

10. This view is well argued by Barnett, although he appears to suggest that Paul's spiritual experiences were 'ecstatic' (*The Second Epistle to the Corinthians*, p.285). But notwithstanding 'I fell into a *trance*' in Acts 22:17, in the New Testament the verb ἐξίστημι never points to spiritual experiences. Should it be so here?

11. Cf. Acts 7:57: 'they ... *covered* their ears'; Luke 8:45: '... the multitudes are *crowding* and pressing upon you'; Acts 28:8: 'Publius was ... *afflicted* with fever and dysentery'. In Philippians 1:23 Paul is shut in between two conflicting possibilities: would it be better to remain in this world or to be with the Lord?

12. Moule remarks that the expression is 'exclusively *subjective*' (*An Idiom-Book*, p.41).

13. Denney, *The Death of Christ*, p.125.
14. ἄρα, meaning 'as a result', 'consequently'.
15. Hodge, *1 & 2 Corinthians*, p.510.
16. Lenski seems to fall into this trap (*I & II Corinthians*, p.1029). He argues that because Christ died for everybody he therefore died for us. Barnett notes that our Lord died on behalf of 'humanity', and that 'The death and resurrection of Christ is the potential reversal of the death on account of the sin of Adam' (*The Second Epistle to the Corinthians*, pp.286,290). The problems raised by this type of interpretation are manifest.
17. John Murray, *Redemption Accomplished and Applied* (Edinburgh: Banner of Truth Trust, 1961 [first published 1955]), p.69.
18. As van der Walt says, 'Man not only needs a clean slate; he needs a full slate. And that he has abundantly in Christ!' (*Antipas Herald*, i. 4).
19. Both verbs are aorists, implying that the death of 'the one' brought about a simultaneous 'death' for the beneficiaries.
20. Athanasius, *De Incarnatione*, 20.30.
21. This interpretation is queried by some. Barnett remarks that 'The debate centers on whether Christ in his death was *substitute* or *representative*,' and believes that 'One can represent, but not substitute for, *many*' (*The Second Epistle to the Corinthians*, p.289, n.9). Is not this an overly scholastic distinction?
22. Again, ὑπέρ + genitive: 'on behalf of' Israel'. *Antiquities* 13.6: 'Jonathan said that he was ready to die for [ὑπέρ] them.' There are very many other examples in the literature.
23. Plummer, *The Second Epistle of St Paul to the Corinthians*, p.174, citing Philem. 13 — 'in your behalf [ὑπέρ σοῦ] he might minister to me'; Moule, *An Idiom-Book*, p.64, citing Winer.
24. There is no reason why the phrase 'for their sakes'/'in their place'/'on their behalf' (ὑπέρ αὐτῶν) must be restricted to the immediate participle ἀποθανόντι, leaving out the more remote participle ἐγερθέντι. I need, and have, a Saviour who rose for me personally. Furthermore, if, as Calvinists properly say, there is such a thing as a 'limited' or 'definite' atonement, is there not also, by parity, a 'limited' or 'definite' resurrection in that Christ rose to confer benefits upon the people of his choice?
25. Cf. 4:3: 'but *even* if our gospel is veiled ...'
26. Cf. John 20:29: 'Blessed are those who have not seen and yet have believed.'
27. In Paul's letters 'according to the flesh' (κατὰ σάρκα) is sometimes adverbial (1:17; 10:2,3; 11:18; Rom. 8:4-5,12-13; Gal.

4:23,29), and sometimes adjectival (Rom. 9:3,5; 1 Cor. 1:26; 10:18; Eph. 6:5; Col. 3:22).

28. It is true that κτίσις can sometimes mean a separate entity, with a somewhat lessened emphasis upon initial creation (Rom. 1:25; 8:39; Col. 1:23 ['humankind']; Heb. 4:13; 1 Peter 2:13 ['institution']). And it is true that here, in 5:17, 'creation' could bear a similar nuance. But one is swayed by the parallel with 4:6. Cf. Eph. 2:10; 4:24.

29. As Vos puts it (Geerhardus Vos, *Biblical Theology: Old and New Testaments*, Edinburgh: Banner of Truth Trust, 1975 [first published 1948], p.299).

30. Cf. Matt. 5:18; 24:35; 2 Peter 3:10.

31. The Greek perfect γέγονεν, 'have / has come into being', implies permanency.

32. Barnett remarks that being 'in Christ' means, among other things, 'belonging to a community of the baptized that confesses Christ' (*The Second Epistle to the Corinthians*, p.296, n.42). Although it is true that all who are 'in Christ' ought to be, and usually are, baptized, does it follow that baptism (however understood) leads in to this blessed state?

33. The noun, καταλλαγή: 5:18,19; Rom. 5:11; 11:15; the verb, καταλλάσσω: 5:18,19,20; Rom. 5:10 (twice); 1 Cor. 7:11. But see also Eph. 2:16; Col. 1:20,21, where a related verb, ἀποκαταλλάσσω, occurs, and Matt. 5:24, where διαλλάσσομαι refers to reconciliation between men. See Seyoon Kim, '2 Cor. 5:11-21 and the origin of Paul's Concept of Reconciliation', *Novum Testamentum*, 39,4 [1997], pp. 360-84, for a detailed consideration. However, I would not agree with Kim when he notes that 'Paul uses the terminology [of reconciliation] never to imply that God is reconciled (or reconciles himself) to human beings, but always to suggest that God reconciles human beings to himself or human beings are reconciled to God' (p.362).

34. Morris, *The Apostolic Preaching of the Cross*, p.215.

35. Berkouwer observes that theological controversy has always centred on the issue of who is the object of reconciliation (G. C. Berkouwer, *The Work of Christ*, Grand Rapids: Eerdmans 1970 [first published 1965], p.257). At the risk of appearing simplistic, one might suspect that the matter is relatively obvious.

36. E.g. 3:3,6,8,17,18; 4:6; 5:5.

37. An excellent example of the tension yet rapprochement between divine love and divine anger is to be found in 2 Maccabees 5:20, in the Apocrypha. The author comments that the temple of God in Jerusalem, 'forsaken in the wrath of the

Almighty was, at the reconciliation [ἐν τῇ ... καταλλαγῇ] of the great Sovereign, restored again with all glory'. Here, the relationship (so to speak) between God and Israel had been disturbed by Israel's sin. Later, the temple was rebuilt 'by the reconciliation' of God. The people are reconciled to God in that the Lord does not look upon their sins. Nor are they rebels. In other words, they are reconciled to him because God initiates the process. Barnett observes that 'Apart from 2 Maccabees, the notion of "reconciliation" is relatively undeveloped within Judaism contemporary with Paul, whether the LXX, the intertestamental literature, Josephus, or the rabbis' (*The Second Epistle to the Corinthians*, p.303, n.10). This, however, does not decide the issue: we may believe that Paul extracts his doctrine of reconciliation from the Hebrew Scriptures and from the teaching of Jesus.

38. The aorist participle δόντος could be in the middle voice, implying self-interest in the giver.

39. Hodge, *1 & 2 Corinthians*, p.519; Barrett, *The Second Epistle to the Corinthians*, p.176.

40. Barnett, *The Second Epistle to the Corinthians*, p.304.

41. The meaning of the Greek, ὡς ὅτι, has been disputed. See also 11:21 and 2 Thess. 2:2, where the words introduce statements which are untrue, or true in part. But the basic sense stands: 'as', 'like', or 'this is how it is'.

42. Cf. Luke 4:44: 'he was preaching'.

43. This third approach was taken long ago by John Gill, *An Exposition of the New Testament* (London: Collingridge, 1853), vol. ii, p.309.

44. Kistemaker, *II Corinthians*, p.195.

45. Murray expounds this well (John Murray, *Collected Writings*, Edinburgh: Banner of Truth Trust 1977, vol. ii, p.149).

46. Cf. 1 Cor. 1:18; Eph. 1:13; Col. 1:5.

47. θέμενος, 2nd aorist participle, middle voice, from τίθημι; not θείς, the active participle, which one might have expected (as in Acts 7:60; 9:40).

48. It is not impossible that Paul is reflecting upon the Septuagint rendering of Ps. 105:27 (Ps. 104:27 in LXX), which says that God deposited *(etheto)* his destructive signs and wonders with Moses and Aaron in the land of Ham. The Lord's deposition with Paul has to do with grace, not judgement.

49. So also the AV, the NASB and the NIV.

50. Gill, *Exposition*, vol. ii, p.310.

51. For the nominative pronoun, ὑμεῖς, see 1:14; 3:2; 6:13,18; 8:9; 9:4; 11:7; 12:11; 13:7,9.

52. Kistemaker, *II Corinthians*, p.200.

Kruse adopts an intermediate position, suggesting that the exhortation 'may very well reflect the language of Paul's evangelistic preaching, but here the appeal is directed to the members of the Corinthian church' (*2 Corinthians*, p.128). Similarly, Barnett interprets the apostolic, 'Be reconciled to God,' as Paul 'admonishing the Corinthians to be restored in their relationships with God ... encouraging them to return to their God and to the word spoken by Paul, the apostle of Christ (see on 6:11-13)' (*The Second Epistle to the Corinthians*, p.311). Likewise Tasker: 'Paul now calls upon all at Corinth, who may hear this letter read out in the assembly and who are still at enmity with God, to accept the reconciliation open to them' (*The Second Epistle of Paul to the Corinthians*, p.90). But the Corinthians, though perhaps dented in their faith, were not apostate. Nor does Paul allow that any were baptized unbelievers; hence the concluding benediction of 13:14, which refers to 'you all'.

53. John Albert Bengel, *Gnomon of the New Testament*, trans. J. Bandinel (Edinburgh: T. & T. Clark, 1857-8), vol. iii., p.385.

54. Lenski, *I & II Corinthians*, p.1050.

55. Neither Kruse (*2 Corinthians*, p.128) nor Barnett (*The Second Epistle to the Corinthians*, p.311) takes this up, both assuming without discussion that Paul is addressing the church. This is surprising.

56. Paraphrasing Denney, *The Second Epistle to the Corinthians*, p.216.

57. $\dot{\upsilon}\pi\acute{\epsilon}\rho$ + genitive, as in 5:14-15. Cf. the assertion in the Mishnah, *Berakoth*, 5.5: 'A man's agent is like to himself.'

58. $\pi\rho\epsilon\sigma\beta\epsilon\acute{\upsilon}\omega \rightarrow$ 'I am ambassadoring' (to coin a phrase).

59. $\dot{\omega}\varsigma \rightarrow$ 'seeing that'.

60. J. I. Packer deals with this issue excellently in *Evangelism and the Sovereignty of God* (London: IVP, 1966 [first published 1961]), pp.18-36.

61. Robert L. Reymond, *Paul: Missionary Theologian. A Survey of his Missionary Labours and Theology* (Fearn, Scotland: Christian Focus Publications, 2000), p.85.

62. Grudem writes that 'I do not think we should rush to criticize an evangelist who tells an audience of unbelievers, "Christ died for your sins," if it is made clear in the context that it is necessary to trust in Christ before one can receive the benefits of the gospel offer. In that sense the sentence is simply understood to mean "Christ died to offer you forgiveness for your sins," or "Christ died to make available forgiveness for your sins." The

important point here is that sinners realize that salvation is available for everyone and that payment of sins is available for everyone' (Wayne Grudem, *Systematic Theology: An Introduction to Biblical Doctrine*, Leicester: IVP, 1994, p.602). With all due respect to Grudem, in statements of this type is there not a blurring of issues? It is one matter to tell unconverted people that faith in Christ is essential and that forgiveness on this basis is available, whereas to inform them that the Lord suffered in their place is another. Peter's closing words to Cornelius deserve meditation (Acts 10:43). Does not Grudem attempt to cut the knot rather than untie it?

63. The Greek is ἵνα followed by an aorist subjunctive, indicating both purpose and achieved result.

64. The terminology behind 'on our behalf' (ὑπὲρ ἡμῶν) is distinct and explicit: Paul now specifies his readers and himself as being among those for whom Christ died.

65. Matt. 3:17; 12:18; 17:5; Luke 23:41,47-48; John 8:46; Acts 3:14; Heb. 4:15; 7:26; 1 Peter 2:22; 3:18; 1 John 3:5.

66. Barnett tells us that Christ was not 'sin personified' (*The Second Epistle to the Corinthians,* p.314, n.65). True. But was he not the mirror of my sinful persona?

67. This view is backed up by Gen. 4:7 (possibly), Lev. 4:24; 5:12; Num. 8:8 and Ps. 40:6, where the Hebrew word for sin could mean 'sin-offering'. Cf. Rom. 8:3; Heb. 10:6.

68. Morris, *The Apostolic Preaching of the Cross,* p.298, citing Adolf Schlatter.

69. 'Made' and 'become' are aorists, denoting point action, a single occurrence. But some manuscripts, such as the *Textus Receptus,* give γινώμεθα, present subjunctive, meaning 'that we might be'. If this is the original reading, the meaning would be that we become and remain 'the righteousness of God'. The essential sense is not different.

70. Cf. Rom. 1:17; 3:21,22.

71. Perhaps a personal note might be appropriate: these negative comments upon some views of some 'Strict Baptists' are made by one who, in the historic sense of the expression, is a 'Strict Baptist', although he does not relish the use of that title.

72. The Strict Baptist articles are cited from Thomas J. Nettles, *By His Grace and for His Glory* (London: Wakeman Trust, 1990) p.389. Gadsby's remark may be found in *The Works of the late William Gadsby* (London: Gadsby, 1851), vol. i., p.256.

Chapter 6 — Paul's pastoral ministry

1. Cf. Rom. 15:10; Eph. 4:8; 1 Cor. 6:16.
2. But see the related noun, πρόσκομμα (Rom. 9:32-33; 14:13,20; 1 Cor. 8:9; 1 Peter 2:8; cf. 1 Cor. 9:12).
3. Matt. 10:22; 24:13; Mark 13:13; Luke 8:15; 21:19.
4. Bengel, *Gnomon*, vol. iii., p.386.
5. Note Acts 13:50; 14:5-6,19; 16:22; 17:5-9,13; 18:12-17; 19:23-41; 21:27-36; 23:12-24.
6. ἀγνότης, found only here and in 11:3, although the latter reading is disputed. Cf. the adjective ἀγνός (7:11; Phil. 4:8; 1 Tim. 5:22; Titus 2:5; 1 Peter 3:2; 1 John 3:3).
7. Eph. 2:7; 1 Tim. 1:16; 1 Peter 2:3; 2 Peter 3:15.
8. First, Paul begins with single terms: 'in much endurance ... in kindness' (6:4b-6a); second, a series of double terms: 'in the Holy Spirit ... in the power of God' (6:6b-7a); third, a number of opposites, each pair of antitheses being introduced by 'by means' of or 'through': 'by the weapons of righteousness for the right hand and the left ... by evil report and good report' (6:7b-8a); and finally a series of adjectives or participles, each introduced by 'as' (6:8b-10).
9. Cf. Rom. 12:9; Gal. 5:22; 1 Peter 1:22.
10. Cf. Gal. 2:5,14: 'the truth of the gospel'; Eph.1:13: '... the word of truth, the gospel of your salvation'; Col.1:5: 'the word of truth of the gospel'; James 1:18: 'He brought us forth by the word of truth.'
11. Cf. 13:4; Rom. 1:16; 1 Cor. 1:18; 2 Thess. 1:11.
12. Hughes, *Paul's Second Epistle to the Corinthians*, p.230.
13. 'In' represents ἐν + dative; 'by', διά + genitive. The NKJV, for example, is vague.
14. 'Glory' ← δόξα. Cf. 'imagine / think / consider / suppose' (← δοκέω).
15. John Calvin, *2 Corinthians and Timothy, Titus and Philemon*, trans. T. A. Smail, ed. D. W. & T. F. Torrance (Grand Rapids: Eerdmans, 1996), p.87.
16. 'Yet': καί; 'but': δέ.
17. 1 Tim. 4:1; 1 John 2:26; 2 John 7.
18. 11:31; Rom. 9:1; Gal. 1:20.
19. 6:9-10 is rich in present participles pointing to each day as it came and went.
20. John 10:14; cf. 2 Tim. 2:19.
21. παιδευόμενοι → 'being disciplined / chastised'.
22. The present passive participle, λυπούμενοι, indicating what was happening to Paul, and not what he was.

23. 11:8-9; Phil. 4:15; Acts 18:3.

24. πάντα can be singular ('everything') or plural ('all things').

25. Cf. Matt. 13:17; Rom. 15:4; Eph. 3:10; Heb. 1:2; 1 Peter 1:12.

26. 'Become', γεγόνασιν, is in the perfect tense: we have become and remain partakers of chastisement.

27. Barnett, *The Second Epistle to the Corinthians*, p.335.

28. Cf. Job 3:1; Matt. 5:2. The Greek is ἀνέῳγεν, third person singular, perfect tense and intransitive, from ἀνοίγω, as in John 1:51: 'You shall see the heavens opened [that is, remaining open].'

29. The verb, πεπλάτυνται, 'enlarged', 'expanded' or 'broadened', in the perfect tense, could be either passive or middle voice. If the latter, Paul could be indicating that he desires his heart to remain open.

30. Acts 9:4; 22:7; 26:14.

31.The metaphorical use occurs also in the Septuagint in Prov. 12:10; 26:22; Jer. 28:13.

32. Barrett, *The Second Epistle to the Corinthians*, p.193.

33. Guthrie, *New Testament Introduction*, p.425. He adds immediately that 'Such unexpected digression would be unpardonable in a treatise, but it is not altogether improbable in a letter.'

34. So Furnish, *II Corinthians*, p.376.

35. See Barrett, *The Second Epistle to the Corinthians*, p.194, and Sirach 13:2,17-18: 'What fellowship shall the earthen pot have with the kettle? ... What fellowship shall the wolf have with the lamb? So is the sinner unto the godly. What peace is there between the hyena and the dog? And what peace between the rich man and the poor?' But Sirach was never at Qumran, and there is no need for speculation about the quarry, if any, from which Paul mined his material.

36. Furnish, *II Corinthians*, p.382.

37. Martin, *2 Corinthians*, p.193.

38. Plummer, *The Second Epistle of St Paul to the Corinthians*, p.204. The contested words are: ἑτεροζυγέω, μετοχή, συνκατάθεσις, Βελίαρ and μολυσμός.

39. Barnett, *The Second Epistle to the Corinthians*, p.339.

40. 1 Cor. 1:12; 5:1,11; 6:1,18; 7:39; 8:10; 11; 15:12.

41. 6:16-17; 1 Cor. 3:16-17; cf. 1 Cor. 6:9-20; 8:1 – 11:1.

42. Philo interprets Lev.19:19 as a prohibition against mismating (*The Special Laws*, 4.203); Josephus, as a prohibition against the unequal yoke (*Antiquities*, 4.228).

43. μὴ γίνεσθε: present imperative — 'Do not continue to be.' Furnish argues that the periphrastic construction — the present

imperative followed by a present participle — means 'Do not become' (*II Corinthians,* p.361).

44. Cf. Matt. 8:12; 22:13; 25:30; John 3:19; Eph. 5:8; 1 Peter 2:9.

45. Another preserved Hebraism, although with a far different meaning, would be 'Sabaoth' (Hebrew for 'hosts') in James 5:4. Belial / Beliar is found as a personal name for Satan in later Jewish writings (e.g. the Qumran *War Rule* 13.2,4 (translated by Vermes as 'Satan'). In 6:15 the Greek Βελιάρ translates the Hebrew בְּלִיַּעַל (1 Sam. 25:25; 2 Sam. 16:7 etc.). A usual English translation of the Old Testament expression is 'man of worth-lessness', joining בְּלִי ('without', 'lacking') and יַעַל ('to profit'). But the Septuagint inclines to the meaning 'without yoke', that is 'lawless': בְּלִי עוֹל (e.g. Deut. 13:13, ἄνδρες παράνομοι, 'lawless men'). The United Bible Societies' Greek text provides Βελιαρ rather than (as the Trinitarian Bible Society's Received Text) Βελίαλ.

46. Philo recounts the consternation felt by the Jewish nation when the Roman emperor Gaius (or, Caligula, A.D. 37-41) planned to erect a 'colossal' statue of himself under the name of Zeus in the temple (*The Embassy to Gaius,* 188). Paul knows that the glory of God has moved from Jerusalem to abide with the Christian fellowships springing up across the world. A similar abhorrence remains as he passes from type to antitype.

47. The expression 'the living God' occurs also in Acts 14:15; Rom. 9:26 (citing Hosea 1:10); 1 Thess. 1:9, 1 Tim. 3:15; 4:10; Heb. 3:12; 9:14; 10:31; 12:22 (cf. Rev. 4:9-10; 10:6; 15:7), and with a similar emphasis.

48. Barnett doubts that Paul cites Ezek. 37:27 (*The Second Epistle to the Corinthians,* p.352, n.44).

49. εἰς x 2 → 'for a father'; 'for a son'.

50. Greek 'almighty', from the underlying Hebrew 'of hosts'.

51. 12:19; Rom. 12:19; 1 Cor. 10:14; 15:58; Phil. 2:12; 4:1; cf. 1 Thess. 2:8.

52. καθαρίσωμεν → 'let us cleanse [once and for all]', aorist subjunctive.

53. The present participle behind 'perfecting' is ἐπιτελοῦντες. In this letter the verb occurs also in 8:6,11, meaning 'to complete', 'bring to an end', 'bring about'.

54. W. E. Sangster, *Why Jesus never wrote a book* (London: Epworth Press, 1956 [first published 1932]) p.43.

55. As observed by Barnett, *The Second Epistle to the Corinthians,* p.359.

56. ἠδικήσαμεν, ἐφθείραμεν, ἐπλεονεκτήσαμεν → 'we wronged ... we corrupted ... we disadvantaged'.

57. παρρησία, 'boldness', 'confidence', can mean boldness of speech or, more fundamentally, assurance; e.g. 'Let us come *with boldness* to the throne of grace' (Heb. 4:16). See 3:12-13.

58. And within this excursus there are (at least) two others: 6:2, a citation of Isa. 49:8, and 6:14 – 7:1. Perhaps the numerous redactional theories fail to do justice to Paul's literary genius, a genius at all times dedicated to the welfare of the Corinthians.

59. Hughes, *Paul's Second Epistle to the Corinthians*, p.266, n.3.

60.Cf. Rom. 5:8: 'But God demonstrates his own love toward us'; 1 Cor. 1:27: 'But God has chosen the foolish things'; Eph. 2:4-5: 'But God ... made us alive together in Christ'; Phil. 2:27: 'But God had mercy on him [Epaphroditus]'.

61. 'By' ← ἐν + dative.

62. The vocabulary of Isa. 49:13b (Septuagint) is akin to that of 7:6. The parallel cannot be accidental. Barnett insists that Paul makes much use of Isa. 40-55 in his overall exposition of comfort in 2 Corinthians (*The Second Epistle to the Corinthians*, p.369, n.19, and elsewhere).

63. Cf. 1:6; 12:19.

64. εἰ καὶ x 3 → 'if', 'if' and 'perhaps'.

65.Cf. Gal. 2:5: 'We did not yield ... for even an hour'; Philem. 15: 'Perhaps because of this he was parted from you for an hour.'

66. Barnett claims that 'The "repentance" called for by Paul ... is not directed to God but to Paul himself, specifically in regard to the Corinthians' attitudes toward his authority (cf. vv. 7 and 11)' (*The Second Epistle to the Corinthians*, p.375). This is difficult. Paul, it is true, represented Christ as an apostle, but never demanded that others genuflect before him.

67. Cf. Rom. 8:27: 'He [the Spirit] intercedes ... according to God.'

68. See Hughes, *Paul's Second Epistle to the Corinthians*, p.272.

69. Cf. Paul's apology before the Jewish mob, Acts 22:1.

70. The background ἐκδίκησις is translated by Kistemaker, probably unhelpfully, as 'punishment' (*II Corinthians*, p.241). But the church did not *punish* the offender.

71. Hence the present continuous infinitive 'to be', εἶναι.

72. Barnett tells us that this interpretation has been 'rebutted' (*The Second Epistle to the Corinthians*, p.380, n.45). Perhaps he travels beyond the data.

73. The construction might be a Hebraism, according to which one of two alternatives is negatived, but only by way of comparison with the other alternative, which is deemed to be more

important. A good example would be Hosea 6:6: 'For I desire
mercy and not sacrifice, and the knowledge of God more than
burnt offerings.' This does not mean that the sacrificial system
was suddenly redundant.

74. 1:12; 3:2; 4:2; 5:11.

75. Inflated self-esteem is mentioned in 1 Cor. 4:6,18,19; 5:2. It
had been a problem.

76. εἰ τι αὐτῷ. The conditionality of the expression is disputed
by some; e.g. Martin, *2 Corinthians,* p.241.

77. 'Fear and trembling': cf. 1 Cor. 2:3; Eph. 6:5; Phil. 2:12.

78. περισσοτέρως is properly a comparative, but probably has
here a superlative force. Cf. Mark 7:36; Phil. 1:23.

79. The sentence does not incorporate a connecting particle such
as 'for', thus demonstrating syntactical discontinuity: 7:16 is a
distinct conclusion.

80. Paul ends this part of the letter on a note of exuberance and
triumph. Notice in 7:4-16 the frequency of words expressing
comfort and joy consequent upon learning of the Corinthians'
response: ζῆλος (twice), σπουδή (twice), μετάνοια (twice), φόβος
(twice); and ὑπακοή (once); παρακαλέω (four times); παράκλησις
(three times); χαίρω (four times); χαρά (twice); καυχάομαι,
παρρησία and θαρρέω (once each).